I0820786

Praise for

LIFE IS SALES

"*Life Is Sales* is a revelation. It beautifully illustrates an entrepreneurial journey, full of internal and external lessons that any businessperson will learn from. Rich exemplifies how entrepreneurship and sales are about relationships and service. Many entrepreneurs get it backward and put growth first—but serve and do the right thing, and scale will come. We can all use our gifts maximally to serve the world, with a little awareness, self-discovery, and purpose."

Verne Harnish, founder of Entrepreneurs' Organization (EO) and author of *Scaling Up*

"If you were ever going to learn sales from anyone, it's Rich Lyons. Not only because he is the walking example of "exponential success," but because he is the living embodiment of a man who learned how to leverage his greatest asset: his heart to serve. As you will see in these pages, leadership is an inside job. Great entrepreneurs think the path to reach their dreams exists on a road map, when in reality it exists in their own mirror. If you're ready to exponentially grow your wealth as well as yourself, *Life Is Sales* is the manifesto you've been missing, written by one of the greatest businessmen and humans of our time."

Jessica Zweig, chief visionary officer at Jessica Zweig, Inc., founder and former CEO of SimplyBe. Agency, and author of *Be* and *The Light Work*

"Through his own story, Rich brings to light the realities, rigors, and rewards of living life with a mission—taking the reader on a thought-provoking journey into the power of purposeful relationships and the compounding value of achieving mindful moments of awareness."

Brendan Witcher, VP and principal analyst at Forrester

"This *isn't* just another sales book—it's a life-changing perspective. Rich and Dr. Bob masterfully connect the dots between sales, business success, and personal growth. As someone who's spent decades leading and growing businesses, I can confidently say this book offers invaluable lessons for success in both business and life. Readers will get practical, actionable strategies not only for sales but also for living a more purposeful life with awareness and choice and intent. Success is an inside job, and Rich examines and outlines a wonderful and successful journey."

Harvey Spevak, executive chairman and managing partner at Equinox Group

"Rich Lyons' *Life Is Sales* isn't your typical sales guide; it's an exploration of how sales principles apply to all aspects of life. He cleverly blends personal experiences with business wisdom, demonstrating that true salesmanship involves understanding needs, building relationships, and empowering others to succeed. Whether you're an entrepreneur, sales professional, or simply seeking a more fulfilling life, *Life Is Sales* offers valuable insights and practical strategies for achieving your goals while fostering deeper connections with those around you. It's a compelling and insightful read."

Tom Ebling, board member and advisor to SaaS companies, former CEO at Demandware

"Great businesses aren't built on products or services, the great ones are built on people and purpose. That's what Rich Lyons understands at the deepest level. Having known Rich for over a decade, I know firsthand he doesn't just sell—he builds real value. He builds companies, relationships, and cultures that thrive. *Life Is Sales* isn't about mere tricks or tactics; it's about leading with authenticity, earning trust, and creating real impact—building real value in business and life!"

Bob Scwartz, managing partner, 47 B Street; board member and advisor, former president, Magento Inc. (Adobe Commerce)

"Rich is an exceptional entrepreneur and business leader. He lays out his inspiring path to success, both personally and professionally, in a straightforward and entertaining fashion, drawing key insights along the way. A great read for any aspiring entrepreneur."

Jeff Barnet, investor and advisor, former COO, Demandware; and CEO, Salesforce Commerce Cloud

"Simply put, Rich is real. Rich is evolved. Rich is a unique leader. Not because he is more talented than others, but rather because of his intention and commitment to develop himself and his company at being the absolute best through the exploration of his 'self' and the service of others. Rich walks his talk. He believes that awareness and conscious choice are the keys to business and life success, and lives the principle that 'sales' is the opportunity to 'serve,' which is one of the most honorable activities a human being can undertake.

Life is Sales is a must read if you truly choose to be better and live your best life. It is a testament that a commitment to your personal development works in business and life, and equally important, that it is a privilege to sell and serve. BRAVO!"

Scott G. Stephen, chief growth officer, Rate; former COO, Playboy Enterprises

LIFE IS SALES

www.amplifypublishinggroup.com

Life Is Sales: A Holistic Approach to Sales, Self-Discovery, and Living a Life of Purpose

For more information, please contact:
Amplify Publishing, an imprint of Amplify Publishing Group
620 Herndon Parkway, Suite 220
Herndon, VA 20170
info@amplifypublishing.com

Library of Congress Control Number: 2024923470

CPSIA Code: PRV0625A

ISBN-13: 979-8-89138-330-2

Printed in United States

To the salesperson in all of us.

LIFE IS SALES

A Holistic Approach to Sales, Self-Discovery, and Living a Life of Purpose

RICH LYONS
with DR. BOB WRIGHT

CONTENTS

ACKNOWLEDGMENTS

To Dave Barr for accepting my offer at Divine and then again to be cofounder of Lyons Consulting Group (LYONSCG). Thank you for being my partner and friend and for trusting in yourself and me. To Norm Alesi, for being a good friend and supporting me in the Entrepreneurs' Organization (EO) and then bringing your expertise to LYONSCG and becoming our CFO/COO. You handled the running of the machine, which allowed Dave and me to sell, sell, sell.

To all the employees of LYONSCG: you are the best in the industry. What we built together—our customer-first culture, our learning organization, our "yes, and" mantra, our karma, our scope busters, our guardians of the culture—will never be replicated and will live with me forever. We defined Commerce Realized! Thank you!

To Dr. Bob Wright for being my corner man, kicking my ass when I needed it, and tending cuts when I was wounded. Thank you for teaching me how to build a culture based on values and principles. To Dr. Judith Wright, for helping me to find the mystic Rich, to question the universe, to break open my rational mind and see things differently, and to yearn for more. Thank you both for holding me accountable to be the husband and father that I wanted to be and proving to me that we can have it all.

To my Senior Sales Lab, Couples Empowerment Group, and Leadership Group at Wright for being on the journey with me, learning and growing with me, and supporting me to be my best.

To Jennifer Foor Stephen for being my sister from another mother. And for being the messenger to tell me what I needed to hear. You are missed. To Scott Stephen for being my good friend—and first Demandware client. You put LYONSCG on track to be the best in the world. And you were and are there for me every day, holding the vision when I questioned it and forgot that we were trying to change the world.

To Karen Smithbauer for being my mom. Thank you for always believing in me, backing me, funding me, and holding me accountable. You were my advisory board.

To Don Delves and Ed Fein, the rest of my advisory board, for listening, questioning, challenging, and believing.

To Harvey Spevak for being our best man. You stood up for us. You're always there for me, listening and lending advice when I need it.

And most importantly, to my wife and daughters. To Morgan and Hannah for choosing me to be your dad. I am incredibly grateful to have two such loving, caring, independent, bright, and intelligent daughters. Thank you for exceeding my high expectations. You gave me a reason to go to work in the morning and a reason to come back home at night.

And to the love of my life, Gertrude. Without you, life would not be so grand an adventure. I can't imagine this journey without you by my side, supporting me, challenging me, and loving me. You are my partner, lover, and best friend. You fought for me, dragged me into Dr. Bob's office, initiated my social and emotional intelligence (SEI) education, partnered to take on our soft addictions and lead a more conscious life, consciously conceived and partnered to raise our children, and authored the discovery of the mystical version of myself that I found on pilgrimages to sacred sites. You have led me to places I would not have gone alone, and you continue to be my light, my star, and the best salesperson in our family. My heart has grown three times larger being married to you and leading our family.

—Rich Lyons

DR. BOB'S FOREWORD

Rich Lyons sees life as sales—a perspective that plays a key role in everything, from his marriage to parenting to business. When Rich talks about sales, he uses the term broadly. As you'll discover, his lens encompasses everything, from business success to taking responsibility for living the life you want and engaging family, friends, customers, and others to flourish in the game of life.

He has mastered the art of helping many different types of people, including his children, nurture their desires and dreams as they develop. Raising strong-willed, successful children meant selling them on values and ways of living while learning and growing with them as they carved their own paths and resisted his will.

Similarly, Rich has applied his sales perspective to customers, even when they occasionally resisted—Rich embraces their resistance to help him serve them better. Meeting the needs of others has driven Rich's growth.

You will also read how he learned to meet his own inner needs, needs he denied initially, especially his vulnerability and softer, sensitive side. You will see how he grew, increasing his capacity to serve others and to live great family, friendship, career, and spiritual lives.

And perhaps most important of all, you'll gain valuable lessons from Rich that you can apply to your own life—lessons that not only apply to selling but also to every sphere of our existence.

Throughout the book, I'll be adding my perspective (my material will be in boxed italics), since I've been working with Rich through much of his adult journey. As his coach and the coach to many entrepreneurs, I can offer insights that come through these varied experiences.

RICH'S FORWARD: THANK YOU

Thank you for the opportunity to spend this valuable time with you—whether your goal is business or personal success (or both), I hope it will help you become a better you as it enables me to become a better me.

I have been called a business superstar, and although the label makes me uncomfortable, it has value as an aspirational term—I hope everyone reading this aspires to superstar status. I wasn't always what anyone would call a superstar; my journey from beginner to superstar contains lessons that can help you on your own journey.

From the time I finished my MBA in the early 1990s to founding LYONSCG in 2003, I was just another business guy. When I finally faced the heart-wrenching pain of selling LYONSCG in 2017 to a global corporation (Capgemini), people started acting differently toward me. Suddenly I possessed the secret sauce, and everyone wanted a taste. Colleagues, customers, and competitors were hanging on my every word, eager to know my business secrets. The mega-dollar sale to a big company attracted a lot of attention, but I would have preferred to keep growing LYONSCG without selling. The velocity of the industry growth and consolidation, however, forced us to acquire or be acquired to remain at the top of our industry.

Before its sale to Capgemini, LYONSCG had won numerous domestic and international awards, including making the Crain's Fast 50 listing four times, the Inc. 5000 listing eight times, *Consulting Magazine's* Fastest Growing Consulting Firms list three times, and the Best and Brightest Companies to Work For four times. We also took home multiple Horizon Interactive, w3, Davey, Interactive Media, Communicator, and Webby Awards. We had been repeatedly named Demandware's Partner of the Year, as well as Innovator of the Year by Magento. We received many top consulting awards and Stevie Awards for women and leadership in business, as well as sales and customer service excellence recognitions.

These accolades, though, paled next to the holy grail of entrepreneurship: selling the firm for a lot of money. This sale marked my passage into the domain of the wealthy and seemingly magically endowed. People asked me variations on the question, "What's your secret?" or "What is the one thing that made this happen?" or "How did you do it?" But, they never seemed satisfied with my answers. They did not want to hear that it took hard work, a lot of failure and rejection, and surmounting incalculable problems. They preferred the fantasy of a solo genius rather than the realities of being a good team member and picking great partners. They especially did not like hearing that I paid my dues, learned business, took risks, used training and coaching, and, above all, discovered how to sell—I knocked on doors, faced rejection, and established a sales culture with everyone focused on the customer.

This isn't false humility. I recognize that I'm a talented guy. But talent alone isn't enough. Sales is the essential element of any business success—and one of the hardest skills to learn. Selling also represented a multifaceted skill because success in sales paralleled success in life.

Life is sales. When I started out in business, I would have said, "Sales is sales, life is life, and never the twain shall meet." I was too good for sales, or I thought sales was beneath me. Over the years, my eyes—and mind—have opened. If we look at what we do on a deeper level, we're far more successful, at work and in life, if we embrace selling. Selling is not just making a sale. It's about intentionally connecting, building a relationship, fulfilling a mission, and serving.

This awareness started about thirty years ago when I was earning my MBA and began attending workshops at the Wright Foundation, an educational and training organization rooted in the human potential movement. Cofounder Dr. Bob Wright has been crucial to my success as a business leader and my development as a human being.

The two events are related. I used training and coaching with Dr. Bob and his staff throughout my career. Later, Dr. Bob and I focused on my leadership and on prioritizing the many choices I faced. I used the Wright Foundation's technologies and methodologies for myself and my employees. At LYONSCG, we followed the Wright Foundation's Advantage-4Sales (A4S) sales curriculum, ran sales contests and sales labs, and used the sales curriculum to train our salespeople. We used the Ideal State Action Planning (ISAP) methodology to teach our customer-facing people to ask better questions and orient to the ideal state for a customer. I trained all of our employees personally on the Wright Developmental Model (WDM), a model that I use every day to be more self-aware and to practice self-management, both traits that allow me to focus more and make better decisions.

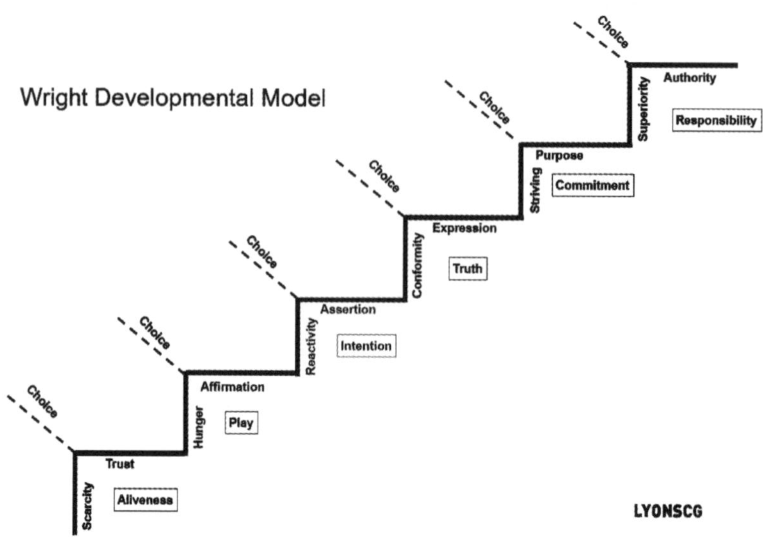

Throughout the book, Bob and I will be referring to the Wright Developmental Model (WDM)—here's a simple explanation. The model fosters awareness. With awareness, we have choice. Without awareness, we fall into unconscious patterns and day-to-day living. The more aware we are, the more choice we have and the better we can sell—and sell in a way that is intentional and fulfilling. The graphic should give you a general sense of how the model works. Don't worry, though, if you're not clear about how it works in practice. At this point, I just want to familiarize you with it (see the appendix for a deeper explanation).

None of us ever really succeeds without other people. Being a CEO can be a lonely position. Dr. Bob provided a critical sounding board for my celebrations, my mistakes, my fears, and my visions. When I forgot my vision and values, he reminded me, with a kick in the ass, if needed. As I tell you about my journey and the lessons it provides, Dr. Bob will offer an "insider's" view. He'll also frame my story in the larger contexts of psychology, neuroscience, spirituality, and other disciplines.

This preface conveys the principles and beliefs that are themes in this book and my life. First, I've come to view business as a blessing and my leadership position as a ministry. If that sounds kind of airy-fairy, bear with me—earlier in my career, I thought the same thing. To perceive business as a blessing rather than a way to make money seemed nonsensical. But through my experiences at Wright, I became more aware of what was going on inside of me. I was given this map, the Wright Developmental Model, that allowed me to better understand myself. It helped me understand my emotions, from fear to joy, and recognize that my choices shaped my life. The assignments I took at the Wright Foundation illuminated these choices, and my responsibility for my life, for me. I would not have become the leader or person that I am without this social and emotional intelligence training.

My engineering mind resonated with the model's rationality, and it made sense of an otherwise chaotic set of thoughts and feelings. It functioned as an internal guide—at any moment, anywhere. I understood what I was feeling when I walked into a meeting and hated everyone. Why was I so angry? I learned how to feel and track these emotions, and I started to "get it." I could understand why I was angry—perhaps I was hurt by a comment someone made an hour ago. That understanding allowed me to "catch up" with myself and then be back in the room and back on purpose. This ability became my superpower; not only did I become more effective, but I also started to see people differently and understand them. They weren't the enemy or the "other." I realized that they, like me, wanted to be heard and affirmed. And I grasped how business was a great way to offer this affirmation.

Rather than picking fights, I began to identify what others needed. My approach to customers changed. Before, I was focused myopically on outcomes—providing customers with top-notch service. Yes, that's important, but I began to consider service in a larger context. Did we treat customers as human beings? Did we establish a real relationship with them? Did they feel better because they had interactions with us as a firm? Were we a blessing to everyone with whom we came in contact? Business was no longer just about selling for me; it was about being a blessing for my people, my customers, and everyone else with whom I worked.

Intention serves as another foundational principle. If you want to know and understand what your intention is, look around you. Consciously or unconsciously, you have intended your life and everything around you. Not an easy pill to swallow. We mess up as salespeople and in many life activities because we forget or are unconscious of our intention and stop taking responsibility for the results that we want. You meet with a customer, and he insults you or says something that hurts your feelings. Your immediate reaction is to get angry or become defensive or mope and obsess about what the customer said. You get hooked by your hurt, and you are no longer focused on your intention—to be a blessing to the customer. The same thing happens in families. Your teenager is sullen and does not appreciate all the efforts you have made on his or her behalf. Immediately, you say something to them that makes a bad situation worse, that flies in the face of your intention to help them feel like they matter.

Focusing and consciously applying intention is a critical principle and skill in the WDM. To move in the right direction, we should focus on the beacon of intention. We can harness unconscious intent by paying close attention to our desired outcomes. We can then apply our intention consciously toward these desired outcomes. When things go wrong, we ask what we have unconsciously intended so we can raise our awareness and focus anew on consciously intending a desired result. We speak of looking to results to identify unconscious intentions. If our intention is unclear, we look around to see our results, creating our intention in every moment. Focusing on intent helps us be more successful salespeople, parents, and human beings.

One of the most dangerous traps for salespeople is based on our fear, feeling like we must win at all costs. Think stereotypical sales guy—a real estate wheeler-dealer or a high-pressure insurance salesperson. They must prove themselves every moment. Failure is not an option. This is a dangerous worldview for all of us. I am not saying we shouldn't strive to win, since that's how I built my business, but I also know that we have an internal and external locus of control. Externally, we drive ourselves to succeed. But internally, we can be on our own side, believe that we are okay, that we matter, no matter what. This gives us an inner calm, even when storms are raging outside or even inside of us. In my life, this ability to remain focused on the outcome, calm and secure with who I am, has made a huge difference. I do not have to prove myself all the time, and I don't have to sell with a maniacal obsession. Maybe I lose a sale here or there. Maybe I decide to pass on a sale because I am not the right partner. But I gain much more than I lose because I establish relationships that last.

Finally, this is no more a sales book than the Bible is a self-help guide. Not to compare what I am writing to the most famous book of all time, but both have a deeper purpose. Whether you are reading this to become more successful, or you want to lead a more meaningful life, this book will help you look beneath the surface of your actions.

One of my big revelations involved shifting from a seller to a buyer mentality. I realized that the artificial line I was using to divide sellers and buyers was illusory; my customers were the same as me. We all have feelings and are hurt sometimes. We all have wants and needs. We are all different, and all the same. If I was selling, I wanted to make sure that it was not myself I was selling—that I was not selling to enhance my self-esteem at the expense of serving my customers.

Before this revelation, the seller-buyer relationship was all about me. Give me credit, tell me how good I am, and buy from me. I didn't feel good about myself, and like a child, I needed constant positive reinforcement and affirmation. A very external locus of control.

Then I pivoted, went deeper, and began to connect with people on an interpersonal level. I looked to see if I wanted them. Sometimes, I'd meet with a prospect or a customer, and we wouldn't even talk about business—we'd talk about our families, hobbies, or beliefs. Sometimes, if we talked about business, it would be the five minutes at the end of the conversation.

In many cases, that is when I closed some of my biggest deals. Because we had established a real, meaningful relationship, my customers trusted me, and I trusted them. We could bypass all the distrust that creates obstacles to getting anything done. We wanted to have a real connection and a relationship with each other.

As an electrical engineer by training, I like to think about life as a circuit and recall Ohm's law. It holds that the flow of current is based on voltage and resistance. My philosophy is to identify and reduce the resistance so that the current flows to the most important circuits in my life. Too often, we have so much resistance—emails and texts, urgent issues, fear of failure, stupid arguments, ego clashes—that we never achieve what is most meaningful and important to us. I have learned how to get the current flowing in the right direction, and I'm writing this book to help you manage the flow in the same way.

CHAPTER ONE

A HUMBLING START

People take many different paths to selling. If I had taken a more traditional path to business and sales, I probably wouldn't be writing this book. More to the point, I would still be looking at sales as less important and limited to transactions rather than as integrated with, and inseparable from, life.

Why did I veer off the traditional business path at the beginning of my career? Veered may not be the right word, as it suggests I left this path on my own. In truth, I was inspired to leave it by my wife, Dr. Bob Wright, and my co-voyagers at the Wright Foundation.

Starting Out on the Well-Trodden Path

I was always good at math. Frankly, I was always good at school and consistently recorded top scores on tests. In middle school, I did so well at math that they sent me to the high school for math classes to challenge me. In high school, they had me enroll in math classes at the local university. Despite doing well academically, I was not a nerd. I was the fullback and captain on the football team, ran varsity track as a freshman, and refused to skip a grade or attend a private school that might have given me more scholarly competition but would not have allowed me to play at the same level in football.

I was planning on attending Michigan State University. Everyone in my family—grandparents, parents, aunt, and uncle—had gone there. I applied and was accepted. Then my father suggested I talk to his brother, my uncle Loring, about my future. During our conversation, my uncle, who worked at General Motors, helped me map out a nine-year plan. First, he said, you are good at math, so obtain an engineering degree. Next, work for a few years and then go back to school and get your MBA so you can become a consultant and write your own ticket.

That sounded good to me, and I decided to buck the family trend and applied late to a superior engineering program at the University of Michigan. I was accepted into the honors college and eventually switched to an electrical engineering major and graduated summa cum laude.

Aside from my contrarian decision to attend the University of Michigan, my life was going according to plan. But after a summer interning at General Motors and being exposed to a lot of engineers and engineering work, I decided that a career in engineering was too dry and dull. I needed a field where I could spend more time with other people and less time with diagrams and numbers. I moved to Chicago and began working for a consulting firm, and this was my first exposure to sales—this was also my first opportunity to use my engineering degree. I developed an environmental database that we sold to law firms.

After a few years as a consultant, I completed my academic education, earning my MBA at Northwestern University's Kellogg School of Management. I was following my uncle's plan, and when I graduated, I was ready for its culmination—securing a plum consulting job with a top company. It seemed inevitable that I would receive a great offer from a great organization, and when I did, I was prepared to accept it.

But something happened just as I was beginning my MBA—the Wright Foundation.

A Broken "Wanter"

Call it fate or call it my soon-to-be wife Gertrude's influence, but I was encouraged to leave my preset path based on a chance meeting. During Gertrude's search for an apartment to rent, she and her roommate visited a place owned by a man named Stan Smith. Though they didn't end up renting the place from him, they did strike up a conversation. Stan was running a growing business similar to the one where Gertrude and I met, litigation consulting, and he needed help. After talking to Gertrude, Stan realized that her expertise matched his firm's needs, and he said he might be hiring soon. One month later, he hired Gertrude.

When Stan learned that Gertrude and I planned to get married, he told her that, as a divorced guy, he had one piece of advice for her, "Work on your communication skills." He told her that he knew a guy, Dr. Bob Wright, who was great at helping people learn to communicate better and that we should see him.

When Gertrude told me about Dr. Bob, my response was succinct: "No effin' way!"

I was a confident, ambitious twenty-three-year-old, and the last thing I wanted to do was get involved in touchy-feely stuff (which is what this sounded like to my younger self). I asked Gertrude if she wanted to do this because she had some awful skeletons in her closet and needed a therapeutic setting to reveal them. Of course, this wasn't her motivation, but at my young age, I couldn't imagine why any "normal" person would seek therapy.

Gertrude is the best salesperson in our family, and despite my protestations, she convinced me to go with her to see Dr. Bob. During that first meeting, I sat there with my arms crossed over my chest as if I could protect myself from whatever penetrating insights Dr. Bob offered. And he did offer those insights, even though on the surface, I refused to betray any enthusiasm or interest in what he was saying. In the back of my mind, I was wondering how he could possibly know so much about me? How could he be so right in his analysis of who I was?

Rich was the most unabashed, cocky person I had ever met. He came from money, he had a guaranteed job in the family business if he wanted it, and he was a former star football player and a genius to boot. So, here was this arrogant little ass. My response to his cross-armed, self-important posture was to laugh at him. Rich wasn't used to someone laughing at him, and that got his attention. I talked about what happens in a marriage and what you have to do if you want to have a great relationship. I got some family history from him, and it became clear that Rich was unconsciously trying to recreate his family history in the present, and his family history was not something he wanted to recreate. Eventually, Rich's dedication to not recreating his family helped him change; as a child he was conditioned to act in a certain way, and he discovered how to escape from how he was conditioned to do what he yearned to do, following a path of growing integrity.

During this meeting, we talked about our upcoming wedding and how we envisioned the ceremony. Dr. Bob asked me what type of ceremony would make me happy, and I said that I was fine with anything that made Gertrude happy. Dr. Bob did not accept that answer. Again, he asked what would make me happy. I responded that I would be happy if the guests had a good time and if Gertrude had a good time.

Like so many guys, I was incapable of articulating my wants if it wasn't a job, money, sports, or some other object, like a car or a sexy watch. I was not in touch with my internal drive, or what I later came to understand as my yearnings. I could only relate to my external desires. Dr. Bob's wife and partner, Dr. Judith Wright, was also a coach, resource, and mentor for me. She termed my condition a "broken wanter." Later,

I understood that this condition was related to my early family life, where I grew up in a chaotic household with fighting parents who eventually divorced. As a child, I thought that if I got good grades and didn't cause any problems, I could keep my mom and dad from getting divorced. But I did not have that power.

I was in a reactive mode, trying not to create a marriage that would end up in divorce like my parents. I thought that anger was bad because I never saw anger constructively resolved in my parents' marriage. So I avoided anger, and conflict, and would not even talk to Gertrude about any of the tougher situations we began to encounter. Dr. Bob was encouraging me to have a proactive vision of what the wedding—and by extension, our marriage—could be.

The reactive mode Rich described causes our unconscious mind to recreate the very things we seek to avoid. Think of the many children who have said they would never be like their parents until they have their own children and begin hearing their parents' words coming out of their mouths.

While I was resistant to what Dr. Bob was telling us, it resonated with Gertrude, and she began attending Wright's transformation labs. I waited until after our wedding when I was accepted to Kellogg and left my job to join a development lab and start doing my personal growth. I had run out of excuses for avoiding the labs. At first, my motivation was competitive—if Gertrude could do this, so could I.

Gertrude's growing communication and engagement ability disturbed Rich. He feared being left behind. With his usual drive, he began additional individual training and learning laboratory groups. In them, he could dig into his unconscious limitations and received assignments challenging his limiting beliefs and expanding his ability to think, feel, and act in more effective ways.

The Most Challenging Assignment

As I took courses at Northwestern and bolstered my business knowledge, I also furthered my social and emotional intelligence and my "personal growth" education at Wright. At that time, I thought of this growth work in the same category as an economics course. It was a subject to master and nothing more—a degree to hang on the wall, another accomplishment. In the labs, I blew through assignments with a "that's done, what's next" attitude.

Until Dr. Bob gave me a non-assignment assignment.

Rich completed his personal development and social emotional assignments at an unprecedented pace. His drive to perform caused him to miss the point of many of the assignments by reducing them to behavioral and not internal skills. He was furious when I told him that he had not learned to enjoy life. He hadn't even considered enjoyment as a skill. "You now have a vacation from assignments," I told him. "Instead, you have to come into the lab every week and report to us on enjoyment and how all this work is changing your life for the better with no assignment or performance outcome to guide you. You must learn to grow from the inside out. If you can't convince us that your life is changing, then you're kicked out of lab." You can imagine how this chronic high achiever took this potential "failure."

Though I thought my lab leader was an asshole for giving me this task, it catalyzed an epiphany: There is a huge difference between completing an assignment and moving on to the next one and learning, growing, and experiencing life.

My perspective began to shift. Before receiving this assignment, I would have told you that life was only about achievement, and that building relationships was not as important as creating positive outcomes. But now, this concept of an adventure and a journey began to take hold. And I began to see what I was missing in life, in each moment and in each interaction.

Do You Want to Be a Real Businessperson?

While receiving my MBA, I considered the possibility of joining the family business. Running the beer distributorship had been an option in my Uncle John's (my mom's brother) long-term plan. It would have been an easy move, but it would not have been the right move for many reasons. Fortunately, my mother had joined the business while I was in school and told me that now was not the right time to return.

Even more fortunate, or so it seemed back then, I had a great job offer from a top company. My impulse was to accept it. Not only was it a great offer, but it also came with a signing bonus. How could I refuse?

Rich came into his leadership group and proudly reported the cherry job offer he had accepted with a top consulting firm and a significant signing bonus to top it off.

He was upset at the question I asked (rather than delivering the anticipated congratulatory communication): Do you want to be a fake businessperson telling real businesspeople what to do, or do you want to be a real businessperson? Though Rich may have been upset by my question, he thought about it seriously. His integrity helped him decide to be a well-rounded business professional and not a high-level slot filler.

I turned down the offer and instead created an ad that I ran in *Crain's Chicago Business*. It advertised that I had just received my Kellogg MBA, and I was looking for a job where I could learn and grow. I approached my job search as if it were a sales job: How many calls am I going to make daily? How many lunches am I going to schedule? How many appointments am I going to make? The first real sales metrics that I ever tracked. I quickly landed a job at a robotics training company, TII Technical Education Systems, where I received as much learning and growth as I could handle.

Over the next few years, my boss asked: "Can you develop an inside sales team? Can you develop an outside sales team? Can you work with a rep network? Can you develop a product?" I did all that and more, including creating a full electrical/electronic training product and an internal company billing system. I also helped the company generate sufficient revenue to become a profitable enterprise—a key goal when I first joined. I could never have experienced these challenges in a big company or as a consultant, like the job offered to me when I graduated.

Rich took advantage of this position to become a real businessman. He was learning business from the bottom up and from side to side. He was well on the way, until his next moment of truth.

The Larger, Deeper Context

Nothing in work, or in your personal life, happens in a vacuum. My various transitions—from single guy to husband, from husband to parent, from salesperson to sales manager—depended on my awareness of all my limiting beliefs and unconscious choices. I learned how to access these issues at Wright, and I'd like to share some of what I learned. In this way, I can put my growth and development in context that supported my awakenings and growth.

As I've noted, I started attending classes at Wright when I was getting my MBA. In the early 1990s, I took Wright's Men's Basic Training workshop. One of its premises was that a new and old model of manhood existed. I recognized that I was rooted in the old model, where men were supposed to be tough and stoic, never show feelings, and never admit that they are afraid. This old model didn't work in relationships because you couldn't talk about your feelings, and you repressed the hurt, anger, and shame roiling inside of you. At the same time, Gertrude was working on her own empowerment as a woman with Dr. Judith Wright and the women of SOFIA (Society of Femininity in Action) and coleading the Woman's Essential Experience with Dr. Judith. Women labor under a limiting model of womanhood—they were supposed to be "nice" and not be overly sensitive or express how they feel. The new model at SOFIA encourages women to be assertive and authentic.

As I became more aware of the old model's limitations, I started running the Men's Basic Training weekends. I became more aware of my feelings and learned how to assess how and why I was feeling something moment to moment. This is where I gained true understanding and began to use the Wright Developmental Model as a map for self-awareness. With awareness, I had choice and gained a great deal of power and understanding. I could see a room differently. I could understand where I and other people were coming from. In the past, I had not wanted to talk about my internal conflicts. I tried to avoid certain subjects, and I saw why I sidestepped them.

My parents fought, and they eventually divorced. I didn't want to engage in the same type of fights that doomed their relationship. Of course, it wasn't the fighting that doomed them but deeper issues—like not fighting for something of value and a lack of responsibility. I began to change as I learned more about myself; I became more compassionate toward others because I was more compassionate toward myself.

Rich was learning to observe himself more deeply and saw patterns emerging that disturbed him. He committed to consciousness in response to his father's alcoholism, as the following resolution indicates.

I had my last drink in 1994. Right before then, I had been traveling for work in Mexico. TII Technical Education Systems sent me and a colleague to Mexico City for two weeks to attend a trade show and support our distributor in the area. Our distributor was a great host, wining and dining us. The trade show, too, was a success, though more like the US auto shows of thirty years ago—it featured sexy women in tight dresses at the various booths.

We did a lot of drinking during our time in Mexico. Remember, I was a guy who was trying to avoid feeling his feelings and his aloneness. Drinking helped me achieve this goal. One night when we went out drinking with our host, he told me that I needed to "have a wife" in Mexico. I explained that I was married, but he kept insisting I needed to have a wife here, and that he had a wife in Mexico and another one in Cuba. We were drinking a lot of beer, I was lonely, and then my host introduced me to a beautiful woman who was at the trade show.

Fortunately, nothing happened, but I realized that it could have, especially after a few drinks. I was behaving as close to unconsciously as is possible for a walking, talking human being to behave. On the flight back to Chicago, I became extremely anxious after thinking about what could have happened. On top of that, my wife and I were supposed to attend a Wright Soft Addiction retreat in Wisconsin when I returned, and that was the last thing I wanted to do. I was embarrassed by my behavior, didn't want to talk about my drinking, and had broken the twenty-four-hour drinking rule (not to drink within twenty-four hours of the start of the retreat). I prayed for a flight cancellation.

Nonetheless, I made it to Wisconsin and attended the retreat, promising myself that I would bury this experience deep in the "vault" and not talk to anyone about it. On Sunday, after the retreat ended, I was driving back with my wife and said, "I've got to tell you something." The weekend had made me aware of my addictions, and my lying, and the hypocrisy of participating in a soft addictions weekend while not sharing addictions of my own. I related the story of being lonely and putting myself in a potentially bad situation. I said that nothing happened, but that the drinking made me vulnerable to doing the wrong thing. And I was drinking to avoid my feelings and acting out.

As I talked more openly about my drinking, I realized that it had been an excuse for my bad behavior over time. At times I would get aggressive in bars and be an asshole and pick fights. At my bachelor party, I was wrestling with many of my friends and trying to dominate them, until one friend stood up to me and elbowed me in the face, giving me a black eye the week before my wedding. Drinking was an excuse for me to let my anger loose. These fights happened more than once. Luckily, no one had beat me to a bloody pulp, since I always seemed to choose opponents who were much bigger than I was.

After my talk with my wife and thinking about my issues with drinking, I resolved to give it up. My wife's mother is a recovering alcoholic, my father was an alcoholic, and many of his brothers were alcoholics—this was a problem in my family. I committed not only to stop drinking but also to live a more conscious life.

Up until then, I focused on external goals: "I'll graduate from the best electrical engineering undergraduate program and get a diploma; I'll go to Kellogg and get an MBA." It was all external rather than internal. I was journeying to the place that I had been running away from. I wanted to show everyone that, unlike my dad, I was successful. In that struggle to prove myself, I had lost sight of what was really important.

Rich was working to get everything over with rather than enjoying the journey. Living life fully, and as an adventure, was the new goal. This episode was a critical turning point toward establishing it. Think back to the difficult no-assignment assignment and how hard it was for Rich. Learning to pause, really pause and bring ourselves fully into the here and now is a challenge for all of us. When we learn to embrace the fullness of being, our doing takes on greater depth. This is an ongoing lesson for Rich, a major theme of his journey.

During this time, Dr. Bob read me an allegorical children's story called *Hope for the Flowers* by Trina Paulus. It's about a caterpillar that attempts to climb a pillar of caterpillars. All are climbing over each other, not knowing what is at the top but compelled to keep climbing. The caterpillar derives no joy from the repeated attempts to get higher but continues to climb. It ends only when he discovers that he can create a cocoon and be transformed into a butterfly who can soar higher than any climbing creature. It was a hard lesson for me to learn that it isn't about climbing the caterpillar pillar but about being true to ourselves and becoming the most loving human beings we can become. I was the caterpillar, and as my consciousness rose, so too did my vision of what life and my role in it could be.

> *"Tell me, sir, what is a butterfly?"*
> *"It's what you are meant to become. It flies with beautiful wings and joins the earth to heaven. It drinks only nectar from the flowers and carries the seeds of love from one flower to another. Without butterflies, the world would soon have few flowers."*
>
> —**Trina Paulus,** *Hope for the Flowers*

Knowing When to Leave ... and What to Leave For

I had learned so much over the preceding three years. It was only in such a small business that I could have written the enterprise-wide software, created the marketing strategy and program, developed the inside sales team, expanded the independent representative network, and helped the company become profitable. At the end of this time, I had taken a week of vacation from my job to participate in a leadership training at Wright. I was learning a lot that applied directly to my job—about teamwork, about social and emotional intelligence, about leadership, and about who I was and what motivated me. I wanted to extend the vacation for another week to go deeper into my learnings. When I requested the extension, my boss said no.

Rich consulted his leadership group about what he should do after his boss told him no. We did an inventory of what he had learned and asked ourselves what else was there to learn at this company. Was his job done? We questioned where his greatest growth opportunity resided. We revisited the question from three years earlier, "Do you want to be a fake businessperson telling real businesspeople what to do, or do you want to be a real businessperson?" If he was serious, only one choice would suffice.

My job at TII Technical Education Systems was done. I had contributed to the success of the firm in many ways and learned all that I could. It was time to move on. I made a values-based decision, an assertive one, to find a place that challenged me even more.

This is a point where many may hurt themselves by reacting. Rich avoided this "reactivity." Sure, he was angry. And he could easily have stayed and complained like a victim or stomped off in a rage. He had worked on his anger and moved beyond what we call reactivity to assertion and began looking for the next challenge and lesson in his development.

I told my boss I was staying at the training for another week. I'm sure he wasn't pleased, but he also recognized that I had made major contributions to the company and that I was leaving it in good shape. I was much better off spending the week on the training than another year at the company. I was confident I made the right, though difficult, choice, given what I was learning and how I was being challenged. My wife and my close friends were supportive of my decision.

In our leadership group, we identified what was next for me: direct sales. In the past, I had managed and developed sales teams and helped to sell deals. But I had never done sales personally—never "carried a bag" so to speak. It was a major transition, and to some a step backward. But I was committed to learning and growing and becoming a true businessman. And sales was what was next.

To take that step, I needed to take a leap of faith and learn to trust. I had to choose to trust my own capabilities and trust that I would find my next right job. I had to embrace my fear, believe I possessed the skills to succeed in an area where I lacked experience, and use my intention to find that next learning environment. This step required humility to take a sales position with a significantly lower salary, especially after getting my MBA and being a company's director of marketing and sales.

Most of us fail to see how many of our plans stem from our fear of the unknown. Learning to risk in the face of the unknown was a challenge for Rich—it represented an unpredictable collection of fear and pain from his early childhood. Fear is the foundational emotion that leads to distrust and living limited lives. He did a lot of exercises to face the unknown and trust life in his growth work. A key lesson for him in trusting came as he had assignments to intentionally look bad and make mistakes—breaking personal rules and challenging unconscious limiting beliefs. He learned from these that the world is more accepting and forgiving than he feared.

The Transition to Complete Businessman—Life Is Sales Begins

Sales was something other people did. It was beneath Rich. Early on he was intent on becoming a consultant or some other type of business leader. If I had even suggested he consider sales at this time, he would have dismissed my suggestion as crazy. When Rich told our leadership group that he had received a consulting offer, and we asked him if he wanted to be a real or fake businessperson, that wounded his ego. This was the catalyst for him to develop his humility as a businessman. Sales would soon develop his humility further.

I had a plan from the time I was in college, and it certainly did not include selling. At Northwestern University, I was in the number one MBA program, and most of my classmates wanted to be in marketing or brand management or consulting. I could have cruised through the more technical, financial-oriented program at the University of Chicago, but I thought I needed the marketing and brand thought leadership skills that Northwestern provided. Not that I liked everything about the program. I had an engineering and math background, and I hated all the group projects and some of the subjective aspects that were part of the curriculum. It was out of my comfort zone, though that's part of the reason I went there. I used to argue with professors about the touchy-feely aspects of the program: "How could you give me that grade?" It was so subjective, and I was rational and objective, believing there was always one right answer that math or logic would identify.

You might have thought I would have learned the value of sales because of our family business—the largest Anheuser-Busch beer distributorship in Michigan. If you think that, you don't understand the beer distributor business. We were the largest distributor in the state of Michigan, selling the number one brand in the state of Michigan: Budweiser.

Rich was not ready to sell in part because, during his MBA program, he was focused on getting top grades, not on relationship building. It was difficult to imagine anyone wanting to buy something from him. He was cocky and arrogant, and that's why I focused on fostering his social and emotional development. It wasn't until he took the job at the technical training organization that he got his first taste of business relationship challenges as he built its call center. He was beginning to see sales challenges from a management viewpoint.

I ran the sales and marketing groups at TII, but I didn't have to sell. I did learn how difficult it was to run an inside sales group, where the salespeople were around my mother's age, and I had to try to break the beliefs that were holding them back.

Rich was so upset by their way of backbiting and bickering that he felt like he wanted to kill them. Their infighting and complaining irritated him to no end. They would give Rich every excuse in the world to explain why they weren't selling as much as they could.

I also had to manage an independent external rep network, which was another challenge because they don't work directly for you.

I was waiting for Rich to become a salesperson. This was the first time in his life that he got a feel for how important sales was to a company. His lessons of trust and social emotional intelligence came into focus here, and sales accelerated his life lessons.

I still did not realize that every successful businessperson knows how to sell, or should know. They may not sell products and services, but they must sell the people they work with and lead them so they work together and do their jobs. I had an MBA from a top school, and what MBAs do is run stuff, which is exactly what I was doing. I was managing people, so I knew that we had to sell more to be successful, that we needed our inside reps to generate more leads. I knew the impact of selling, but I didn't see myself actually doing it.

People don't know what they don't know until they're beyond what they know. During this time, Rich had a holistic view into every aspect of a business. As a result, he could no longer deny the importance of sales. When he and the head of the company parted ways, he asked me what was next. That's when I said, "If you're serious about being a businessperson, you have to learn to sell."

This had never come up before. This was the first time Dr. Bob and I spoke about my role in sales. It wasn't until much later that I developed my theory and practice of sales and began applying it to all aspects of my life. But without being aware of it, I was already engaged in selling. I created the *Crain's* ad that helped sell a company on hiring me. I developed a training product and sold people on using it. But it was only when I asked, "What's next?" that I was willing to consider selling as something that I might actually do as a job and something that I might learn to do well.

Wright Developmental Model (WDM) Takeaways

- Be able to identify your fear and make friends with it (Level 1). We all have fears. Fear sets limits on what we can and cannot do in relationships, tasks, and even our self-esteem. If you don't identify your fears, you will never understand and expand your limits by addressing these fears (like asking for the close or the raise).

- Choose to trust (Level 1). You choose trust by doing the things you are afraid of—using your fear to indicate the next level or skill to master by stepping into the discomfort of your fear. For some, the fear is public speaking. For others, asking someone out. Some people fear just saying what they want—remember me and my broken "wanter" behavior. I ignored a lot of fears that needed to be expressed. I needed to pursue my wants and not leave that work to my wife, Gertrude.

- Believe in yourself and your capabilities. Be on your own side (Level 2). To be on your own side, you must develop an internal dialogue that encourages you. Rather than criticizing, opt for supporting—a skill we can all stand to develop.

- Identify your anger and reactivity (Level 3). The function of anger is to get away from danger and pain or to acquire a desired outcome. For me, being angry means being vulnerable. Most of us see anger as effective in sports but do not know how to use it effectively in love and business. I worked hard just to identify my anger since my entire persona was to act like I was above everything.

- Use your anger to assert your will and be intentional in terms of what you want and get it (Level 3). Think of situations where you are frustrated and angry. See if you can harness the anger to stay in a relationship with others and get what you want—a skill that will serve you mightily if you have not already mastered it.

CHAPTER TWO

FROM NOVICE TO SUPER SALESMAN: BECOMING COACHABLE

Searching for a sales job represented a major change in my life, the start of a transformation that is ongoing today. At the time, I was focused on finding an organization that would give me the chance to learn how to sell. Though I had experience managing salespeople, I'd never had to call on customers, experience rejection, demonstrate resilience, and find a way to close a sale—and then do it all over again the next day. I was never accountable to a personal quota, and I was never dependent on commission as a major part of my income.

In my life and my career, I had never experienced significant failure. As a salesperson, I was about to encounter repeated failures on the way to success. It was all part of winning in sales—no failure, no success.

Finding the Right Place to Sell

I began networking, looking for people in the tech industry who might have a connection to a company where I might learn how to sell. Tech seemed to be the right industry since I had a degree in electrical engineering. It was also the mid-1990s when the tech industry was taking off. With my MBA from Kellogg and work experience at the technical training firm, I was an attractive job candidate.

I interviewed at Whittman-Hart, one of the fastest-growing consulting firms in the Chicagoland area at the time. It had multiple practice areas in tech-related fields. They had an IBM products group, did Oracle and SAP enterprise resource planning (ERP) implementations, custom software development and networking, and so on. Importantly, the company was transitioning from a "body shop" (also referred to as staff augmentation) to a solutions-oriented sales organization. The former type literally provides bodies with desired skills for customer companies, which they manage, helping to build or support existing or new systems. A solutions-type company goes beyond staff augmentation to offer strategies, tactics, and other value-added services. And part of this value-add includes taking responsibility for the results and success of the project.

When I began the job at Whittman-Hart, I was unaware of a key piece of information. The company had never developed a new salesperson from the "outside" successfully. And, it did not have a sales manager. Not knowing these facts, it seemed like an attractive position because, as Dr. Bob pointed out to me, Whittman-Hart was one of the IT consulting organizations that invested in training. I was more likely to learn at Whittman-Hart than at other places. And learning how to sell was the goal. I met the CEO, Bob Bernard, negotiated more vacation time up front (I had learned my lesson), and took the job.

I had coached a key Whittman-Hart staff member from the time it only had twelve employees. The company saw the quality of its consultants as a key differentiator. As a result, it invested in ongoing technical training to ensure it continued to have the best consulting staff possible. Little did I know then that that dedication did not extend to sales employees.

The formal company training was fine. I spent two weeks attending a new employee orientation, one week learning all the practices and offerings, and one week on selling. I was good at absorbing information and problem-solving. After the company provided us with tools and data to help us sell, we conducted a role-playing exercise to demonstrate what we had learned. I remember being in a room with a video camera focused on me, the teachers and my colleagues watching from another room. I had to come up with a solution based on the situation the "customer" was describing. It was pressure-packed. I later learned that it's easier to deal with a real customer than to have peers watching your every move.

Our organization turned us loose after that initial training, and we received little support or guidance thereafter. The company gave us some accounts and told us to make calls and schedule meetings. Initially, the company's CEO was managing sales, and his feedback was limited to "Good week" if you had three or more meetings or "Schedule more meetings" if you had fewer than three. This feedback was written on a weekly calendar printout and put in your physical mailbox—no pipeline reviews and no other metrics to track or report on, just the requisite three meetings. We also had a highly ambitious dollar sales quota to meet, but in terms of daily or weekly feedback or support, there was almost none.

While the company gave novice salespeople an account list, these accounts were generally the worst ones. Of course, this is every salesperson's lament. If you have ever seen the David Mamet play or movie, *Glengarry Glen Ross*, you'll recall one of the salespeople, Shelley Levene, complaining, "The leads are weak." The complaint? The senior salespeople had all the good accounts locked up, whether they were working on them or not.

Unexpectedly, finding three people weekly who would agree to meet with me was daunting. At the Wright development sessions outside of work, we had a sales support group with participants like me who worked for a variety of organizations. One guy sold insurance, another financial services, a third carpet cleaning, and so on. We began to set goals around "dials" (calls made or emails sent in a day or week), contacts, and meetings scheduled. We held competitions among ourselves, with financial and other consequences for winners and losers. We competed against each other, as individuals, and as teams, setting new goals every two weeks and tracking performance. In this way, we ensured accountability for our sales efforts.

I had outsourced my sales training and support and accountability to Dr. Bob and the sales group. They were pushing me past my resistance and the low company activity expectations, especially the three-meetings-per-week goal. I thought three meetings were a lot, but Don Delves, a member of the group, helped me shift my perspective when he said, "Everyone has to eat breakfast and lunch every day. That's ten meetings a week."

We also worked on changing our perspective on relationships and connecting with people. Typically, salespeople focus on one individual per account. We explored the value of meeting multiple people in a given account. Not only do multiple contacts in an account help you provide better customer service, but they also help you establish deeper and stronger connections with a customer. What if you only have one point of contact, and that individual leaves the company? We looked at how to create three-by-three-by-three relationships—connections with three different people at three different levels and in three different departments in a company. Instead of being satisfied with selling one thing to one person, you could open up a variety of selling opportunities by creating a diverse group of connections. And the warmest leads are always existing clients.

Everything we do at Wright is based on assignments geared to reveal and challenge limiting beliefs. Most of us have many limiting beliefs about sales, and one of our Wright sales lab assignments addresses this. The journey began with a gum-selling competition; sell as many sticks of gum as you can, in as many ways, for at least twenty-five cents a stick. Initially, Rich's fellow lab participants outsold him, and he resisted the assignment. But then his competitive nature kicked in, and he embraced the activity. Another early assignment was to get people to give you things. Like most people, Rich feared being judged and failing. Again, Rich denied his fear and saw this as beneath him and resisted, even as other participants with far less education or business experience carried out the assignment with sometimes spectacular results—a carpet cleaning salesman without any college education was given thousands of dollars of goods, from a car to home appliances.

Another assignment was to explore your beliefs about sales and to create a job history. Rich needed to examine his limiting beliefs about sales and about people. He saw the world as one of challenges, a dog-eat-dog competitive environment. This was far from the friendly, loving world of affiliation and rapport he was to build years later.

At Whittman-Hart, though, Rich's struggle was psychological—the company's three-meetings-a-week goal posed a significant barrier. He did not have the network that the other longtime industry professionals possessed—a network that allowed them to walk the halls of businesses like Boise Cascade or United Airlines and just take orders for programmers. He resisted our repeated suggestions to set up more meetings.

We had to push him for one meeting a day, and he was psychologically blocked from reaching that goal consistently—after all, he thought, setting up a single daily meeting exceeded the goal for everyone else in the company. However, what he learned was that it was not a level playing field. His colleagues possessed many great contacts to his none. To say he was resistant is an understatement. Like other salespeople, Rich would minimize activity unless a greater fear like being fired caused him to up his game. There were guys in our group making seventy-five dials a day and going to many meetings daily. Marty Goldman, the carpet cleaning salesperson, was a tornado of activity, meeting with prospects at least three times a day (as a note, we have used first names only when we do not use a person's real name in the narrative).

People in the group were challenging me to have more meetings. I tried to explain that our company only asked us to have three, that it just was not part of our culture to have a larger number. Then, the CEO promoted a buddy of his to take his place as the sales manager. He'd started with me in my sales training class, and he started to pay more attention to metrics and numbers. I was not doing that well, and the new sales manager let me know it. I was on the bubble, and he threatened to put me on a plan—a performance improvement plan (PIP as we used to say).

I knew I had to do something differently. My reality shifted. Fear kicked in, and I really started listening to what people in the Wright sales support group were telling me.

And then, I had a breakthrough. I finally saw how sales was about activity. It was about metrics and tracking that activity. I began doing more dials than I had ever done before; up to five hundred every week. We had established a dashboard in our sales support group, and I became a beast about tracking my numbers, recognizing this was the key to success. The breakthrough also involved the number of meetings I scheduled. Instead of three meetings a week, I scheduled five. Then I ramped that up and even had five meetings in one day.

The breakthrough, though, really occurred as I was driving to meet with a client on the north side of Chicago, Outboard Marine Corporation. As I drove, I passed numerous industrial parks with the names of many companies on the side of each building. I thought: Holy crap, look at all these potential customers! I'd pass a sign, pull into the parking lot, and call the number of each company: "Hello," I'd say, "I'm on the way to see my customer at Outboard Marine, so I'm in the neighborhood. Do you have fifteen minutes to see me?"

Some of them said yes. Sometimes we'd meet in their lobby, and they'd give me those minutes to tell them about what I was offering. Now, I didn't want to be a door-to-door salesman. Who does? But this was working.

The day Rich scheduled five meetings using the door-to-door method—seeing names on billboards while driving and calling the featured companies—was the day he challenged his limiting beliefs about success and discovered what working efficiently and effectively really was. He was on the way to tapping his full potential as a businessperson and salesperson, using his challenges and sales to continually stretch his potential and challenge his limiting beliefs.

This was likely the beginning of Rich's awareness of the possibility of sales to stretch himself and fulfill his potential—life is sales. He would go on to realize how part of his leadership was actually selling, even selling himself. In his marriage and parenting, he realized that selling was all about creating mutual benefit for others and achieving his desired outcomes while meeting the desires of others.

My thought processes shifted—if I could do five meetings in one day, maybe I could do twenty-five in a week. From that point on, everything started working. I had one success after another, and within five years I was promoted to sales manager.

Learn from the Masters

I would be remiss if I didn't acknowledge two individuals who modeled the selling behaviors that I adopted and adapted: Jack Duffy and Cadi Nones. They'd take me on calls, and I'd observe them in action. This wasn't company policy. Nor was it my policy; I didn't want to ask one of the company's star salespeople if I could tag along. Dr. Bob, however, encouraged me to overcome my resistance. Fortunately, I heeded his advice, and my time with Jack and Cadi turned into on-the-job training that was more helpful than any classroom exercise.

Jack took me on a sales call to one of his customers, Boise Cascade. When we entered the office building, Jack walked down the hall and seemed to know every single employee he passed, calling out their names, asking questions about work and family, telling jokes. He knew everyone's stories, and sometimes he'd stop and engage in conversations with people as if they were old friends. He would even play golf with them.

This was completely foreign to my experience.

Jack introduced Rich to relationship and organizational depth and to a much deeper idea of sales as interpersonal, meaningful relationships. Rich had never considered that, in sales, he could go beyond being trustworthy to friendship. He was on the way to developing lifelong friendships and deep mutually beneficial partnerships—even with industry competitors. Respect and caring became his new approach. He learned to enjoy relationships and selling became a result—not the narrow aim of relationship.

I never realized that I could have a real relationship with customers, that I could tell them jokes and talk about our kids together. If people needed something at Jack's accounts, they would immediately call Jack rather than anyone else. They trusted him implicitly. He basically lived at his accounts, even had an office there, and it paid off. I had perceived the seller-customer relationship to be purely transactional, and Jack helped me learn that it could exist at a deeper level.

Ultimately, Jack's approach became outdated at Whittman-Hart, which had switched from selling staffing to becoming a solutions-focused organization. For all of Jack's brilliance at creating strong relationships, he didn't have a lot of experience doing strategic plans and solutioning for customers. Customers began expecting more from Jack and the other salespeople at Whittman-Hart than just bodies. This transition to a new way of operating and selling was difficult for people like Jack, accustomed to the previous approach.

Cadi was my other mentor. She took me to one of her accounts, and we were sitting in the lobby waiting for a meeting. I stared into the distance and looked at a magazine, anxious for the prospect to arrive and nervous about how the meeting would go. From the moment we checked in and I sat down, however, Cadi was on her phone. She must have made at least ten calls in the five minutes we were waiting. One after the other, she followed up on earlier exchanges of information, set up additional meetings, answered questions. When our customer came out to get us, she was in the middle of a conversation: "Sorry," she said, "I have to step into a meeting, but I'll call you back as soon as I'm done."

I watched her and thought to myself, "You've got to be kidding me." Cadi was an animal when it came to dials. From her, I learned the value of maximizing your time. If you could make ten calls in five minutes, think what you could do in a spare sixty minutes per week or 240 minutes per month. Potentially, you could increase your dials by thousands monthly!

In the Wright sales support group was a guy named Marty. Like Cadi, he took dials to another level. He would sit in the bathtub, the yellow pages in one hand and a phone in the other, and he would make hundreds of calls. If he could have made calls in his sleep, he would have. Again, I saw how an unwavering commitment to metrics and numbers and making calls and setting up meetings could pay off.

Rich was beginning to learn that sales is first a numbers game and that skill does not replace numbers. But numbers caused him to develop skill and to sell a lot more. He became the most diligent numbers tracker I have ever trained—even in his future as a CEO.

My realization about numbers helped solidify something that Dr. Bob talked about—how our minds create artificial barriers to performance. I resolved to break through my barriers, making activity my number one goal. I started tracking everything I did—every dial, every contact, every meeting, every opportunity. I compiled a ton of data, and I knew to the nth decimal point how much every dial and every meeting was worth.

Dr. Bob became my unofficial sales manager, offering the guidance that I wasn't receiving at Whittman-Hart. We did pipeline reviews, strategized about accounts, and set up next steps. Members of my sales support group would motivate me by having contests: Tim Brennan, a member of the group, and I used to bet that whoever made the most dials would receive a free lunch from the other.

One of the dangers in sales—and in all areas of life—is magical thinking. How many times have you heard someone say, "I'm going to do better tomorrow … or next week … or next year"? Salespeople do this all the time, resolving to double their sales. Resolve is great, but it's nonsensical to think that you can double your sales without doubling your activity or having some strategic breakthrough. I used to tell my salespeople what each of their dials was worth—I had calculated it down to the penny—and I'd show them on paper how many more dials and meetings they needed to do if they wanted to double their sales.

At that point in my career, I was a beast in terms of the metrics. And it helped me become one of Whittman-Hart's top salespeople and eventually, the sales manager over the largest and most successful territory in the country.

It seemed like the sky was the limit. At least it did until the bottom fell out.

Whittman-Hart made a major acquisition in 1999. It merged with another company, USWeb/CKS, and renamed itself marchFIRST. It had gone from a $30 million to a $1 billion company during my tenure. At the time, we had a great deal of Year 2000 (Y2K) and dot.com business. But the dot.com bubble burst suddenly, and Y2K turned out to be a lot of prep for nothing. The company had also spent a lot of time in the preceding years acquiring expensive real estate, and it had spent money in other ways—for starters, simply changing the name to marchFIRST cost the company around $50 million.

One year after the name change, marchFIRST went bankrupt. It was a shock. I and others had significant shares in the company, and we had never sold them because we believed in the company vision. It was inconceivable that the vision would not be realized. Then, overnight, our shares were worth nothing, and we were all out of work.

Looking back, it's clear that the company was ahead of its time. It took a more holistic approach to selling than other competitors—an approach that was ill-timed because of the dot.com bust. Even the intention of the acquisition, the combination of an IT consulting firm and a network of creative agencies, was ahead of its time. I ended the Whittman-Hart era with a much better understanding of sales—and myself.

WDM Takeaways

- Learn to trust your metrics (Level 1). This is more difficult than you think. Use your fear as motivation to act, not as an excuse to hide out. Translating numbers to behaviors facilitates this process. First, recognize that the numbers need to be accurate—trust yourself to keep good numbers. Second, hold yourself accountable to numbers like dials when there is not a one-to-one correlation between any one action and result. As I say, "Activity begets activity"—we must learn to trust activity and learn to be better as we put in the numbers.

- See sales as an opportunity for engagement (Level 2). Recognize that you can create stronger, deeper connections when you establish relationships with several people at a company rather than just your primary contact. When fear or hurt shuts us down, we do not see the opportunity for warmth, fulfillment, fun, and, yes, sales. But even if we do not close a deal, we can still be fulfilled by full engagement.

- Be willing to be different and break the mold (Level 4). We easily get addicted to doing what others do—note how I needed to step out of the Whittman-Hart model to succeed. Be willing to seek out supportive people who will hold you accountable and tell you the truth.

- Strive to be your best, and break through your own limiting beliefs (Level 5). Don't accept your own excuses—excuses that gain power when you believe in limitation. Find sales training and coaching that will help you to become your best.

- Use your anger to make breakthroughs and to be your best, not to defend your position or your weaknesses (Level 3). Remember the lessons in intention—use anger to motivate and to get what you want, and not to punish. We do not learn when we turn our anger in on ourselves.

CHAPTER THREE

MANAGING AT A HIGHER LEVEL

When marchFIRST went bankrupt, Andrew "Flip" Filipowski's Divine Interventures acquired it. Flip was outspoken, a deliberately provocative entrepreneur, and a leader in Chicago's technology community. This was the first time I had ever been part of a company that had been acquired. I had also never worked for such a charismatic, outspoken, and high-profile boss in a culture that was far different from the ones I'd previously experienced.

Managing a sales team that sold services from marchFIRST, as well as software and hosting from Divine, was challenging, but I was in a good position to succeed. After acquiring marchFIRST, Divine also bought a hosting company, a departure for a company that had previously sold software and now needed to sell services. Unlike the company's other sales managers, I had experience with both. I was soon leading the most profitable sales group in the company. Though selling services was our primary mission, we ended up selling more software and hosting than the other two groups, which primarily sold software only. We knew an important secret to selling: relationships matter most, not products.

The good news was that, once again, my group was highly successful. The bad news was that Divine was going to suffer the same fate as marchFIRST. At the time, though, I was about to learn another lesson in my life-is-sales journey.

In the high-flying Divine culture, Rich proved to be one of the few multi-skilled, high-level contributors. Joining a product company gave him a view of another sales and management approach. Historically, Rich disdained braggarts. He was reactive to them. He had matured beyond reactivity; his self-possessed style allowed him to operate independently. Divine's braggadocio style motivated him rather than resulted in a great deal of judgment and distance (as it would have in the past). He was amused instead of disgusted and, most importantly, worked even harder to assert his perspective and build the strongest sales team in the company. We call this self-validated intimacy. He was becoming truly independent in his values and way of being.

While some of Divine's executives acted like superstars, they caused Rich to consider how a real business superstar should act, furthering his evolution into a self-effacing superstar. Rich hadn't been an immediate natural as a sales professional. He needed to turn himself inside out to develop his high-level sales skills. Because Rich had invested in his own development, he possessed the knowledge necessary to educate his staff in their personal development for enhanced performance. He was beginning to formulate his vision of a company's learning culture. He was beginning to define his style of business leadership, which included teaching and facilitating staff development.

The Pot Calling the Kettle Black

Divine wanted me to manage and not sell. As a result, I learned what it was like to be responsible for leading a group of salespeople like myself—or at least like I used to be when I first started selling at Whittman-Hart. I experienced an aha! moment that demonstrated to me how far I had come. Salespeople would enter my office and start grousing: "How come David gets all the good leads?" And, "My numbers are down this month because no one knows how much time I have to spend researching companies so I can be prepared for my calls." And one of my favorites, "The delivery team is messing up my project, so I have to hand-hold the client to keep them happy, and I don't have time to prospect."

The pattern of victimhood was uncomfortably familiar. People told me with great sincerity how they were being unfairly treated, how the playing field wasn't level, how they would perform much better if they had better leads, more support, improved products, etc. As I listened to the pile of excuses, I had to admit the truth: They were me. I used to make the same excuses and whine about the same issues. This is a great example of my reactivity coming back to bite me. I had learned a lot about intention and how to get out of victimhood by taking responsibility, and it was time to teach my team the same lesson.

This was a turning point in Rich's development as an intentional salesperson. From this point on, he allowed himself no excuses and became without question the most focused salesperson I have ever coached. Rich and I went on sales calls together for the Wright Foundation. When we were selling to an insurance company, I missed the point of the company's most foundational need and lost credibility in the meeting. Rich stayed on point with them, and the CEO tried to hire him afterward. He was beginning to radiate a confidence in himself that increased customer trust.

As I noted in the last chapter, karma comes back at you. I was now in a position to face what my sales managers had experienced from me in the past. Still, having been there and done that, I was in a good position to coach my people and hold them accountable. I had heard it all before because I had said it all before. One of my salespeople, however, presented a difficult managerial problem. Doug was a prima donna. He was the top salesperson in the company and delivered two and sometimes three times as many sales as other staff. He was a superstar salesperson and acted like it. He was savvy about how to curry favor with the people who could help him—he'd give prized Chicago Cubs tickets to the favored few. Doug was like a big, fast speedboat: impressive to view from afar, but someone who left a wake that would drench those nearby. When we started at Whittman-Hart at the same time, we were both intensely competitive, especially with each other. Once, our rivalry almost led to a fight in the company parking lot.

When I became his sales manager, my point of view shifted. Doug was challenging at times, but his problems ran deeper—he was not a decent human being and could even be brutal to some people. Sure, I understood that he was cocky and had problems, but no amount of coaching and conversation could get him to change. He was verbally abusive, knowing that he could get away with it. Right off the bat, we had a number of skirmishes, but things came to a head when he asked me to fire a fellow salesperson. Doug had been giving Randall a great amount of grief about one thing or another, and finally, Randall was unwilling to tolerate one more abusive word. He said to Doug, "I feel sorry for your children, having to live with someone like you."

Doug stormed into my office and demanded that I fire Randall. I asked him to tell me what happened, and Doug did so with great drama, ending by saying, "I'm the top sales guy here; he can't talk to me that way." I told him I needed to hear both sides of the story, but he said there was no other side to hear, insisting again that I fire Randall. I said I was not going to fire him and that, if he wanted, he could take his case to the human resources department and file a formal complaint.

Doug stormed out of my office with even more anger and frustration than when he entered. He went over my head and negotiated a deal where he no longer had to report to me and got his own office. He was that good and that important to the company. Many years later, after Divine was long gone, my boss, Kevin, apologized to me and admitted that he should never have undermined my authority in this way.

Doug was probably Rich's best teacher, and the way Rich responded to him demonstrated how Rich always chose culture over clothes, being good instead of looking good, and supporting the hard-working team members rather than kissing the self-important superstar butts. Doug was the company's number one performer—he was the clothes. But the culture Rich was trying to build was based on values, and Doug's bullying behavior was antithetical to Rich's values. It takes a lot to get Rich to fight, but when he does, it's about someone violating his values.

Rich was going through a lot of changes during this time. Divine was segueing into consulting. Doug, like Cadi and Jack from Whittman-Hart, was a body shop salesperson. So Doug was struggling not just with other people, but with a larger transition.

Rich was still learning and growing with feedback from his staff. A few of Rich's people were with him from the time when Rich had started selling, and when he tried to coach them out of this victim mentality, they'd say, "The pot doesn't get to call the kettle black." He was facing his own karma once again, and it helped him develop and make difficult decisions in the face of displeasing others. This is Level 3 of the Wright Developmental Model, the level where we learn to harness our anger to conscious positive intent and develop from reactivity to assertiveness. At this level, we react against until we learn to harness the anger in our reactions and drive toward desired outcomes—the same emotion harnessed to a more desirable outcome. Rich had to deal with his own reactivity and his over-identification with his salespeople. He really sympathized with the whining and complaining. He had not yet gotten over his desire to have everyone like him. He was angry at them but did not know how to express it effectively—we call this harnessing his intent. He needed to learn how to use his anger effectively to assert his will and intend positive outcomes—and do it while strengthening his credibility and alliance with his salespeople.

I remember trying to hold people accountable, and one guy saying, "Dude, you know you used to have the same complaints as I do; you used to do the same bitching and moaning." That was a huge wake-up call. I asked myself if I really complained as much as he was suggesting. After examining my past lack of accountability for my actions, I realized it was true. Though I had grown, I still had more growing to do.

I challenged Rich at this point. Until Doug got himself removed from Rich's group, he was lobbing hand grenades into Rich's team, creating all sorts of problems. It was a conundrum: Doug sold a lot, but he also created a lot of counterproductive tumult. It was a question of culture versus volume. Rich was responding, not acting in a reactive mode with Doug. But he never stood up to the guy. He managed Doug at great cost to the culture and his own credibility. It's worth noting that years later, despite Rich's battles with Doug, Doug still liked and respected Rich and even wanted to come work for him. Rich would never allow a hotshot to disrupt his business again until the culture was strong enough to handle a disruptive, self-centered high performer.

However, Rich was still facing his desire to be affirmed over his desire to be satisfied. He had been avoiding other people's anger at a high cost. He saw that cost and did a great deal of internal work to strengthen himself so he could live closer to his values, no matter what others thought. He was developing what we call, "a stronger sense of himself," an internal locus of control. He was starting to be on his own side at new levels. He learned to care about people and serve people without needing them to be nice to him.

And these lessons helped with my relationships at home. Like at work, I needed to hold high expectations for my kids and sell them on operating with self-respect and integrity, especially when they were in victimhood and drama and said they hated me. My values and a certain level of awareness and containment helped me to keep an even keel. Just as my salespeople pointed out my flaws, my children delighted in reminding me that I wasn't perfect and still had gaps to fill. I was hurt by this and had mixed emotions. I liked my children's assertiveness, but in the moment, it was hard to take at times. But I would remember that my job as a dad was to raise contributing members of society, not to be a friend.

Transforming Rather Than Complaining

You don't sell in a vacuum. Every organization has different products, services, policies, and culture. As I was gaining experience as a manager of salespeople, I began to develop a greater appreciation for all the factors that influence individual and sales team effectiveness. I learned not only how to manage someone like Doug who was difficult and whom I hadn't hired, but also someone like Dave Barr, whom I had hired and trained and who became my initial partner in LYONSCG. In the past, I had set sales goals for my people. Even before I hired Dave, he had assessed his accounts and presented me with a plan for how much he thought he could sell. I saw that I did not need to treat all salespeople like children.

Salespeople can be territorial. They guard their accounts fiercely and feel like they have to fight to keep other salespeople from stealing their accounts. Overtly or not, companies condone these attitudes and actions, and, as a result, integrity can be low.

Territoriality can be a reflex—like children at a candy store stuffing themselves and their pockets with more than they can eat—and salespeople are always clamoring for more territory even when they can't handle the territory they already have. One reason Rich was a good sales manager was because he didn't cave to people's demands for more accounts. He put customers first, and he never gave in to internal politics.

As businesses grow, however, the balance between territoriality and empowerment becomes complex. A degree of uncertainty exists about who gets which accounts and what's fair and best. That's when values become paramount.

My approach evolved, and the value of fairness shaped the system I helped to create. Early at Whittman-Hart, I was working in an irrational system: people had their names on more than two hundred accounts and didn't do anything with them. That's why the new salespeople (like me) were so angry. Over time, we created a rational system. We decided you could only have your name on fifty accounts. If you wanted a new account, you had to throw one back in the pool. Another value involved documentation. If there was nothing in the Salesforce.com CRM notes, no activity, then we'd take the account away and give someone else a shot. This was a rational system.

As aggressive as Rich was as a salesperson, he wasn't greedy. Rich knew how to guard his territory, but he also developed the maturity to ask himself what was right rather than grab as much as he could. Rich understood the truth about territoriality. He was operating in a culture where territories were given away; some of his colleagues did not develop their territories but would not let Rich serve accounts within them even though he had strong connections and preexisting contacts.

Because of his personal development and the SEI work he was doing at Wright, Rich's capacity for self-reflection was beginning to pay dividends. He was expanding his capacity to establish high-quality rapport, even with complaining sales prima donnas. He still valued culture over raw results.

Every salesperson wanted the good territories that the senior salespeople had been sitting on forever. But they were not going to get them. If they remained in their self-pitying, complaining mode, they'd never succeed. But if they adopted a transformative mentality, they could.

When I started making calls to companies in industrial parks that I passed on the highway, I began to see opportunities in places that I'd been blind to when I was a complainer. Once my eyes and mind opened, my perspective shifted. I was learning to choose and to operate from a new paradigm of abundance; the leads were everywhere. The possibilities were endless. I tried to coach my people to make similar shifts rather than whine about the good leads.

Sales, like life, isn't always fair. To succeed, though, people need to learn to pivot, to adapt, to find alternatives to their routines and practices, and to break through their own limiting beliefs. For instance, back at Whittman-Hart, Todd was a salesperson who had closed some big accounts and was highly successful. The CEO then declared that his accounts would become "house" accounts. A house account is one that no longer has a salesperson attached to it and would no longer pay out commissions. Because Todd was making too much money, management viewed him as a threat. Many companies make this critical mistake when they are not sales-driven and sales-focused. They fear the cost of salespeople and commissions and try to drive their compensation down. In reality, a company should be thrilled to pay their salespeople a lot of money because that is a sign of success. The more the salesperson makes, the more the company makes (assuming the compensation plan is structured properly). Paying salespeople fairly and well assures the sale of profitable projects. It is a win-win!

Rich had learned the hard way that it was a limiting strategy to place an unfairly low ceiling on a sales professional's income. He operated from a win-win perspective and wanted his salespeople to win and make a lot of money. In his whining days, Rich had seen his success punished repeatedly by sales goals being raised and commissions being lowered in the face of sales success. He did, however, structure a tiered commission structure where the sales commission reduced over a period of time as he began adding account managers. Over time, his account management program was to sell as much, and sometimes even more than, his business development staff.

This "house account" structure was a radical change in policy, and it happened almost overnight. In the past, salespeople would "ride" or "milk" their big accounts. No sunset clause existed, so they could take significant commissions from accounts for years. We did not even have an account management team, so the salesperson could milk an existing account forever and never have to open new accounts. If you landed some major accounts, you really didn't have to sell new ones.

For Todd, the changed policy was like an insult, and although his first impulse was to quit, he stayed because he still was making good money. From his perspective, the change in policy was outrageously unfair—the rules of the game had been changed midgame. Yet Whittman-Hart needed to create more motivating sales compensation plans, and one move in that direction was to not allow salespeople to rest on their laurels.

Over the years, I worked with Dr. Bob to evolve a viable account management system, but the seeds of this system were planted at Whittman-Hart and nurtured at Divine. I saw how allowing salespeople who brought in accounts to receive commissions on them in perpetuity could be de-motivating. Too many companies allow their salespeople to coast—especially their best salespeople. Eventually, Dr. Bob and I developed a system around a sunsetting provision, one that allowed salespeople to reap the benefits of bringing in accounts but placed a limit on the duration of these benefits. In this way, they felt fairly compensated but also were motivated to keep bringing in new accounts. At Divine, we started testing this type of concept, which didn't endear me to everyone.

Rich really liked being the nice, popular guy, but it had been hurting him. Fear of being different and rejected limits people from hitting their heights. Rich still let people know he loved them and wanted to belong, but he clearly also wanted to be different. He became more assertive, taking away accounts from people when they didn't develop them—a major leap in his development. He was also unwilling to accommodate Doug's demands, his top salesperson. And at the same time, he was building a strong relationship with his longtime sales hire, Dave Barr. Dave's values, beliefs, and actions aligned with his own. As he learned to be a better sales manager, Rich found support from within with affirming self-talk as he faced increasing disaffirmation from his staff. By understanding himself and others, using the Wright Developmental Model, Rich understood his needs enough to develop them. He used this map of development for himself and, over time, for his staff to help optimize each person's possibilities.

I began to worry less about how others would view me. I was becoming a more effective, influential communicator, bringing rationality to my expression. I was increasingly able to harness my anger into more creative intent and harness my anger with reason. People still liked and respected me, and I was a master at containment.

Rich did not give in to most impulses; he would contain a knee-jerk reaction and be able to strategize. Most people act without his level of strategy and positive conscious intent. As a result, others had no clue when he was angry and felt like hitting someone. This is a key skill we would all do well to emulate.

Prior to my becoming a sales manager after Whittman-Hart, I had been held hostage by the top producers. The organizations at both Whittman-Hart and Divine were afraid to change their systems, convincing themselves that their best salespeople would leave if they stood up to them or changed how they were rewarded. Their compensation systems didn't just have a financial effect but also impacted the company's culture in a disempowering, fragmenting way.

Over time, I reduced the number of accounts people could have. I wanted them serving a few accounts better rather than a lot not as well. I had tough conversations with my people along the lines of, "I'll let you have this account for six months, but if you can't crack it in that time, I'm going to give someone else a shot." I also mandated that if you wanted to take on a new account, you had to sacrifice an existing account. During this time, we started to build a vision of a useful customer relationship management (CRM) system. We forced salespeople to enter data by not paying commissions if they did not enter meeting notes and customer information in the system. These were big steps in my growth, mandating that my folks do the right thing even if it meant displeasing them.

Rich found this task difficult because he was still developing the inner strength to do what was right even if it was unpopular. He was still thinking like a salesperson. He'd run the gauntlet as a salesperson. Whittman-Hart was erratic in compensation policies, placing people in charge of sales who were inexperienced and had no idea what true relationship selling was. The organization would increase his sales goal by 30 percent, sometimes more, after he hit his previous goal. At times, the company upped it in the middle of the year. This was unfair, but Rich always rose to the occasion and met all of these challenges, which left him feeling like a salesperson deep inside.

I over-identified with my salespeople. I protected them. I needed to evolve beyond that as a sales manager and start thinking about what was best for the business and ultimately the client. That's when I started introducing changes, like giving another salesperson a shot at a stagnating account. Again, it was a rational response—if Jack isn't able to break into an account, maybe it's time to give Sue a shot and see what she can do.

When I was a salesperson at Whittman-Hart, I met with Dr. Bob every two weeks, and we would review my pipeline. We'd assess where a prospective account was within the pipeline—from making an initial contact to closing the deal. Sometimes I focused on adding to the pipeline, and other times I concentrated on moving items further along in the pipeline or closing them. We even focused on assignments that got people to say no and moved them out of the pipeline. Ironically, these were often the times of the highest close rates. This was self-imposed accountability with Dr. Bob, and it was essential to my growth. As in any sport and in life, we all need coaching and feedback to get better.

At Divine, I began weekly pipeline reviews with the individuals in my group. We'd assess if a pipeline was "healthy" by answering the following questions:

- How many total opportunities are in the pipeline?
- What is the total value of the pipeline and the weighted value (percentage probability multiplied by the anticipated value)?
- What goals have you set for opportunities?
- What is the stage of each opportunity (unqualified lead, qualified lead, demo, proposal, finalist, verbal, etc.)?
- Is an opportunity progressing from one stage to the next? How quickly is it progressing? When was the last time it "moved"?

These pipeline sessions were reality checks. Too often, salespeople have a lot of opportunities in their pipelines, a significant percentage of which aren't real. I created binders for each salesperson that charted all these pipeline factors, ensuring that people were accountable for their progress, or lack thereof, on accounts. Our weekly sessions also included conversations about next steps. I'd ask, "What are you going to do this week to move this account further along?" We'd determine what additional actions they needed to take to penetrate an account more deeply. This ensured that a salesperson wouldn't place all his bets on one individual at the account and that he'd create relationships with two others at different levels and in different areas of the organization (the need for three-by-three-by-three relationships). We'd create action plans for movement, and if no action occurred by the next week, I'd take the account out of the pipeline.

I can't overemphasize how difficult it is for salespeople to move accounts out of the pipeline. Having a large number of opportunities in the pipeline provides them with security—false security, but that's not how they see it. Taking an account out makes them anxious. As a sales manager, however, you want some degree of anxiety and discomfort—it provides energy and motivation.

More than that, though, you want salespeople to view their pipelines realistically. When you question someone about an account where nothing has been happening, they automatically respond, "Oh, that one's hot; it's about to close." Generally, that's a pipe dream, not a realistic view of the pipeline. Cleaning out the pipeline helps you view it strategically—when it's too full, it's difficult to know what to do, what is missing, what needs more focus.

Dr. Bob taught me that movement in the pipeline is important. You have to have proper stages. If things aren't moving, either the deal is dead or the salesperson is having a challenge and getting stuck at a certain stage in the pipeline. It then becomes a training opportunity.

He also taught me the value of a weighted pipeline, assigning percentages to the likelihood of a given event happening. If we were a finalist for an account, we knew it had a 50 percent likelihood that it would close. All this helped me use the pipeline as a highly effective training tool—it fostered accountability. I could sit down with my salespeople and say, "You told me that this account was going to move in a few weeks, but it hasn't. Why not? What's going on with it?"

I learned how to assume different roles during this period—as a manager, a coach, and a teacher. I grasped the influence I could have over others and how I might help them become successful. At the same time, I still had a lot to learn and room to grow. Dr. Bob talked to me about owning my own satisfaction rather than expecting other people to satisfy me. I was at a transition point where I wasn't satisfied with the way my people were producing or the way they were following my coaching. I began to learn this hard lesson: I could not will someone to be successful. I could give them the tools and the training and all the secrets of success, but they had to want it and do the work.

As a businessperson, Rich was beginning to develop systems that allowed him to have greater influence with more people. He was giving tools to his people that helped them feel more successful. Though he had started to face his authority issues, he still had a ways to go before he was comfortable being a boss. He always felt like he was his own guy, but he would whine and have problems with authority figures or staff who did not respect his authority: he'd do his job well but be resentful and respond to other people's actions rather than choosing his own course of action from his desire and intent. He succeeded because of his anger; it allowed him to thumb his nose at those in authority. As a sales manager at Divine, he became the authority. He was still thinking like a salesperson, so it was a tough transition to becoming a boss.

Up until this point, I still wanted to be liked by everyone. I had an external locus of control. I was looking outside to others to see if I was okay. But when you start holding people accountable, not all of them are going to like you. I was managing people who were my buddies.

At the same time, I wasn't willing to make a complete commitment to transformation. I was still afraid to implement certain policies. For instance, I used a spreadsheet and had my own metrics, but I wasn't requiring my people to do the same. Transformation requires a lot of time and mistakes, thinking and learning, and breaking through limiting beliefs. We all need coaching and immediate feedback and external accountability. We would never dream of winning an Olympic medal if we didn't use coaches and compete against the best we could find.

Rich was transforming faster in his personal life than his professional one. His children were challenging him, and he was going on spiritual pilgrimages where he was beginning to see business from a mystical point of view—based on his view of electrical circuits. Good business was like an efficient circuit with little energy loss.

At work, he ran into challenges as a leader and a manager. Managers need to keep the machine running, and leaders need to take the organization forward into its possibilities. I coach managers to see themselves wearing five hats: trainer, coach, supervisor, team leader, and manager of the area. That's a lot of hats, and it takes time before people are comfortable wearing all of them and knowing which is appropriate when. At home, though, Rich was motivated to change faster, in large part because he did not want to be his father as a parent. He invested a great deal in his daughters. They always knew what he liked and what he didn't like and they knew what his limits and boundaries were, when they could stretch beyond what he said he wanted and when they needed to toe the line. They were also becoming independent beings chafing at the demands. Here again, life is sales: Rich was stretching himself, expanding his skills of communication, influence, teaching and so on.

My first daughter was born in 1996 and my second in 1998. As my kids became toddlers, I was transitioning into a managerial role at Whittman-Hart/marchFIRST/Divine. At the time, I was attending fathers' groups at Wright and listening to men with older children talking about the mistakes they were making as parents. Combined with my experience of my father's mistakes, I was compelled not to repeat these same errors. I held high expectations for my daughters from the beginning. I needed to sell them on their potential (life is sales). But I did not hold similarly high expectations for the people who worked in my group.

Rich began attending fathering groups before his first daughter was born. As a father, Rich didn't have to deal with larger abstractions. As a trainer and coach, you sometimes need to say things five or ten times before people get it. As an individual performer, it was tough to get his head around this idea. As a father, though, he didn't have to deal with multiple variables. His role was clear, and his authority was absolute.

A Not-So-Divine Ending

During my tenure at Divine between 2000 and 2003, things were going well professionally. Just as my consciousness was rising, so too was my success as a sales manager. Though I wasn't in Divine's inner circle, and I kept having managers installed above me, my group was outselling everyone. Divine was focused on acquisitions. After the dot.com bust, it was scooping up companies for pennies on the dollar. We were soon a $1 billion company with 10,000 employees.

Eventually, though, we went bankrupt. Part of the problem was that the company was overextended financially—Flip had a bold vision, but maybe it was too bold and unsustainable with available resources. Part of the problem was that the company was overstaffed, especially with past employees and friends of Flip. People who were getting high-level positions weren't always the people who were generating the best results. I'm all for loyalty, but it should go hand in hand with performance and accountability, and at Divine, you didn't always find both.

Around this time, I began to realize that love isn't always soft and sweet. From a business perspective, you must hold a higher vision for your people and not just hold their hand or baby them. You have to be willing to feel uncomfortable as you demand accountability. I saw the parallels with the vision Dr. Bob helped me and my wife set for our marriage. Part of marriage is soft and sweet—you're supportive and empathetic. Part of it is holding an inspiring and challenging vision for each other—you challenge your partner when he/she isn't living up to your shared values and vision.

So yes, as a manager you have to encourage and praise, but you also have to hold a higher vision for your people and make sure they understand this vision and are inspired and challenged by it. They may lose sight of that vision, but you have to remind them when they do. This is not always easy, but it's always necessary.

This was a great learning to take away from Divine and apply to the next stop on my journey: my own business.

WDM Takeaways

- Harness anger. Rather than just an emotion to thwart others, anger can allow you to get what you want (Level 3). Harnessing anger means growing in awareness—to be able to contain anger like a steam engine harnesses steam. You intend positive outcomes just as the piston in the steam engine transforms the steam into mechanical power.

- Be aware of how you feel. Awareness of how we feel in the here and now allows conscious choice rather than knee-jerk reactions. Sometimes containment is the best choice vs. reaction (Level 3). Express your feelings later, but you don't always need to in the moment. Consider your goals and the purpose of the meeting you are in. Keep clear on your intent.

- Recognize your fear so you can choose to trust yourself and take risks (Level 1). Fear is an effective tool and can provide great information, but it is not an excuse for inaction.

- Choose to be different rather than conform at times. Express yourself and tell the truth (Level 4). You can't be liked by everyone, and you won't be an effective leader trying to always be liked. Recognize that sometimes it is easier to feel angry (Level 3), than to acknowledge your hurt (Level 2) or your fear (Level 1). Awareness is the key and can give you more choice and more personal power.

CHAPTER FOUR

FROM SALES PROFESSIONAL TO ENTREPRENEUR

My new life began with no job and worthless stock. I went from being wealthy on paper to having shrinking assets and no income to support two young daughters. At Divine, I really felt good about being the only regional sales director who consistently made my numbers. My staff members were great, my clients were great, and I was doing well as a sales director. But now I was on my own. For the first time in years, no one was providing me with sales goals, and I no longer had anyone to manage. I faced a fork in the road: I had to decide between working for another company or starting my own business.

After Divine ended, Rich wavered at the crossroads, unwilling to acknowledge that the choice would not go away. Though various organizations wanted to hire him, Rich did not rush, taking time to clarify his path. He became increasingly clear that he did not want to work for someone else again. If he decided to be an entrepreneur, he would be learning a whole new game—it would be analogous to re-learning how to walk after a paralyzing injury.

I had always wanted to start my own company, but I had doubts. Maybe now wasn't the right time, and maybe I needed the experience of one more job. But as I began interviewing and considering other companies, I had a revelation that led to this chapter's title. Actually, the title is just the first part of that revelation: the other part was that I could lose money on my own. Why did I need someone else to tell me how to do it? I had just gone through a couple of billion-dollar bankruptcies. What was I afraid of? My traditional view on security had just been blown up.

The more I thought about it, the more I realized that I didn't want to start working for someone else and have little or no equity or say—to allow someone else to control and possibly lose my value. Why couldn't I do something for myself? The more I asked this pivotal question, the more I was compelled to put the question to the test. I could start a business. Deciding to go it alone as an entrepreneur, I asked myself: What do I want to sell? What did I want to learn next?

Answering these questions involved a major transition. I was learning how to walk again. Selling for myself raised a host of challenges. If I were the boss, who would I complain to about the new sales quota, the staff I needed, and on and on? Nothing was the same anymore when viewed from the top of an empire consisting of myself.

Selling as an entrepreneur is a sea change in both thought and action. Rich needed to return to his beginnings in sales. He needed to learn the basic disciplines anew from a self-driven motivation perspective. Rich was embarking on a journey of becoming a new type of salesperson—only this time, a self-directed salesperson facing a whole new range of challenges: technical, skill-based, and unconscious. In terms of this last challenge, Rich had to confront monsters of fear, doubt, and the great unknowns that arise from the unconscious mind. He was facing his existence—alone. What got him to where he was would not get him to where he was going. Rich's ideas about selling needed to evolve for himself as an entrepreneur as well as for his staff. Think of a switchback path that takes you zigzagging up a mountain. What gets you to one turn will not get you to the next turn, and Rich was making monumental turns.

This transition to entrepreneurship was when I really became a sales professional. The journey was long and rewarding. In my first job after my MBA at TII, when I managed salespeople, we were selling a product. At Whittman-Hart, I was selling a service, and at Divine, I was selling services and products. This was the first time I needed to set my own aggressive meeting and dial goals, to break through my limiting beliefs rather than respond to someone else's demands. Here's the harsh truth that salespeople face: no one wakes up each day excited about making cold calls. No one thinks to himself, "Woohoo, I'm going to make these cold calls, go to these meetings, and face rejection after rejection. Awesome!"

So, if you aspire to be a good or great salesperson, you can't let that truth deter you. You have to set minimums for dials and meetings and always meet or exceed them as if your life depends on it (because it does). You can't control everything. As every salesperson knows, some days are going to suck. No matter what you do, you strike out. But what you can control are the dials and meetings. If you can go home at the end of the day and say, "I met my minimum for dials," you'll be fine. Sooner or later, your efforts will pay off.

Whittman-Hart, however, didn't hold me accountable for developing these hard skills—quantifiable competencies (as opposed to soft skills that are difficult to quantify). That's why I set my own goals and standards and outsourced my accountability to a Wright sales lab. I developed hard skills like learning how to track sales and asked to be held accountable for blowing through my excuses and rationalizations. I cycled back through the soft skills, like building rapport and understanding different personalities, after acquiring the hard skills. It wasn't just about scheduling so many meetings a week. To sell well, you have to understand why you're doing it, your purpose. It's too easy to get stuck in the mindset of "I just want to sell" and ignore what the customer wants. Are you willing to walk away from a sale because you don't believe it's right for the customer? This is all about the soft skill of purpose.

As I discovered I was meant to serve and help others fulfill their purpose and mission, I faced another, bigger challenge: to sell myself on selling, each and every day. I was truly beginning to see my life as sales, starting with myself first, my family and others second. Too often, salespeople look at their work as a job rather than as a way of life. They see sales as selling X amount to keep their job and X-plus to make good money.

These salespeople are really missing out. There's so much more to it than numbers, driving results, and closing. Soft skills like time management, self-care disciplines, and establishing high-quality rapport carry over to every sphere of life. Learning the soft skills and hard skills helps us as sales professionals develop into more well-rounded and, ultimately, much more effective, happy, and successful salespeople. We become much more effective and successful in all areas of life from self-care to relationships, from service to spirituality. Remember, life is sales!

Of course, I didn't know all this when I started working at Whittman-Hart. My wife and daughters were always going to be my most demanding teachers of life is sales, because I couldn't fire them when I didn't like the lessons they taught me. I had to do a lot of sorting and other personal work to achieve win-win outcomes—especially the ones where the girls did not see my approach as win-win.

Rich is very intentional. He was not just a straight A student in school. He took his entire life on as a purposeful project and was training to earn straight A's in all areas of life. When he engaged in conversations with colleagues, customers, and all of us at Wright, this intentionality prompted him to ask critical and important questions. He began to learn that it wasn't just about the hard skills of sales and business as he worked to have all his relationships flourish.

Rich's values never shifted from his focus on closing the sale and results, but his evolving perspective helped him to see the sale as just one facet of an integrative transformational process—living a full, well-rounded life. A big transformation came in becoming a sales manager. Then he further transformed to partnering even more deeply with clients and software partners on their success through project management and client realization of results. He also discovered he was no longer a buddy-buddy guy as he set compensation and goals for others.

Many salespeople miss the opportunities to serve and transform. They see sales through a narrow lens. They often work to live and forget that work is a primary playground for facing challenges and enjoying life. They miss the opportunities to become something more than they were before. Remember, Rich was going on a sales call to Outboard Marine and had the epiphany that he could call the companies whose signs he spotted on the side of buildings—everything started to change. This was facilitated out of the partnership of his fellow sales lab mates.

After his epiphany that life is sales, Rich began to see how his personal development meshed with his professional development as a salesperson. He began studying in Wright's father's program, wanting to be as successful as a dad as he aspired to be as a salesperson.

Author Daniel Pink says "to sell is human" (the title of one of his bestselling books), but he's coming at it from a researcher/journalist perspective. Rich speaks as someone on a transformational journey. For him, sales is a golden path to personal responsibility and service, not just to himself but to others who make a similar commitment—who also choose to develop themselves as sales professionals and as well-rounded human beings.

At Wright, we always talked about how to assess your intention—"Just look around you"—that is your intention, either conscious or unconscious. Intention is the principle that leads to results. During early childhood, usually in our terrible twos, it surfaces. Consciously or unconsciously, we all create situations in which we find ourselves, based on the choices we made to get there. I went through a lot of learning to discover this truth in sales. I was stuck, creating a victim-oriented reality from the limiting beliefs of the Whittman-Hart sales culture—its three-meetings-a-week rubric. My sales lab challenged me constantly to break out of that mindset. With their encouragement, I could take action when I saw a company's name on the side of a building and realized I could call them. I was telling myself at that moment that I could change my intention and change my reality—I needed to do something different to break through my limiting beliefs.

I was in a transformational lab that Dr. Bob was leading (I decided to take on my personal growth and SEI education) at first only out of fear of losing my wife. I worried that if she grew and changed at a faster pace than me, it might destroy our relationship and I would be abandoned—my greatest fear. I was always late for this lab. I had all the excuses: a call ran late, traffic was bad, etc. Dr. Bob asked me, "Was your intention to be on time?" "Of course," I said, "I intended to be on time." Then he asked me, "If I were to give you $1 million to be on time next week, do you think you would be on time?" I said I would come the night before and sleep here to be sure I was on time.

And as I said it, I grasped what intention was really about. Intention is not a yes or no. Rather, we can measure it more on a scale from 1 to 10. I was not anywhere near a 10 in terms of my intention to be on time. And because of my desire to be liked and please everyone, I was unwilling to tell the truth. Salespeople often don't think this way. They are no different than the rest of us, preferring the easier path rather than the most effective and fulfilling one (the latter rarely being easy). This is the victim mentality, a topic to which we'll return. This mentality is the opposite of the life-is-sales philosophy.

I was discovering that I had to become a victor over myself and my own drama and victimhood. There was some truth in the response from

Alec Baldwin's character in the movie version of *Glengarry Glen Ross*, when he said, "You're weak." Previously, I was not choosing to find the strong way, to make sales happen and strengthen myself as much as I could. Instead, I settled for an excuse. Now, I began to take responsibility for everything that happened in my life. No more excuses, and I empowered Dr. Bob to help me stick to this no-excuse commitment.

Sales increasingly transcended the act of selling and grew to become a guide for relationships and other aspects of my life. It became a mirror, reflecting who I was as a human being. It enabled me to discover my limiting beliefs, to partner with people, and to do the right thing. In the following chapters, you'll see themes of integrity and doing what I say I'll do. Life is sales took on a larger perspective in my life and was key to my development as a businessman and a person.

I discovered that you don't always receive payment for what you sell, but you can be rewarded in other ways. For instance, I sell people on a vision—my employees as well as my children. I sell them on what they can become and their full potential.

And I'm always selling. If I'm not, it means I'm not in touch with my yearnings, my needs. That's why I'm always asking myself, "What's my intention?" and "How important is it to me?" I use the Wright Developmental Model as a map to keep myself aware of my current state and to allow myself more choice in my life.

Think of it in terms of karma. Something like cause and effect. If you put yourself out there and do the right things, that goodness will come back to you. When I am in touch with my fear and choose to trust, I feel more alive and engaged in life.

In sales and in all of life, karma does not bite us in the butt if we take responsibility, learn, and grow. We break through the artificial limits we've set unconsciously: "I'm not experienced enough to get that big account; I'm not well-known enough to get an appointment with someone at the executive level; I don't know enough about that industry to make a sale to their market leader."

To get past these limiting beliefs, salespeople need to set up consequences—penalties and rewards. We need to force ourselves to take risks, fall down, and get back up. If you can motivate yourself not to do X and to do Y, you'll push past the barriers that limit your success. Hold yourself accountable and make sure someone else is demanding accountability from you. If you're allowed to just get by without consequence or measurement, your limiting beliefs will gain strength, and you will not learn and accomplish all you can. Set big hairy audacious goals (BHAGs) as coined by Jim Collins and Jerry Porras in *Built to Last*. Sometimes, this is the only way to break through limiting beliefs. We will talk about this more as we describe the founding of Lyons Consulting Group (LYONSCG).

Don't let rejection take you down. Feel the hurt, embrace it, and learn and grow from it, becoming stronger and more resilient. Great information is contained within rejection and objections. Many salespeople miss this truth. And it happens to the best salespeople. Push past rejection—it's just one more barrier that stands in your way.

I've talked a lot about numbers—number of dials and meetings—and they're critical. But that's just the ante to get you into the game. Achieving success is also about developing an appreciation for what exists beyond the numbers—the relationships you develop with customers, the sense of serving others, and the meaning of the work you do.

If you can do all that, then you'll discover that karma is on your side. In the long run, that's the best advantage any salesperson can possess. Karma doesn't always operate in a logical, balanced way—one good deed does not always lead directly to a corresponding good outcome. Rather, if you keep doing the right things, then the positive outcomes will happen eventually, if not immediately.

Good karma comes to those who are open to it. They learn from experience as they take full responsibility for their lives. I was learning to trust in people and life and generating a lot of good karma—positive feelings, friends, and unexpectedly beneficial surprises when I most needed them. I was using the Wright Developmental Model to assess my feeling and to make choices in line with a greater purpose that I was discovering. I wanted to maximize my potential, and the impact I could have on the world. I was working hard in transformation lab to identify and break through my limiting beliefs, realizing that I was the only thing holding me back.

Doing my personal work paid off after things became urgent. The Divine bankruptcy call was a rude awakening. Even though I knew the company was in trouble, I thought I had more time. After all, I was leading the company's most profitable services division, and we were even selling more software than the software teams. I assumed my accomplishments offered me more protection than they did. I hadn't realized the extent of Divine's financial problems. It had acquired many software companies in a short period, and the company's failure to use the sales disciplines I had instituted in my folks, along with the financial downturn in the economy, resulted in a financially overextended company.

Let's put Rich's sales experience at Whittman-Hart/marchFIRST/Divine in context. He was much more than a tech solution salesperson. His self-awareness, combined with his insight about what was going on in the heads and hearts of those to whom he sold and with whom he worked, allowed him to establish especially effective rapport. He was also a particularly good student in all areas of his business life. In his leadership and sales trainings, he worked with a wide range of salespeople, in industries from manufacturing to metal coating; he worked with many types of specialists, from marketing consultants to designers; and he worked with a diversity of products, from financial instruments to replacement windows to carpet cleaning. He really knew the world of sales from multiple perspectives—the inner experience as well as a variety of business perspectives.

He had become a real businessman. Now he needed to become an entrepreneur, and what got him to this point would not get him to the next phase successfully. He was at the turn of the switchback, and it felt like he needed to go back to go forward.

My changing approach to sales wasn't limited to my profession. The effect of my evolving perspective had a positive effect on my life at that point—on my relationship with my kids, my wife, and our partnership. As I learned to sell, I learned to live my life with increasing satisfaction and fulfillment. That meant selling them on coming along on the journey with me. I wanted everyone to learn what I was learning about living a satisfying life.

Becoming more expressive was an integral part of living a satisfying life. I was no longer robotic as a parent. I stopped avoiding engagement in tough conversations with my wife. My relationships with friends became closer and more vulnerable than in the past. A parallel exists with work: Just as a business prospect's objections are an opportunity to gather more information, spousal disagreements and fights became an opportunity to communicate what matters and to understand the other person's point of view.

Reflections of a Sales Professional

As the previous section has shown, that uncertain time after Divine's bankruptcy gave me time to think long and hard about my career development as a sales professional. Thankfully, I still had the valuable learning environments of my leadership group and my sales lab to help that development.

Rich is not just blowing smoke here. His purpose began to clarify as service, learning, and growing. Competition brought out his best and forced him to adapt continuously. He was in a sales training laboratory, learning from and with other very dedicated salespeople. Their accountability and competition every two weeks were fierce. Pride went into teaming with *each other and beating the other two teams even though there was only $120 at risk every two weeks. That is actually $120 in cash payments for the winning team, and $60 that had to be paid out if you lost ($20 per person).*

I had become a believer and a beast in terms of sales metrics—I tracked everything. Every morning, I drew a table in my sales notebook so I could monitor my dials, contacts, meetings, proposals, wins, losses, etc. I carried this book everywhere and transferred the numbers at the end of the day or the end of the week to an Excel spreadsheet. I still have spreadsheets going back to 1997, and every year after. This discipline made me better over time, as the data I had to analyze grew. I also learned a lot about partnering with customers and allies. Networking and rapport became key to my success. I continued to evolve a purpose to serve, which involved truly caring for others and not just myself.

Rich learned this caring as a sprinter. Every summer we had a men's leadership week, and we would do foot races, arm wrestling, and numerous physical competitions. Rich was one of the fastest sprinters, and he was known to push himself so hard that upon crossing the finish line, he would heave his guts out.

Rich was "striving," and fear drives strivers at a certain point in their lives. At this point, we only feel affirmed if we win. We look at competitors as enemies. So when Rich raced, it was life or death to him. He was at the most basic foundational level of our existence (fear). He was willing to barf at the end of the race, to punish himself, because of how much fear was coursing through his system. Everything was a pass-fail event for him, with his self-esteem and self-love on the line with every event.

Life was not nourishing for Rich at this level, and he wanted it to be nourishing. He began working with great focus on a lot of issues in his life—he learned to trust and to do his best out of love rather than fear. As a result, he had a breakthrough at our men's summer leadership training event where he ran another race—this time a quarter-mile competition. This time, though, another racer was just about as fast as Rich. They battled neck and neck the entire distance, and Rich won but not by much. This time, though, Rich didn't barf at the end of the race. Even more important, he cared about and valued his competitor—he no longer viewed this guy as the threatening enemy who would reveal his flaws. Previously, Rich ran fearing he was not good enough and always to prove himself rather than for the joy of the event. He realized he was being drained rather than nourished. As he developed an understanding of his prior motivation, he began enjoying all he did with greater nourishment—he even called it running from love.

I learned to enjoy more than running. I was starting to relish the adventure of life. Life became more than a pass/fail event, as I decided to engage and live life fully vs. trying to avoid failure. I even loved keeping statistics and used my data to determine how much a dial and a meeting were worth to me and how many dials and meetings I needed to make to achieve my goals. This activity eliminated excuses and gave my mind a rational framework to overcome my own barriers. I was learning soft skills as part of my SEI education, and I used the WDM to understand myself, which allowed me to understand others. I began to develop rapport skills that allowed me to shift my sales style to match the customer I was meeting with based on that customer's personality. I could change my level of energy, my language, the amount of detail I shared—all to develop a deeper and more satisfying relationship with my clients.

Here's an analogy from my electrical engineering background that helped me develop as a person and as a professional. I was starting to integrate the different parts of me into a coherent and consistent purpose. It starts with Ohm's law: V=iR. Voltage (V) equals current (i) times resistance (R). We are all circuits, and life is a circuit. We always want to increase our voltage (purpose). But if we take our purpose as a constant, then we want to increase our flow (current) and reduce our resistance. To the extent we live life fully, the resistance in our circuits is reduced and aliveness (current) expands and flows. Similarly, in any interaction, I can lower my resistance and work to establish high-quality rapport to reduce another person's resistance.

How can we all be a better channel for life to flow through us, so we can realize and maximize our potential? I found the answer when I reduced the resistance in running and enjoyed stretching myself from care rather than fear. The concept of potential energy, the energy stored between two oppositely charged plates, is also relevant. Think of me and the guy I was racing. Could I increase my capacity to store and apply the charge in the race? I can similarly contain energy and then direct this energy to do the greatest good in sales and all I do. Containment is a key factor for me. This is conscious intent. Can we intend where we put our energy and our focus, or do we just react to what is the loudest or most urgent, but not the most important or purposeful?

I seek potential maximization in all my relationships and for myself—whether it is with my children, my wife, or a client. In any situation, I strive to turn potential into reality. And I bring this focus and intent into the sale.

Rich began seeing his job in life as reducing his resistance to Spirit and Life. Here, we see the mystical Rich. Rich and his wife Gertrude began attending spiritual pilgrimages to sacred sites each year. His spiritual perspective gave him a sense of love or caring that he likened to the electrical current that was flowing through each relationship. He began to see sales as helping people reduce their resistance to the flow of life.

Let's look at Rich's relationship evolution from a different perspective. At Wright, we teach how certain concepts guide us in business and life, and one of them is mutuality. Borrowing a phrase from the satiric group, the Firesign Theater, "I think we're all bozos on this bus." We all have value, and no one is inherently superior to anyone else. A related concept is that of net givers—when everything is added up, we give more than we take. Rich embraced these concepts, and they had a profound effect on how he worked with staff and clients.

I intended to win every deal, but this intent existed within a larger context. If the deal was not right for us or for the client, walking away could be a win. We might not have the skill set to help the client to be successful, or the client may not be ready for the project and our methodology. And we were never going to be the least expensive company, but we were the best and were committed to delivering predictable results. Although it killed me to lose deals, it was the right outcome at times. As I used to say after a loss, "They will come back." And they often did, after a poor experience with a competitor, or after growing large enough to be able to afford us.

Rich went through internal turmoil as he learned to not compromise quality and cost. He was running his business to optimize benefit for the client and his staff. He came in to coaching sorting opportunities, trying to determine which ones to pursue and which ones to let go. Consider, too, the contrast between optimal and maximal. The latter term refers to trying to obtain as much as possible. Optimal is about doing what is right and fitting, while maximal is often not what is wanted and needed. Rich became skilled at helping companies optimize their online sales. For a while, Rich used a bridge as a visual symbol for his company, and it was appropriate—he wanted to help companies transition from where they were to where they could be. This was an optimal approach. If a company wasn't interested in optimizing—and if they lacked the resources to pursue a maximal strategy—then he was up front about why they shouldn't hire him.

Rich was more interested in what's best for the other person first, and his staff second, rather than what was best for him, and he trusted that in the long run, this approach would benefit both parties equally.

We continued to modify our methodology, and we added training, enabling our customers to be successful. I would always say that the implementation was the easy part (for us at least). But the real work started after we launched, and we wanted to be sure that the customer was ready. We truly were committed to the customer's success. And to our company's success, and to our employees' success. A win-win-win.

His capacity to envision for others expanded. This included his employees and everyone he encountered. He and his wife worked on this. They even began leading couples' groups. He was learning that teaching others deepened his knowledge—learning to practice what he taught.

I'm always selling. If I'm not, it means I'm not in touch with my yearning, my needs, and tapping the potential of the moment. Not what I want, but my deeper yearning. Our deeper yearnings have to do with existence, connection, influence, belonging, commitment, and our desire to be the captain of our own ship. Ultimately, our deepest yearning is for love. That's why I'm always asking myself: What's my intention, how important is it to me, and what is the highest purpose? I use the Wright Developmental Model as a tool to identify my current state and facilitate more choices in my life.

We can build up goodwill through our actions. By learning to operate in good faith with the world, we are operating with growing integrity—even when it means doing something that does not seem to be in our own best interest. Trust in the universe. If you put yourself out there and do the right things, good things will come back to you. This is Level 1 of the Wright Developmental Model. When I am in touch with my fear and choose to trust, I feel more alive and engaged in life.

When Rich talks about growing in integrity, it's a concept that goes back to existential philosophers like Jean-Paul Sartre. In good faith, we are willing to support others and potentially lose, as Rich learned in his running race. Good faith begins with being honest with ourselves—and being honest, authentic, and up front with others. We have referred to this as a soft skill, but it can be very hard work. It was a long journey for Rich before he was able to even acknowledge that fear was always present for him, as it is for all of us. Learning to recognize his fear of being a failure, he made friends with it. This deepened his relationships with others. By getting in touch with this fear, he could capitalize on its natural ability to inform him of danger as well as possibilities. By being aware of his fear, he could do a cost-benefit analysis of the risks that he might take.

Here's a story that demonstrates how bad faith can surface and what to do about it when it does. Our tradition during men's leadership week was to perform a humorous skit at the end of the week related to what we had learned. My group created a skit about Dr. Bob—it was intended to poke gentle fun at him, but not only was it not funny, but it was also hostile.

Dr. Bob halted the skit before it was finished, and other men verbally attacked us for what we had done. It was a terrible feeling. They were attacking us for showing bad faith. At that moment, I thought that this was the last time I was ever going to attend one of these retreats.

Dr. Bob, though, stopped the attack. He told one of the people who was particularly incensed that we were there to learn and grow and that no one should demonize anyone else. "We all have bad faith," Dr. Bob said. There was a pause in conversation as we all began reflecting on our own bad faith and where it came from.

All of us traced our bad faith back to early childhood experiences involving fear, hurt, and even physical abuse. Then Dr. Bob asked a question: "Why would you want to wipe out anyone?"

I told myself I would never want to do that, it wasn't who I was—I was the nice guy. I didn't even get the notion of wiping out someone—"canceling" them in today's jargon. I told myself I'd never been wiped out. But, in fact, I had been; I just wasn't conscious of it. The more I thought about this concept, the more I was driven back into my past. I experienced a moment of spontaneous regression—essentially, I was re-experiencing an abuse from my childhood.

As Dr. Bob later explained, many aggressive high performers take refuge in performance and react to tamp down their deeper hurts; they hope winning will stop the helplessness of early childhood abuse. It explained why I wanted to wipe people out, why I had this anger that sometimes bubbled to the surface, especially when I had been drinking earlier in my life. Normally I wasn't hostile and aggressive, but sometimes these feelings emerged—such as the skit we created about Dr. Bob.

I was missing an essential piece. I had grown up in a chaotic environment with an alcoholic father, but I convinced myself that I had had an idyllic childhood. I discovered at this leadership retreat where my bad faith originated. It's not that we have to demonstrate good faith all the time. As Dr. Bob told me, if we can be 51 percent good and 49 percent bad, that's a good goal. The key is learning how to be more of a net giver than a net taker.

To foster this awareness, you need to do personal work and dig deeply into your unconscious and your limiting beliefs, identifying where they come from. This is the only way to unlock your potential, and I needed to unlock it, especially as my time at Divine was ending.

Rich was facing a moment of truth after the collapses of marchFIRST and Divine. He was good at what he did. This was very affirming. Also, he was deeply afraid for his future and his family. He had built an excellent reputation in a diverse community of businesspeople, and many were eager to hire him or go into business with him. This was a period of significant affirmation and uncertainty. The sudden end of a previously thriving company was shocking. It was also financially frightening because Rich had a young family to support. A great deal of his unfinished business was surfacing. Could this lead to another in a series of failures like his father had experienced? It was also a time of healing as he took stock of how his life was different from his father's.

As I pondered my next steps, the option of starting my own company was particularly scary given my father's business setbacks. Dr. Bob and I talked about this possibility, but I wasn't sure the time was right. Other organizations were looking to buy pieces of Divine, and when that happened, opportunities would arise—for instance, an investor asked me if I was interested in running the services division of its potential Divine acquisition. I was also talking to other companies that were thinking of starting Chicago offices and were considering hiring me to lead their Chicago operations. Over my time at Whittman-Hart, marchFIRST, and Divine, I had built a strong network of relationships, providing me with a myriad of options. Like a lot of relatively young professionals who had enjoyed some early success, I had reached a crossroads, and I was not clear which way I should turn.

WDM Takeaways

- Recognize that intention (Level 3) exists on a scale of 1 to 10 (rather than being a yes-or-no question) and assess where you are on that scale based on your behaviors. And remember, if you want to know what your intention really is, look around you. Consciously or unconsciously, you create your reality.

- Strive for things in life. In this way, your true purpose will begin to emerge (Level 5). Swing at everything in front of you, and trust that things will work out in the end. Start to pay attention to what you like and don't like, as your true calling will begin to emerge through action.

- Take responsibility. As we achieve more and become good at things, we establish a certain level of superiority (Level 6).

The challenge is to take our skills and gifts and use them to author our life and own everything that happens. No more victimhood and blame, but full responsibility.

- Face yourself. Sales allows us to confront rejection and hurt, if we are brave enough to look in the mirror. Hurt is not a bad thing (Level 2). We all are hungry to be affirmed and acknowledged, and ultimately to be loved. Sales gives us the chance to "get on our own side" and affirm ourselves and keep engaging in the adventure of life.

CHAPTER FIVE

BURNING THE CANOES

My choice was not just between working for myself versus working for others. It was also about which job would best facilitate my development as a person and as a professional. As I wrestled with my choices, I decided to set up an LLC, Lyons Consulting Group (LYONSCG), as a way to fill the interim period between jobs. The business concept was relatively simple. I had a lot of established customers who were looking for technology people, and I knew a lot of quality tech specialists. By playing matchmaker, I could serve both parts of my network.

In the beginning, Customer A would call me and say something like, "Rich, we need this type of tech specialist to help us develop or install a new system." I would then call Tom who had this expertise and was looking for work. Tom would tell me he charged $75 per hour for the work, I'd tell Customer A it would cost $95 per hour, and I would take the $20 difference as my compensation.

This work entailed little risk, and I could do it in my spare time while I continued to explore other job opportunities. At a certain point, though, it sank in that although other companies were presenting me with good opportunities, no one was offering me equity in their business. They wanted to capitalize on the extensive network of contacts I had built over the years, but they weren't willing to provide compensation and ownership interest that matched what I brought to the party. It dawned on me that perhaps I might expand and explore what my "side" business could become.

I reached out to Dave Barr, who had worked with me at Divine. It took quite a bit of conversation and visioning before he convinced himself to join me. With Dave becoming part of the company, I was making a commitment. It was time to set an overarching goal. Remember those BHAGs? I learned about this concept in Wright's men's leadership group. We also studied the Jim Collins books *Built to Last* and *Good to Great* where he wrote about BHAGs and how good-to-great companies used them to drive themselves beyond complacency. My BHAG was to build a $50 million Midwest-based IT consulting firm by the time I was fifty. As you may know, BHAGs aren't necessarily realistic goals but audacious ones to which you aspire. I didn't think I could reach my BHAG, but it was a supremely motivating target.

At first, we were a body shop, providing temporary technology experts to companies that didn't want to hire full-time staff for a given need or project. Our original differentiator was that we would be a customer's single point of contact for all their technology needs, and I had a network of great consultants in a variety of fields. It didn't matter what they needed. We found a way to provide it. Even if we had to turn to a competitor to meet a customer's needs and forego our commission, we'd do it. I didn't know it at the time, but this was the beginning of LYONSCG's philosophy and value that we would do whatever it took to meet the customer's needs.

At the beginning, my joking refrain was that I'd been through two different billion-dollar company bankruptcies, now I can go bankrupt on my own. But we did not go under. In fact, things went well initially, and I hired a few more salespeople and a great recruiter to find great consultants. We grew, and I made the neophyte entrepreneur's classic mistake: I was subsidizing the business and not paying myself.

Rich and I disagreed on him not paying himself. I encouraged him to keep an accurate accounting, especially the money in back salary the company would owe him. His unpaid salary represented a loan to the company. This included sales commission and fees for administering LYONSCG. This is a common mistake that entrepreneurs make. They think money paid to themselves is profit when it is really an advance on money the company owes as salary, commission, and service delivery time.

In terms of subsidizing the business, Rich was making the right move. It was way too early to take on additional debt. He was maintaining control in this way. And he was willing to bet on himself by extending his credit. One beginning entrepreneur's mistake is to go for outside capital before proving the business model, a mistake Rich avoided. He was betting on himself and his own track record. It was scary for him not to have that infusion of outside cash, but it provided him with freedom to operate the business as he wanted. Without additional outside money, Rich was also acutely aware of every dollar taken in or spent—not a bad motivator for a new entrepreneur.

The tragedy that I see in entrepreneurs is paying good money for branding and marketing before they have anything to brand, anything proven to sell, and customers they know will buy their product or services. They begin marketing and branding before they have anything to market or brand.

Rich possessed a major skill many entrepreneurs lack: sales experience. He was already an expert. I've given sales presentations to rooms of more than one hundred entrepreneurs, and when I asked how many of them are salespeople, around one-third raised their hands. The failure to develop sales skills and recognize that businesses won't succeed without sales produces much entrepreneurial suffering and failure. LYONSCG was not mature enough to bring in outside money (later his mother did provide some funding, but it was "friendly" money and not subject to the same pressures that come with other outside funding). He was learning business lessons and keeping the business on track simultaneously.

Burn the Canoes

Given my education and professional background, I wasn't naive about business. But no one had ever taught me about cash flow. On paper, the company looked great. We were obtaining more customers, which meant more hires. As entrepreneurs grow, however, they often experience a timing gap between what they're taking in and what they're paying out. We were struggling to pay our bills, which seemed impossible unless you understood the nature of cash flow—you can be profitable on paper but not have collected the money you need to operate in the immediate present. (This is a common entrepreneurial failing, one that motivated me to start the Lyons School of Transformational Business, a school aimed at helping entrepreneurs understand many of the business skills they may hear about but aren't taught in traditional business schools.)

I took out a home equity loan at one point to cover the gap between income and expenses. I wrote personal checks to cover rent and payroll, and each day Dave and I examined the mail, anxious about whether we received any checks from customers.

I didn't know what to do. Should we slow our growth? If we slowed things down, then we would have more cash on hand and be more profitable. This sounded sensible, but it didn't sound like what I wanted. My vision was to be the best, to grow the business. I saw a window of opportunity in the marketplace, and I knew the window would close if we didn't move quickly. I had a phrase that I repeated during these years, one that Dave hated but that captured my philosophy: Burn the canoes.

Imagine you're the captain of a ship in the eighteenth century and you need to take an island from your enemy. You arrive on the island, facing a fierce force, and during the battle, you're tempted to retreat. But if you burn your canoes when you arrive on the island, there is no retreat. You're 100 percent committed to your plan— there is no back door and no turning back.

Burning the canoes wasn't an act of suicide but rather faith in myself, my team, and the plan. I was convinced that we could serve our customers differently and better than our competitors. Initially, our point of differentiation was a little fuzzy, but it clarified over time. From the start, I wanted the company to be more than salespeople trying to sell customers something.

Everyone talks about wanting to serve customers, doing whatever it takes to do what is right. But not everyone can act on this belief. I resolved that our company would turn that belief into action. If customers called and they needed something we couldn't provide, we referred them to people who could help them. We were becoming trusted advisors and partners with our customers. Sometimes we wouldn't make any money from doing this, or make less money, but we made a lot of friends. Creating strong and lasting relationships struck me as critical, and these relationships served as the foundation of our success.

Rich's investment in relationships paid off. One of those relationships was with Kathleen Coughlin (O'Malley), who was brilliant at finding the best people for Rich's clients. He brought her on staff, and she was critical during this early phase of the business. Rich's company offered only the highest quality tech personnel. The company carefully vetted folks it sent out and only sent out people a second time if they received glowing feedback.

Beyond relationships, Rich saw the value in keeping his overhead low. That meant keeping staff small and using contractors to supplement. Because he wasn't tied to paying internal people whether they produced or not, Rich had his choice of contractors, and he picked the best ones, eliminating those who were less capable. When he did start hiring full-time employees, he was able to hire only the best, people he had worked with and had good feedback on. Having the top staff was another differentiator. He also expanded beyond the body shop model and started doing project management.

Satisfaction Guaranteed or Your Money Back

We evolved as a business in a variety of ways. As we became more confident in our ability to deliver what our customers needed, we began to offer customers what was essentially a money-back guarantee. No one was doing this, especially in a services business. We needed a way to differentiate ourselves and to prove that we were indeed customer-focused.

How could we guarantee customer satisfaction? We used the best contractors, and as more money became available, we hired the best contractors as full-time employees. We looked to hire not just the best, but those individuals whose values matched our own.

These changes happened organically, as did our expansion into project management. We observed that some of our customers weren't doing a great job managing the bodies we sent their way, so we offered to help them manage these resources. It made perfect sense for our customers to maximize the value of people, to guarantee an outcome, and it made perfect sense for us as an organization.

I don't want to make this sound like it happened overnight. It was a learning process. Initially, I thought I could hire any salesperson and make him or her successful. Just as some doctors have a God complex and think they can heal anyone, I was convinced that I had the power to transform anyone into a stellar salesperson.

I was disabused of this notion when I hired Al and Tim. I couldn't figure out why they weren't producing. I'd given them the benefit of my wisdom. To my shock, they couldn't use it to become successful. Then

I hired Abigail and Lois, and we paid them a lot of money, thinking they'd produce in line with their salaries. Dr. Bob had warned me of the dangers of this idea; he'd suggested we base part of their compensation on the number of dials they made, but I said no. Again, they weren't producing, and I finally heeded Dr. Bob's suggestion and told Abigail and Lois that we'd reduce their compensation if they didn't make a certain number of dials. They threw a fit but complied, and, eventually, they thanked us.

It took me a while to learn how to hire and manage salespeople effectively. Part of the problem stemmed from what Dr. Bob refers to as my hero complex. From the time I was a kid, I took too much responsibility for other people's successes and failures. I'd come home from kindergarten crying because the class got in trouble, and I'd assumed it was all because of something I did. In the same way, I thought I could help my parents stay married if I got good grades and was a good child.

This carried over to business. I became over-responsible. This was especially true at Whittman-Hart, where I maintained a salesperson's mentality as a manager. I treated my people as if I were still one of them, indulging their complaints about leads. I didn't hold them accountable, and once I started hiring people for LYONSCG, I still struggled to hold individuals like Al, Tim, Abigail, and Lois accountable.

But I was learning the necessity of doing so. And Dave helped me understand what I should expect of our salespeople. He was someone who carried his weight.

That's a wonderful term. Many centuries ago, if you weighed 180 pounds, you were supposed to be able to carry 180 pounds. There was a shared expectation, which created alignment.

Rich learned several key lessons during these initial years of hiring and managing salespeople for his company. For instance, he discovered that it was useful to hire salespeople whose lifestyles demanded they make significant money—they possessed inherent motivation to do whatever it took to be successful.

He also discovered that there was a difference between salespeople at an established company like Whittman-Hart and a new company like LYONSCG. At an established company with strong products and services, excellent salespeople are drawn to working there and can hit the ground running. At a new company, it takes time for the company to mature, for people to want to work there. In the interim, entrepreneurs have to climb a learning curve. For Rich, he had to learn the benefit not just of hiring talented salespeople, but of hiring individuals who could make everyone—salespeople and customers—better.

Our hiring breakthrough came when we brought in Steve Krol. Besides Dave, we'd never hired anyone who could be a supervisor. More specifically, Steve possessed the experience and expertise to handle process, delivery, and project management. It was a big leap for us to recognize the value of hiring someone with managerial abilities who could help us serve customers better, and it foreshadowed an even more critical hire that would take place in a few years.

This was to be a key aspect of Rich's strategy: growing in response to the customers' needs. As customer needs expanded, he expanded services, which caused him to stretch LYONSCG's capabilities, even when he had no idea how they would do what they promised—yet. When people asked Rich, "Can you do it?" he invariably answered yes. He was willing to say yes to things other people would say no to. Others said no because they hadn't done them before. Rich didn't care that there was risk involved. He said yes, and his affirmative responses helped expand the business, further defining his company's service ethos—to focus on the customer and the customer's needs, not the company's. Growth plans were emerging out of customer needs, not good ideas. Expanding business services required him to establish a learning organization that embraced challenges as opportunities.

Rich and his company built their business skills along with their confidence and self-esteem to take these risks. He was not cavalier in saying yes. Instead, he was highly intentional, using these opportunities to expand his company's capabilities and develop its culture of possibility.

Saying yes, of course, has its limits. We couldn't continue to say yes to everything because as good as we were, we weren't good at everything. We learned to say yes often, but we also learned how to wait until the time was right to say yes. In the beginning, though, this affirmative approach served us well.

Initially, we were working with external recruiters. I had built an extensive network of these outside groups, and they would find the people that our customers requested. The problem, though, was that it added a layer of fees to the process. When we hired Kathleen, she managed the external recruiters. After a while, though, she started recruiting directly and eventually brought this function in-house. By taking on the risk of employees, and doing it ourselves, we could make a higher margin.

Dave and I were good salespeople, and we began using our contacts to our advantage. We discovered that we often knew someone—or we knew someone who knew someone else. As Dr. Bob suggested, even when customers requested that we recruit someone outside of our area of expertise, I said yes. I was sure that even if I didn't know this individual, I possessed a large high-quality network that someone out there could do the job. I was willing to reach out to competitors, if that's what it took to help customers meet their requirements. I believed in "coopetition," especially back when we were a small company, and I would gladly pay competitors if they could help us complete an assignment. As you might imagine, these relationships could become complicated, but it was worth it if we could satisfy our customers' needs.

Too often, salespeople focus on the sale rather than on winning friends, influencing people, and being a contributor to their world. At Wright, we teach the Wonders of Intentional Influential Networking (WIIN). We identify four WIINS here. The first win is for yourself. You have the benefit of warm, supportive interactions and an opportunity to contribute to others and find opportunities for yourself. The second win is a win for those with whom you interact. We speak of being a net giver; you are always seeking to contribute to others, and you use your network as a blessing to benefit those whom you deem in need and worth it. The third win is for your organization. And the fourth win is for our world. At the Wright Foundation, we speak of a world that works for everyone in our purpose statement. We ground these concepts in network science, a term that originated with the US Army and that describes the links between diverse nodes in complex systems. It led to a predictive model that the Army used to find Osama bin Laden and Saddam Hussein.

Another example of Rich's fantastic networking is what brought him to the ultimate focus of his business: eCommerce.

Selling Screen-to-Screen Instead of Face-to-Face

Around 2005, we started moving into the eCommerce sector, becoming more involved with the Demandware platform. How we made this transition says a lot about the nuances of selling—achieving a close is not always a direct line between pitch and sale but requires indirect paths through relationships.

Playboy magazine was one of our first business intelligence/data warehousing customers, and I had a strong and long-standing relationship with Scott Stephen, who was in charge of *Playboy*'s eCommerce initiatives. The company intended to build a shop-the-bunny site, with *Playboy* bunnies recommending items; the site was meant to compete with online sites like Victoria's Secret. *Playboy* selected Demandware as its platform, and Scott told the Demandware people that they wanted LYONSCG to do the implementation because we were already working with *Playboy* and knew its systems. The Demandware people refused, claiming that the timeline was too tight, and the process became complicated, especially when a new "partner" was involved. Scott essentially told Demandware, "Look, we trust LYONSCG, and if you don't use them, we'll use another platform."

While Rich believed in burning the canoes in his commitment to business development and the customer, he NEVER burned a personal relationship. His relationship with Scott exemplifies how he learned to connect with others, establish rapport, and build trust. Rich is an extraordinary networker and partner builder. Your network is your net worth, and Rich was rich by any standard.

We completed the implementation, and it helped us form a strong relationship with Demandware; we became one of its first implementation partners. Before this, Demandware was doing all of the implementations on its own. This positioning changed the game for us. Software as a Service (SaaS) became hot in the market, and we were at the forefront of companies that could implement Demandware. Integrating the legacy backend of a company to an eCommerce frontend is challenging. A retailer that wants to get into selling online has a plethora of systems it needs to integrate into the online process, from catalog data to product imagery to inventory and price. There are other backend systems to coordinate, such as point of sale (POS); order management; and picking, packing, and shipping. Don't forget about messaging customers, informing them that the company has shipped their orders, handling changes and returns, etc. And finally, there are the branding issues—making sure the brand message and experience get conveyed properly online.

Companies needed us to be both technically proficient and creative in our integrations/implementations. We rode the first wave of eCommerce, working for well-known brands such as Hello Kitty, Frederick's of Hollywood, Warner Brothers, and many others. We evolved into other well-known brands such as GoPro, Beats by Dre, Vineyard Vines, Patagonia, Kate Spade, and Titleist.

We committed to training our customers on how to use the system, and they trusted that we would provide support as needed. We started codeveloping with customers that had strong IT departments, which wasn't common in the industry at the time, helping us build trust.

Rich is what I would call a pragmatic perfectionist. He was pragmatic—he knew he was a great salesperson, so he stayed in his lane. Rich is also a pragmatic visionary, and his vision drove him toward his picture of perfection in service—service as he would want it. This led him to drive great technical and customer support.

Being able to provide strong technical support and great customer focus drove the company from the beginning. Unlike his larger competitors that would bring in a complete package and elbow client employees aside, Rich chose to conform to each company's needs and honor the people they worked with who were on the in-house eCommerce team. He was befriending the people other implementers would have fired and replaced.

Demandware's internal implementation teams and other external partners never grasped this "secret sauce" in Rich's approach—conform to customers as you respond to their needs and partner with their strengths. His implementation standards were peerless in the industry, and he repeatedly was awarded top prizes nationally and internationally for Demandware. No year since this time has Rich's company fallen below 94 percent on-time and on-budget delivery. His major competitors were often below 50 percent on time, on budget. His hard skills in sales were translating into hard skills in business management.

Growing Pains, Business Gains

We then began moving from subcontracted implementer for Demandware to true partner. Demandware was transforming into a software company, focusing on developing software and not providing implementation services, which forced a partner program. This shifted the dynamic between seller and customer. It was exciting, but it was also scary. While I was shouting, "Burn the canoes!" I was also investing a lot of money. I saw an industry window that was closing fast, and we needed to be nimble, agile, and aggressive to take advantage before the window closed. At one point, we took out a bank loan and incurred long-term debt—I couldn't keep funding the business on my own. And we had to take a line of credit based on our receivables for working capital.

It was tough, especially when you have customers that don't pay for sixty or ninety days (despite having a contractual agreement that they'll pay in thirty days or fewer). For a small, rapidly growing company with more salaries, increasing healthcare benefits, and higher rents to pay, it was touch and go at times.

Especially at one particular time. We had contracted to do a major business intelligence project for a customer, and we lacked the skill sets necessary to do it on our own. I brought in a group that possessed the expertise—they were former Whittman-Hart colleagues who had started their own company a few years before I started mine.

We worked out the financial arrangement, and they completed the first phase of the project for our customer. As we entered the second phase, I received a call from my contact at this former Whittman-Hart group—I'll call him Mike. Mike informed me that they were not going to be able to pay us the amount specified in our contract. Mike explained to me that they had looked at the margins they needed to make, and they were getting to be a big company and needed more money to grow even bigger and start new offices. For these reasons, he said, they were reducing the amount they were going to pay us.

I was furious. A deal is a deal. I told Mike that I didn't care how big his company was, or how big it wanted to get. On top of that, I had referred him to my customer. He was acting as if it were his customer, and he was doing me a favor. Mike was trying to screw me, and he may have gotten away with it if I hadn't forged a strong bond with that customer. When I explained the situation to the customer, with whom I now had a trusted relationship, he told me he'd talk to Mike. What the customer said was, "Listen, you know we work with LYONSCG. If you're trying to screw them, I'm going to kick you out."

This story illustrates a core principle that I was trying to instill in our culture: Do what you say you'll do. Have integrity. Invariably in sales situations, someone will try to take advantage of you. If this happens, you can't simply react and respond in kind. You have to trust people until they prove they're not worthy of that trust. This is Level 1 in the Wright Developmental Model. I was choosing to trust—risk—and believe that the world wanted the best for me, even when I was getting screwed. Admittedly, this can be a tough value to embrace when you're angry at someone for an unscrupulous action. But if you think long term, you'll realize that people who maintain their integrity are the ones people respect. This respect is what cements relationships for the long term.

Rich still has a relationship with the people from the firm that tried to hustle him. He gave them what we call a logical consequence. He fought, but not in an underhanded fashion. He also wasn't deterred by his firm's lack of expertise in a given area. Some people would have caved when a partner showed bad faith. But he did not, and he strengthened himself and his firm as a result.

LYONSCG was unusual because of its sales-driven principles and strength. Rich's early leadership training was principle-based, and it helped him develop the principles and values at the heart of his company's service culture. The leadership principles, which are closely aligned with Peter Senge's "learning organization" concepts, were aliveness, engagement, intentionality, and truth. From them, Rich created his corporate principles: collaboration, responsibility, excellence, engagement, and joy. The company's values also emerged from these early leadership lessons: client-focused, integrity, commitment, independence, and value experience.

Tech companies are usually either sales-driven or technology-driven, but not both. Too often, sales-driven companies are not technologically excellent. Rich's commitment to integrity in service, along with his electrical engineering degree, drove him to develop internal systems excellence focused on the best results for the client, not the engineer—a very unusual quality in sales-driven companies that do not understand the wily ways that engineers can make their life easier while taking away from customer service orientation. Later, we'll explore how this quality was critical as LYONSCG grew and faced increasing diversity of service and expansion.

At this point, I brought together my individual and business purposes—who I was as a person and what I wanted my business to be. I wanted to synchronize my principles and values with those of my clients and employees. While through eCommerce we strove to realize and maximize our clients' potential online, I also wanted to realize and maximize my own and my employees' potential. This confluence of concepts was crucial to all of our development.

Rich established a sales-driven culture right from the start. How LYONSCG went to market is particularly instructive. The vast majority of companies go to market either over-adapting to customers and compromising their values, or they go in with sharp elbows, saying, "Get out of our way. We are the experts." Rich went to market doing what he needed to do to get work, selling what he could sell, while filling in customer needs. He did not replace client staff, which made friends and allowed deeper partnerships with clients so other firms had trouble displacing LYONSCG. The large firms often wanted to replace staff so they could run the whole show without interference. This meant that customers' staff were essentially pushed to the background or even fired.

Rich differentiated himself from competition by encouraging his clients to hire and develop excellent staff, allowing his excellent people to partner more deeply with customers. This is as opposed to how a firm like Accenture often works, where they essentially say, "Get out of the way and let us take over. We'll get rid of all these people. We'll do everything for you."

We wanted to train and empower our customers' people. We were one of the few consulting firms that codeveloped projects in tandem with a customer's team, which required clear and continuous communication. We were always looking to be better. We were always iterating.

In many sales-driven companies, the downside cost is that engineers design mechanisms and processes that are suited to their own needs. Rich made sure that engineering as well as project management processes were client-focused and never just convenient for engineering.

We had to walk a fine line between the best practices we'd developed and knew worked and the customer's culture and methodology. Sometimes we were too rigid about adhering to our practices. At other times, we were too flexible and bent too far in the direction of the customer's culture and processes. We had to strike a balance.

Being a good salesperson involves a lot more than products or services—not an easy concept for sales professionals to accept. When we began partnering with Demandware, its head of sales used to tell new salespeople that they should accompany me on a sales call because I could "sell ice to an Eskimo" and sell their product better than any of their reps could. I didn't know more about the product than anyone else nor did I have the best spiel. I was good at aligning what I was selling with what was best for the customer. In fact, I communicated to customers that I wasn't selling a product but a solution that would simplify their lives and help them sell more online.

Crucial to these aligned solutions was a process we call Ideal State Action Planning (ISAP)—a process Rich mastered. Too many companies get stuck arguing about present-state problems that they haven't defined fully. ISAP helps avoid this mistake, identifying and analyzing liabilities and assets in great specificity and depth. Rich trained his entire company to find out the real problem—to measure it and collect data on it. They'd explore different pathways to solve the problem and then pick the one that worked best. Though the ideal state is difficult to reach, this planning process helped the company get there. It provided a way to consider all aspects, issues, and developments of an ideal state and measure them going forward.

When we did a project, we needed to know what we would get out of the project. We needed to measure the current state against the ideal state at the beginning. If we didn't know why we were doing something or how we were going to measure our outcomes, then we would be setting ourselves up for failure. We came to understand that alignment was critical. For this reason, we began asking clients how we were going to define success for a given project so that we could obtain alignment and stay aligned.

It is remarkable how many companies engage in projects without clarity on their current challenges and ideal state outcomes. By clarifying the strengths and weaknesses and the ideal state with precision, we partnered with clients at unusual levels of depth. We became vision holders and a trusted advisor. When we found a path to move toward the ideal state, we knew what the right course of action was and had better alignment with the customer. We were also in a position to manage expectations. Even on deals we lost, where our price was higher than competitors, we were sometimes brought back in to clean up the mess of the company initially hired—thereby winning lifelong trust with individuals and firms.

Most salespeople lack this mentality. At Whittman-Hart, marchFIRST, and Divine, I saw salespeople make calls and essentially ask prospects, "Do you need this?" If they said no, they hung up immediately. Typical product sales. This is a very different mentality than the consulting sales approach, where you're offering creative ideas as well as products and services and becoming a trusted advisor, whether or not you win the job.

I learned the hard way that it's difficult if not impossible to turn software product salespeople into sales professionals who sold solutions and consulting. At Whittman-Hart, I worked with highly successful salespeople who sold people but not solutions—they couldn't see beyond the product. They couldn't take their customer relationships to the business outcome level. As good as they were at convincing someone to take people, they either weren't interested or capable of more complex, higher-level solution selling.

Rich wasn't the first person to discover eCommerce, but he did bet on the right horse at the right time—Demandware. His competitors in this category tended to sell single solutions, and Rich looked at selling deeper and wider. He looked at a customer's strengths and weaknesses and personalized his approach. He developed much deeper partnerships with more people and disciplines within each organization than the norm, and he also began to see even better ways to serve his customers.

Instead of taking the simplistic approach of replacing retail selling with eCommerce, Rich assessed what customers needed—and what they didn't need. He developed holistic solutions that met customers' needs in more than one way. As a result, his customers felt understood within a deeper partnership context. This deep partnership served as a foundation, allowing his service offerings to expand naturally and organically in response to customer problems and needs. It also helped produce a top account service department that fit their services to exactly what the customer needed—NOT what Rich's company needed. This focus required that Rich become a preacher of sorts, delivering the gospel of customer focus like no other.

Soft Training for Hard Results

With our increasing success, I saw that we had a lot of potential for growth if we could help our people go on the same journey that I was on. As we began to expand our sales team, that meant shifting their perspectives on selling. And it meant outsourcing our sales training to Wright. By having Wright bring accountability and some hard and soft skills training to my people, I could better strategize and manage our sales processes to best meet our customers' needs.

I was involved in developing the curriculum that Wright used for our sales training. For hard skills, we focused on metrics: tracking dials, meetings, and so on. Sales is mostly a numbers game, so we wanted to give our people the ability to capitalize on the numbers.

Most salespeople "get" the value of hard skills like metrics, but whether or not they develop the disciplines to practice these skills, they also need to learn about the soft skills, many of which can only be learned through trial and error. A critical element of the Wright training was teaching them about personality styles and how they affect the selling experience. Our people learned how to read a customer's personality style and shift their own style to fit it. This was the type of training that helped us differentiate ourselves from competitors. It freed me to manage and optimize sales because Wright drove the skill disciplines and accountability in the learning laboratories and taught seminars such as the foundational Wright SEI training, Cooperator/Analyzer/Regulator/Energizer (CARE) personality style training, and the Ideal State Action Planning visioning, planning, and problem-solving technology seminars.

CARE allowed staff members to understand each other more deeply, adapting and responding to clients' and team members' personality styles. By doing so, they could work together more effectively. We seriously invested in this and other training methods, especially those that involved social and emotional intelligence that would help us and our clients deal with difficult situations.

Our competitors weren't using this type of training. They weren't looking to understand customers. Our folks learned to see their own and customers' personalities through the CARE profile lens. Our salespeople established high-level rapport and penetrated accounts both widely and deeply.

We also developed business practices that firms our size were not using. Though it took a while to establish, we brought in a consultant who introduced us to the strengths, weaknesses, opportunities, and threats (SWOT) process. SWOT helped us analyze whether a given action was something we must do, something we should do, or something that would be nice (but not absolutely necessary). It also helped us drive our projects for the following year, maximizing our potential. Our competitors weren't implementing SWOTs every year, so this gave us an advantage. We weren't doing these things to be trendy or because I didn't believe in the hard skills. We wanted everyone at LYONSCG engaged in the success and direction of the company. Everyone participated in the annual SWOT process, which was critical to our success.

We did it because life is sales. The ability to excel at selling and to grow LYONSCG depended on our awareness of ourselves (strengths and weaknesses) as well as our customers and the marketplace (opportunities and threats). With everyone participating in these processes, we maximized our strengths and limited our weaknesses. Sales excellence requires insight, analysis, and reflection. Most of all, it requires learning.

Peter Senge, author and systems scientist at MIT, talks in his book *The Fifth Discipline* about how the only real competitive advantage in business is the ability to learn and grow. I grabbed onto this concept of being a learning organization. This training and our focus on continuous improvement helped us become one. We were giving people tools to ask questions of customers, to listen deeply to what they heard, and to change, if necessary, to meet their needs. We wanted to recreate ourselves continuously, to ingrain in our culture that we had to keep getting better or we wouldn't continue to be the best.

Rich had participated in countless hours of communication training. He was also deeply trained in problem-solving, with an eye to an ideal state vision. He practiced what he preached when he talked to his staff about excellence in technology and service. He didn't just participate in our senior sales lab but also led sales labs. It taught him the importance of accountability. Most salespeople don't want to do the hard work that involves the numbers.

A key part of the sales lab trainings Rich participated in involved learning how to use all the available metrics. The labs taught Rich the value of continuous learning, and he applied this lesson in his organization, creating a learning culture. They acquired new knowledge and grew, developing new skills and ways of doing things as part of the culture. At this time, in his trajectory, a new aspect of Rich's brilliance as a leader was emerging. Even more so, he was developing the skill of applying assignments that he would eventually translate into annual themes for his firm.

Rich picked themes around which his entire organization could focus its attention and develop enhanced excellence. He began a practice of introducing new themes at the beginning of each year to align the people in his ever-growing company. "One Team" was one of the first themed years and reflected the emerging values and principles of his firm. Another training was Wright's Consultative Professionalism which introduced the concept of "yes, and." Here, the firm learned to engage with customers more deeply, not just simply saying yes or no. This led to LYONSCG learning and growing with customers and developing ever-deepening partnerships that led to more add-on sales than new client sales.

Life is sales was an overarching theme, promoting a life of learning and growing, deepening relationships, expanding understanding as well as engagement skills in all relationship areas—our relationships to self, family, friends, coworkers, our society, and our higher power.

The "yes, and" training was more than teaching people never to say no. Its impetus was our realization that we were being too accommodating of our customers, saying yes to everything they requested. We were losing money on projects, giving away services for which we should have been charging. To instill the "yes, and" approach, we implemented a yearlong "Scopebusters" theme, inspired by the movie *Ghostbusters*. We made a campy movie that was a lot of fun but also conveyed the "yes, and" concepts. We created and distributed T-shirts to our people with the "Scopebusters" theme to serve as a reminder for the year. We wanted to communicate that while we couldn't just say no, we could say yes *and*—with the understanding that we would also need to talk about how our yes might affect the budget, timelines, and priorities.

This effort changed the conversation internally. The Scopebusters theme kept us conscious throughout the year that we couldn't let things get away from us by responding with an unqualified yes to every customer request. This emphasis helped us make "yes, and" part of our culture. Our people were learning to really think through add-ons and make sure we were appropriately compensated. As we introduced our salespeople to sales labs and the LYONSCG culture to the concept of a learning organization, accountability was critical, following through with what you say you will do and having others keep you honest and focused. We allowed no excuses—the worst salespeople are afflicted by magical thinking and reasons, really excuses, for not performing to promised levels. They convince themselves that they will double their sales next year by doing the same things they did this year. If you want to double your sales, you need to double your activity or have some brilliant new strategy. This is what the numbers tell us. Combined with being aware of and able to read personalities, our folks developed the skills to make big leaps in productivity. As they produced more, the company grew significantly and started changing in ways that took us into a new realm of success.

WDM Takeaways

- Recognize that safety and security are a choice. Choose trust, and believe that the world wants the best for you. You can choose to trust in each moment, then choose again when you forget (Level 1). BHAGs are an effective way to break through your fear and your limiting beliefs.

- Don't fall into scarcity and make the mistake of not paying yourself as an entrepreneur. Don't fall into scarcity and forget that sales is about service (Level 1). Figure out a way to solve your customers' needs, even if it is not something you can provide. Use your network.

- Strive for accountability. Sometimes you need to break out of your conformity and wanting to be liked by everyone. Tell the truth (Level 4). Give people feedback tied to a vision of who they can be. Help them to maximize their potential.

- Don't burn bridges, as you never know where you will run into someone again. Manage your anger and reactivity—turn it into assertion and intention (Level 3). Remember what you are going for and come up with a win-win solution.

- Align with your customers' purpose in every project, and be sure you understand what the definition of success is. Commit to making your customers successful (Level 5).

- Learn to say yes and no, at the right times (and sometimes "yes, and"). Reactivity can be harmful if you always live from no (Level 3), but conformity and always saying yes can be harmful as well (Level 4).

CHAPTER SIX

THE BEST AND WORST THING THAT COULD HAPPEN

Initially, we succeeded because we were selling a wide variety of digital solutions with knowledge and integrity. Eventually, with an ever-evolving marketplace, this wouldn't be enough. Businesses, like people, need to learn and grow. As salespeople, we tend to stick with successful formulas. Experience, however, taught us that blind adherence to formulas is a bad idea.

When we launched our own business, Dave and I developed a strategy that helped differentiate us and attract clients. We became adept at solution selling, establishing rapport with customers, earning their trust, and understanding their needs.

I know we've described the ideal state action planning (ISAP) and strengths, weaknesses, opportunities, and threats (SWOT) assessment and planning processes. The solution selling that Rich just referred to was grounded in these processes, and it's worth understanding how remarkable these multipurpose tools are.

In terms of ISAP, recognize that people struggle to identify their ideal state and therefore find it difficult to move from past or present states to the ideal one. A density of data exists in the here and now that causes confusion, making it difficult to map a path from present to ideal. It's also challenging to articulate the ideal state in an empowered way—a way that is actionable and provides values and standards against different pathways. The ISAP process helps do all this.

In conjunction with ISAP, SWOT harnesses the power of the mind for many objectives. It's especially valuable for client alignment, providing insight into what they are thinking and feeling about strengths, weaknesses, and so on. This process often helped customers clarify what they really needed, and it gave Dave, Rich, and their people a much broader view of the client. They really dug into what was going on in the company that made it want what it is that it said it wanted. They provided a demanding process to identify the ideal state toward which the client was using the current project. They examined pathways, including the project at hand. Rich and Dave developed an unusually intimate perspective of their clients, which gave them an inside track.

Because our people learned both soft and hard skills, they could develop real relationships with our customers, shattering the "used car salesperson" stereotype.

We created partnerships with Demandware and other platforms and third parties that were tremendously beneficial. Demandware's salespeople knew that we could help them close deals. Not only did we have referenceable customers, but customers also viewed us as an "unbiased" third party. Obviously, we leaned toward the companies we partnered with and always went with the company that brought us in; but because we sold other platforms, customers perceived us as more objective in our recommendations. Even though we sold certain products, we stayed agnostic as to what we sold the customer. I recently sold a major project to a customer for whom I had declined to bid on four years earlier. At that time, I told them that I did not think that what we had was the right fit for them. When they eventually came back to talk to me, they cited that initial instance and said how much that instilled their trust in us.

All this fueled our growth, helped us expand our staff, and increased our revenues. We reached new heights as a company, and then everything threatened to come tumbling down.

The Financial Crisis of 2007–2008

The subprime mortgage scandal in 2007 triggered crises among banks throughout the country. Though the government bailed out the biggest financial institutions, smaller ones went under, including our bank, Amcore Bank. Before shutting its doors, the bank called in our loan and our line of credit, which was nothing short of catastrophic for our business.

Like many fast-growing, entrepreneurial companies, we couldn't keep up with our growth and expenses—increased salaries, equipment, and so on—without a line of credit and a long-term loan. Our cash flow was insufficient to meet our needs because we were always paying our employees faster than our clients paid us. We could have slowed our growth down, lowering our expenses and avoiding the need for loans, but that wasn't my vision for the company. My BHAG was to become a $50 million company by the time I was fifty, and there was no way to achieve that goal through slow, cautious growth.

At first, our line of credit was based on my home equity loan. As we became more successful, we took out a longer-term loan to fund our growth and maintained a line of credit as well—we could draw money based on 80 percent of our eligible accounts receivables. This helped us hire more people, buy more computers and software, and meet other payments that grew as the business grew.

We were left high and dry when Amcore went out of business. During the financial crisis, entrepreneurs were dropping left and right, and despite media reports that money still existed for small businesses, all I saw were small companies desperate for money and unable to get their hands on any.

As Samuel Johnson once said, "When a man knows he's going to be hanged in a fortnight, it concentrates his mind wonderfully." Our company was facing death, and as unpleasant as the situation was, it forced us to examine who we were and what we wanted to be. Until this point, we were trying to be everything to everyone. Salespeople don't like to say no. We honestly believed that we could do everything and that we could do everything well. No doubt, many of our prospective customers were dubious about this grandiose claim. They would ask, "What are you good at, really? What is your specific area of expertise?"

With the economic downturn and the failure of our bank, though, we couldn't maintain our wide range of services and survive. We acknowledged that the enterprise resource planning (ERP) and IT side of our business was drying up; companies didn't want to spend on the "cost" side of their businesses during precarious financial times. We also realized that companies were willing to spend on eCommerce and digital because these were areas that could boost revenue.

We became a focused eCommerce digital agency, and, hard as it was for me, we turned away any business that didn't fit this area of expertise. Though difficult, it was absolutely the right thing to do. We changed our messaging, who we hired, and how we trained our salespeople. In hindsight, it's clear that these changes and an increased focus saved our business and put us on the path to great success. At the time, however, nothing was clear. When you're running out of money, you think the end is near. Fortunately, we had someone willing to invest in us: my mother.

Rich was forced to challenge his "never say no" approach to service. He had to react to events with a great deal of self-examination and then formulate a plan of action in a new way—aligning his staff, thinking, and market-facing moves to create a viable company identity. He chose to focus on a rapidly growing area and let go of the rest. It's never easy for salespeople to shed services and products that they've developed, and Rich resisted this course of action for years. But market pressure and his financing forced him to do something quickly, and this financial challenge presented a huge opportunity to drive the business forward . . . with a little help.

Selling Mom on the Business

At the time that our bank closed, my mother was in good financial shape, having sold the largest Anheuser-Busch beer distributorship in Michigan. Still, asking my mom for money wasn't easy. I considered going into the family business (at one point my mother's brother had been running it and wanted to bring me in as president). This might have happened if I had not started my growth work, and my mother had not decided that she wanted to run the company.

A business owner's relationship with investors can be complex, but when the investor is your mom, it's even more complicated—you're dealing with an individual on multiple personal and professional levels. I am so thankful for the growth work my mother and I have done. For that reason, my mom and I decided to do even more coaching, individually and together, to help us confront the issues that complicated our relationship and to stay clear with each other. We needed to understand each other even better to take this step—why we did what we did years ago as well as in the present. This counseling was critical. In business, you're always going to have differences of opinion with investors, and if you have underlying, unaddressed personal issues, the issues will only exacerbate these differences.

At Wright, we are big proponents of finishing unfinished business, recognizing and challenging unconscious limiting beliefs, and expanding our range of behaviors into realms that would have been otherwise unconsciously prohibited. This includes addressing the foundation of our unconscious empowering and disempowering beliefs, especially those installed in early life by parents and caretakers. When leaders and team members stay blind to these issues, they often have either authority issues or fail to work to their potential. We call it doing your "parent work." Rich did his. He discussed the issues resulting from the unspoken problems from his childhood and his mother discussed hers.

Our experiences from years ago cause us to live out what we have avoided unless we learn to recognize and deal with it. For Rich, this meant addressing not only his fear of failing at business as his father had, but also facing his mother's seemingly never-ending unhappiness during his youth. Rich had worked extensively on each of these. In fact, he entered therapy with his mother around this time, both in Michigan and in Chicago. Rich used the same process in his emotional/personal life that he used at work, working toward his ideal state.

Many people avoid the emotional work of facing their unconscious issues and stay stuck with limiting beliefs about the world that can prevent them from being their best selves. Borrowing money from my mom meant I was once again dependent on her, but this time I was ready for an adult-adult relationship. In my earlier personal development work, I had walked away from family wealth and was afraid to step back into it. The counseling work I did with my mother years earlier provided enough separation that we could enter this new financial relationship with honesty and mutual accountability.

One of the most difficult challenges I see in my peers is understanding that they're in a cage, the bars of which were constructed when they were small children. Unless they acknowledge this constraint, they will continue to live inside this cage and never reach their potential—no matter how much worldly success they attain. When they build their business, they will unconsciously recreate the challenges they faced personally. For this reason, we need to understand the template inside of us. I call it the matrix of unconscious beliefs, rules, and stories that were set long ago—the template that determines why we do what we do. Fortunately, I learned early on to test the bars of my own cage and eventually escaped.

For instance, Rich needed to create order out of chaos, a product of his difficult childhood with very young parents still in college. This wasn't all bad. In his business, he created order out of chaos, establishing processes and values that served his clients and his employees well. But these childhood issues also have a dark side. Rich had to deal with boundary confusion, differentiating between his own needs and those of his mother. For instance, his mother wanted (eventually) for him to return and run the family business; he had to learn that her need was not the same as his.

We bring all these limiting beliefs with us to the workplace, and if we're not conscious of them, they can be harmful. Many entrepreneurs avoid family work and become entangled financially with family members. As much as we may deny it, we all have unrecognized, unconscious limiting beliefs that stand in the way of us fulfilling our potential. Some of our unconscious beliefs are empowering, while others are disempowering. These unconscious beliefs form the substance of what we consider ourselves to be and not to be.

Rich came to see himself as a savior, doomed to being a good boy—he was limited by this confining role. When Rich began his parent work, he recognized and broke family rules, myths, and beliefs through assignments. The most challenging assignment involved telling difficult truths to his mother. He had to say things that were critical to her that would engender guilt trips in response; she would blame Rich for "hurting her feelings."

Rich had done a great deal of this work before he was willing to fully trust himself and his mother and borrow money from her. This made the conversation about a loan much easier and led to Rich including his mother on his advisory board. With Rich and on her own, his mother had begun doing her coaching and growth work and approached loaning money to Rich as an investor, holding Rich accountable.

Years earlier, my mother had been hurt when she wanted me to return to the family business, and I said no. I was hurt because of her response to my saying no. In therapy, we revisited this event and the earlier time when my uncle wanted to bring me into the business. We both realized that we had very different perceptions of these same events. Eventually, we acknowledged each other's perspective and made peace with it. I explained to her that I wanted to do something on my own and that returning to the family business would have been the easy way out. Her business was already doing well, so I saw no role for me there. How much of an impact could I have had? Once she understood my point of view and I understood hers, we could move forward personally and professionally.

My mother joined our advisory board as an investor, and we met quarterly. In the beginning, it was a challenge for her and for me. Our business was very different from her business. We were not a cash business, and we reinvested almost every available dollar back into the business, content to be marginally profitable. Initially, my task was to help her become comfortable with what we were trying to achieve, and the opportunity ahead—and that we were going about it the right way.

Joining my mom on the advisory board was Scott Stephen, my fellow MBA student and career-long friend and customer from *Playboy*, who opened the possibility of eCommerce and Demandware to LYONSCG, as well as Don Delves, an executive compensation expert and member of my leadership group. My mom also brought in a financial consultant, Ed Fein, and we appointed him to the board since my mother frequently used this type of consultant in her business.

I ran the advisory board meetings, and our main goals were to report on the sales and financials of the business, monitor the staff and our culture, and track opportunities and threats. I've alluded to the SWOT process, an analytical process that Norm (one of my Entrepreneurs' Organization (EO) forum members who consulted with us and eventually joined the company and became a key contributor to our success) brought to the LYONSCG culture. One way our board helped us manage risk was by addressing a potentially huge problem: 80 percent of our business at one point was represented by one platform, Demandware. As a result, the board urged us to add other platforms, which we did—Magento in 2009 and Hybris in 2012. Putting all of your eggs in one basket is a common tactic of small businesses. But it makes companies vulnerable to a single catastrophic event. Our moves to establish other platforms and relationships helped provide some protection from that vulnerability.

Rich's competitive nature and focus on excellence caused him to become an unusually disciplined entrepreneur, a trait he brought to the crafting of his advisory board meetings. His board members had a wide array of skills. In addition to Dave and folks from Rich's leadership group, he brought in a consultant that Scott had worked with, Ed Fein, to give his mother an outside, objective partner on the board. They invested time and focus in preparing for the board meetings, and the formal reporting process imposed structure and accountability. Rich would bring the vision, Norm would bring the financials, and Dave would report on sales.

Rich also tracked opportunities and threats from meeting to meeting and would not remove threats from the list unless they were resolved. Rich had already started developing significant financial discipline long before forming this board. He knew that he would need planning and accountability. It is this understanding that caused him to bring in Norm as a consultant initially, and partner and CFO/COO eventually. I had advised Rich against bringing in such a high-priced consultant. This would prove to be one of two times where I was very mistaken, and Rich proved me wrong.

We placed an even greater emphasis on planning—we started creating and tracking three-year plans, which besides helping us stay on course, pleased my mother greatly. Norm provided the financial controls and really kept the company focused so that Dave and I could focus on sales.

This freed me up to craft the company vision and principles and focus on culture and alignment.

External Changes, Internal Principles

Even though our positioning and services were undergoing a radical shift, we retained certain core values that had always been critical to our success. From the beginning, I was committed to having the clients' best interests at heart and guaranteeing their success. We liked to say that while our competitors budgeted for lawsuits, we budgeted for client accommodations.

As the business evolved, so did our principles. Our customer commitment, unbiased independence, and insistence on hiring the best and the brightest didn't waver, but we added principles that reflected our growth as a company.

We became a more collaborative culture. As we grew and developed different practice areas under our eCommerce/digital banner, we needed to learn how to work across functional boundaries to create teams in which the whole was greater than the individual team members.

We emphasized responsibility and people being accountable for their actions (rather than making excuses or blaming others).

Throughout these years Rich was constantly expanding and refining his delivery mechanism. The way that his architects, project managers, and, eventually, account managers interacted shifted over time. Rich needed to stay constantly aware of the internal development and delivery processes because the developers tended to want processes that benefited them. Rich was constantly meeting to make sure that all processes internally stayed focused on the client. With each major expansion of services from search engine optimization to becoming a full design agency and service firm, there were new processes to be designed—and Rich never wavered in his focus on the best interest of the client even when there might be greater efficiencies.

Too often, people become wrapped up in achieving goals, then coasting. We realized that our only competitive advantage was our ability to continuously learn and grow. We always tried to put ourselves in our customers' shoes. We talked about how work was a long journey rather than a single destination, and how we had to strive for consistent excellence.

We promoted engagement. It wasn't enough to be competent. It wasn't enough to do a good job passively. We wanted our people to be active participants—to engage fully and consistently in their work.

We talked to our people about joy. Work shouldn't be drudgery. We wanted them to take pleasure in their tasks, to feel great when they did something positive.

We also made it clear that a principle we used to emphasize—balance—was no longer a principle of our evolving company. As wonderful as the concept of balance sounds, it's not a realistic value for consultants. When you're helping a customer whose site has crashed, you may spend days doing nothing but trying to fix it. Balance goes out the window in these situations. Instead, a more accurate and compelling principle became "work hard, play hard." In fact, when we hired people, we told them that this was a more appropriate value, and that balance was impossible when you're neck-deep in crises or racing to meet deadlines.

We needed the customer to see us as a dependable partner, and we faced two challenging problems in this pursuit. When a customer asked if we could do something, we would either say "No, we don't do that," or "Yes, whatever you want." Well, "no" closed doors, and "yes" often put us in an impossible hole—it taxed our capacity to do an impossibly wide range of work. As we described in the previous chapter, this led to our consultative professionalism training and "yes, and." We worked to say "yes, and," giving a provisional yes but added that we needed to get back to them about what it would take in time and resources. We needed to confirm the impact on budget and schedule. This became a big driver of our sustainable growth, along with the principles of responsibility and the value of putting the customer first.

Rich began putting into practice life values and principles. The "yes, and" concept was just one of them. These values also included purpose, service, one team, and caring for others. He integrated this annual focus into all-staff meetings, and everything he did. His perspective on work and parenting shifted, and he came to perceive himself as a vision holder and inspirational leader. Rich translated this perception to everyday work realities with employees and his family and friends. He developed new trainings every year and one of them was a training he called Responsibility Realized, in which he trained all of his staff on the Wright Developmental Model and the principle of responsibility.

His annual themes provided a unifying focus for his people to engage in with customers. He talked frequently to his people about customer awareness, teaming, vision, values, and core operating principles.

His personal life began to join up with his professional life—he was experiencing a unity of vision at work and home. He wanted his family to realize and maximize their potential just as he wanted his employees and clients to do the same. His family was a learning organization too! He and Gertrude attended every parent-child, family, and couples activity they could. They ended up leading most of these activities.

I put our purpose, principles, and values in our promotional materials and on our website:

The Values and Principles That Guide Us

VALUES:

Client Focused—We always put clients first.
Integrity—We always do the right thing.
Commitment—We stand by our work.
Independence—We are unbiased.
Value Experience—We hire and attract the best people.

PRINCIPLES:

Collaboration—We work together as ONE TEAM with our clients and each other.
Responsibility—We are each individually accountable.
Excellence—We always strive to be our best.
Engagement—We are all active participants.
Joy—We work hard, and we play hard.

I really believed in our purpose, principles, and values. We offered a money-back guarantee as a symbol of these guiding concepts. Little did I know how devastating and amazing this guarantee could be.

From a Gutter to a Strike

Just as the call of our loan and the collapse of our bank challenged our growth, so too did another seemingly catastrophic incident that occurred a few years later. One of our clients was a bowling shirt company, and we were running into issues with the Magento platform; when customer service people tried to make changes to the site, it slowed down the site's frontend performance. Our client was upset, and we flew to the Los Angeles headquarters of Magento and met with the company's president and founder to try and solve the problem.

Our team in Ukraine worked with Magento's team in that country to separate the frontend and backend, the crux of the problem. We needed to supplement our US team, as we couldn't find enough skilled folks in the US, and US labor rates were exorbitant. We reluctantly hired offshore in Ukraine, which turned out to be a great advantage in this case. But solving this problem did not prove to be sufficient, as our client was actually facing market challenges, too. Our client told us that sales were off, and they no longer were interested in launching the new site to sell their products. Furthermore, the client decided that they wanted to take us up on our money-back guarantee.

Though we always made this guarantee to clients, no one had ever acted on it because we made sure that they were satisfied with our service. In this instance, however, despite us satisfying the original concern, their lagging sales, over which we had no control, caused the client to request a refund. This was not the intent of our money-back guarantee.

As painful as it was, I wrote a big check and sent it to the client. I was so terrified that I immediately called Scott, in tears, and said, "I think I did something that could end my company." I saw two huge negative consequences as a result of my action. First, there was the financial fallout—we were giving money back that was crucial to our business plans. And second, I anticipated reputational consequences. We were unable to launch the site for our client, and I figured this failure would ripple through the industry, tarnishing our company. But I knew giving the money back was the right thing to do. It was a question of integrity, and as much as I hated to part with the money and feared it could put us under, failing to do so would have violated our principles. The money-back guarantee was a promise that we made to all our customers. Scott understood that it was a question of values, as did Norm. I had to face my fear and stay true to my values.

After sending the check, the president of Magento, Bob Schwartz, became a friend for life. The move was perfectly aligned with how Bob thinks about business and customer service, and it established a deep trust between us and in LYONSCG. Bob knew that no other SI's would ever do this, and he began to send us companies who trusted him to connect them with people who would do the right thing.

This was one of many turning points for Rich, where he relied on his integrity and made a decision based on his principles. Rich was learning to trust the world and to believe in goodwill being more important than dollars and cents. Some would say that he created good karma. Rich had studied principled leadership and developed a strong belief in doing unto others as he would have them do unto him. These principles, along with

Rich's deep sense of integrity, acted as headlights guiding him through these and many other major fears related to seemingly unsolvable situations. For solutions and resolutions to these situations, he also relied a great deal on Norm, who was constantly assessing and arriving at a huge variety of solutions.

We were about to attend a big eCommerce and retail trade show, and we had planned a major promotion for the show featuring our client's bowling shirts with the LYONSCG logo printed on them. We attended the show (though we obviously didn't do the bowling shirt promotion), and I knew that many attendees would be aware of what I thought would be perceived as our failure for this client. I felt like I should tell them the whole story, including how I gave the client their money back.

Most of the people who heard the story could not believe it, and respect for us was going through the roof. No one gives big sums of money back to clients, they figured, especially when we had done the work we had promised to do. My fear that word would spread that our company was incompetent, and I was an idiot, was not realized.

Instead, this refund became the stuff of industry legend. Though many in our industry were aware of our money-back promise, few believed that we would honor it when a large sum of money was involved. When we did, they realized that we walked our talk and lived our values.

This story reached many in our business, and it attracted new customers and new employees in a way that even the best marketing campaign couldn't. Trust and integrity are powerful magnets, drawing clients and employees toward us in a way that all the boasts and promises could never have.

As a postscript to this story, we ended up changing our guarantee. Though we still guaranteed we would fix problems for free, we limited the money we would give back to the specific work with which clients were dissatisfied. We recognized that offering an unconditional money-back guarantee made us vulnerable to the unscrupulous.

The other postscript is that this incident became part of our culture. It became a living symbol of our willingness to satisfy the customer, and it made everyone conscious of this value.

WDM Takeaways

- Continue to choose to trust the universe and look for messages and direction even when you experience terrible news and events (Level 1). With intention (Level 3), even seemingly negative events can lead to positive directions and outcomes.

- Understand that truth and integrity are key to all relationships (Level 4). Try to keep all your relationships clear and without secrets. Be willing to accept that other people may experience the same event differently and have very different feelings than your own.

- Embrace the fear of accountability (Level 1). Resist your hunger to be liked and patted on the back (Level 2)—engage with others who require you to be your best. Create an advisory board to keep you accountable and on purpose.

- Do the right thing and take responsibility even when you fear the consequences (Levels 1, 6); recognize that by abiding by your purpose, and principles, and trusting, you may lose in the short run but win in the end (Levels 1, 5). Karma is the friend of those who do the right thing.

- Be willing to write down your mission, purpose, and values (Level 5). Let people know what you stand for so you can be held accountable and lifted up when you forget.

CHAPTER SEVEN

GLOBALIZATION AND PROFESSIONALISM

After the "bowling shirt client" episode, our company's directional arrow surprisingly pointed upward. Like a lot of relatively young companies, we struggled with focus, direction, and finances. We tested different strategies and tactics and made mistakes, but we learned from them and bounced back.

We emerged from these experiences stronger and with a clear sense of the company we wanted to create. We were "professionalizing" the business. Norm, who became our COO and CFO, was critical to this process because he was skilled at annual planning, the SWOT methodology, continuous improvement, and running a business—his growing involvement with the business paralleled the business's growth. Norm seemed to have a crystal ball when it came to budgeting and forecasting.

As strong as my network already was, I knew that to expand the business, I had to expand that network even more. I joined the Entrepreneurs' Organization (I actually met Norm there), and it introduced me to new business owner contacts and friends.

Rich has a great capacity to network and make friends with clients and other professionals, building strong relationships with trust—a huge factor in his success. He is also hungry to gain knowledge, which pushes him to learn each time he meets new people. Over the years, I have marveled at the difficult situations he has faced—often emerging with friendships intact out of the engagement, a theme you will see repeated in his story.

The Value of Professionalizing and Focus

What was the best use of our time? This was a question that both Dave and I struggled with for quite a while. This may seem like an obvious question, but it's one that entrepreneurs often overlook. They become so caught up in their day-to-day tasks that they don't take that step back to ask: What focused activities would yield the most bang for our buck? We concluded that the company would benefit the most if Dave and I spent more time on sales and less time on operations and delivery—that's what we hired Norm and others for.

We had been so far down in the weeds building a business, we couldn't see the bigger picture. When we'd sell a project, we felt compelled to make sure everything rolled out smoothly. That meant visiting clients to ensure projects were being implemented properly and that the clients were happy. All important tasks, but they took time away from selling, and selling was what made our business tick. Our combined sales and customer focus made our business different from others.

Norm took the professionalization of the business to a whole new level. He was great at solving client problems and maintaining strong relationships as they professionalized their operations even further. Professionalizing often means hiring skilled professionals. They started to hire project managers. Rich agonized a bit about whether these project managers could be trusted—trusted to do as thorough and committed a job as he would do himself. It was a leap for him—a leap for any entrepreneur. His partnership with Norm was key. He knew he could trust Norm to oversee projects. This was a point in the business where Rich was redefining their delivery systems as they attracted larger clients and had to get increasingly complex teams up and running. It was a time of experimenting with different ways of achieving this goal, of trying to get the most out of these teams.

It's important to remember that Rich's undergraduate degree is in electrical engineering. He's trained in systems, in how things work together and flow toward a desired outcome. So, methodology comes more naturally to him than other entrepreneurs.

LYONSCG was owned by a sales professional with great engineering skills but who never delved into the details of the inner workings of eCommerce more than necessary. This allowed Rich to focus on building his business—another differentiator from most entrepreneurs. The all-too-common problem that entrepreneurs face is what I call the entrepreneurial feast or famine. After a sale, the entrepreneur dives into delivery and drops their sales discipline. Once the delivery is complete, the entrepreneur is now terrified and scurries to sell more business. After selling more business, the entrepreneur once again dives into delivery and forgets about sales.

This is another element of life is sales. When we understand this and we understand entrepreneurial feast or famine, we begin to develop the disciplines of sales and set a floor below which dials, meetings, and proposals will not fall. Ultimately, sales must remain primary to drive growth and force change. Many feast-or-famine entrepreneurs never learn this lesson. The successful entrepreneur must maintain minimum daily dials, conversations, and meetings goals at all times, placing sales at that essential first part of the day position.

We started assessing how we might reuse elements from one project to the next. Part of being a professional delivery organization is recognizing that you don't have to reinvent the wheel with every new client. We asked ourselves how we might iterate on the delivery process to make it better. This concept of continuous learning became our theme and our way of gaining a competitive advantage.

Becoming more disciplined was rapidly becoming essential for our company. After our bank went under, and we borrowed money from my mother, we started growing quickly and needed to impose discipline on the growth process. Where were we going to invest next? What must we do to maintain our advantage? Where were we willing to take risks? What threats existed and how could we deal with them? Because we didn't have infinite resources, we had to be disciplined.

The Complexity of People and Projects

Our projects became not just bigger, but more complicated. As positive as this development was, it also increased our risk—there was a greater chance of making mistakes and the mistakes were potentially more costly. We needed to manage the projects more effectively to reduce risk and increase the chances of success, which meant hiring the right people with the right expertise to be even stronger project managers.

Before Norm joined LYONSCG, Dave and I were trying to juggle selling, managing customers, hiring project managers, and servicing accounts. It took us a while to integrate everything into a coherent strategy for our company. We needed a methodology going forward, or we'd be all over the map in what we did and how we did it.

This is where reusing project elements came to the forefront—one of our methodologies involving learning how to reuse the tools we created. "Reuse" became an integral element in how we did business. Typically, we would launch an eCommerce website for a company and create a feature with a specific function for that company's site. We take this method for granted today, but back then, it was an innovation. If the client was a furniture company, we would design a configurator—a way for site users to configure the type of couch they wanted. This was not part of the typical eCommerce packages we sold but a customized tool we added. If people were interested in buying a sofa, they could use this tool to choose a color, a size, the type of wood, and so on.

But for each client, we didn't need to build a new configurator. What if we could take that configurator code and turn it into a module that different clients could then reuse, which we could adapt to different applications? If we could achieve that objective, we could reduce our costs (because of scale), increase our profit margin, and bring our customers' products to market faster.

The problem, of course, is that we were in a run-and-gun phase at this point, so it was a challenge to start creating the structure to scale a reusable methodology. But we committed to planning, and this put us on the right path to professionalize this aspect and others of the business.

I should point out that this was an extraordinarily complex process, and that it took years. Rich yearned for this, and what's impressive is that he never let go of this reuse idea even though it took five years to put everything into practice. But when Rich finally realized his reusable methodology, he could bid lower on jobs and enjoy higher margins.

To create this methodology, we had postmortem meetings after every single project, attempting to identify anything new or unique that we might use again. We didn't just focus on innovative things, we also looked at every aspect of a project—if we came in over budget, was it because we messed up? If so, did we need to feed this error back into our scoping and pricing practices and change them for other projects?

Their review system was state-of-the-art, and it was part of a superior project management system. Many young entrepreneurs, especially ones who enjoy some success, are impatient. But for many early-stage entrepreneurial businesses, it takes time, even years, for an idea to come to fruition. It's like a loose tooth—you know that it needs to come out, but it takes a lot of time and wiggling before it finally does so. This "watchful waiting"—staying current with innovations in the industry and in one's business—is essential.

During LYONSCG's early growth stages, the company tested a variety of concepts and programs. It started hosting, then attempted to do search engine optimization, then considered partnering with a design firm, then brought the design function in-house. It was juggling a lot of balls. Most impressively, Rich timed everything with almost preternatural precision. He knew the right time to stop an experiment and the right time to go all in on something else.

Besides having an exquisite sense of timing, Rich is insightful and agile as a leader. Few entrepreneurial companies discover how to store, retrieve, and redeploy elements of what they develop for a client. This requires an in-depth ability to identify the common elements of the company's services and offer them to different clients and see the direction of the market. It also requires the flexibility to find ways to adapt things rather than to make them new each time—the trap so many entrepreneurs fall into.

I would complain to Dr. Bob about the methodology before I hired someone to help me with it—how it was a pain to implement properly, how it took so much time to create and refine the processes. I was chasing deals, trying to sell, and so as important as methodology was, it seemed a lower priority. In response to my complaints, Dr. Bob worked with me repeatedly to fix and refine the methods if they were damaged or broken. Easier said than done. That's why I hired people who could operationalize and professionalize the business even more than I already had. Of course, once I hired them, they became billable, and the salesperson in me wanted their hours billable to clients rather than non-billable (even though they were working on processes necessary for the business).

Many entrepreneurs tend to focus their time and energy on either delivery or selling to the detriment of other functions. I might have "gotten away" with this behavior if not for Dr. Bob challenging me and my willingness to work on what he recommended. I realized that I needed help. Coaches like Dr. Bob provide support, they challenge you, and they help you articulate and stay true to your vision. The best advice I could give any entrepreneur is: Hire a coach who will nurture you when you are down and take you to the mat when you are being stubborn and need a kick in the ass. We all become so myopic about the business that we fail to see the value of anything that is tangential to direct revenue. Hiring a good coach can push you and ensure that you remain true to your vision. The coach can provide the far-reaching perspective and hold the vision while you work on sustaining the business today and planning and building for tomorrow.

Timing Is Everything

Let's return to my earlier point about loose teeth, about how Rich tried different strategies and knew when to jettison one and double down on another. All this exploration helped foster the company's emergence. Rich constantly faced seemingly impossible choices and a myriad of possibilities. Should the company do hosting? What about search engine optimization? Account management? Rich kept collecting data and refused to move until he had enough to bet strongly on a move. No matter how hard I pushed him, he bided his time until he knew it was time for action. This give-and-take dynamic is an essential aspect of the coach-client relationship. Rich also mined his leadership group for input and other sources of knowledge that he used, such as the Entrepreneurs' Organization (EO).

Entrepreneurs often act too soon or too late. In part, that's because they're managing their business in a kind of frenzy and not allowing ideas to incubate and emerge compellingly at the right time. Rich was selling like crazy now, managing accounts, and the business was growing.

An apt metaphor is the development of a fetus from an embryo. If you've ever seen time-lapse film of this development, you'll witness alternating expansion and contraction as an egg is fertilized, organs develop, and the shape of the fetus evolves. Rich was watching his business develop similarly. He had to focus on growing one aspect of the business while letting another part fade away. In these early years, the business, like a child growing up, looked different from week to week and month to month until it finally emerged.

While all this was happening, Rich was talking to others, learning, growing, and making friends, expanding his network, and hiring people from that network. Talented individuals really wanted to work with him rather than other companies that might have more resources or offer more prestige but lacked the LYONSCG principles and values. This is how he won the war for talent. People sensed Rich's commitment to quality, to customer focus, to a clean, solid logic, free of the usual mistakes, in large part because Rich listened carefully to his people.

Rich and I developed a dynamic relationship where I would constantly push him for product and service expansion. I cannot overemphasize the importance of entrepreneurs making the move on what feels right for them and not doing what their coach tells them to do when their coach tells them to do it. They are the ones on the battlefield fighting the enemy in hand-to-hand combat. Developing that relationship of mutual trust takes time, however. An entrepreneur must always remember that they're paying the price for the choices they make. Rich was very good at taking responsibility and sensing the right moment and not moving until he was ready. His friendships and alliances often provided the information necessary to make the right moves.

I was building alliances, which paid off down the line when we expanded the types of platforms we offered. I even made friends with competitors. I'm someone who doesn't like to burn bridges, that's not my style. You never know when someone can help you. That doesn't mean that I like everything people do as part of a business relationship. Who likes getting screwed on a deal? Remember when we brought an outside group into a deal, and they reneged on the established terms of the relationship? One of the people who was a member of that group was Ron. Ron ran a Salesforce business-to-business practice, and he brought me into deals. We are still friends. Why? Because we trust each other. He respects me as a person and knows my integrity is real. I didn't burn the bridge with Ron even though I was upset by what happened, and that connection has paid off as a friend and in business.

It's not that I don't get pissed off when someone hurts my feelings or backstabs me. But I'm able to take a step back and look at a given situation strategically. Awareness is key, as is my use of the Wright Developmental Model in the moment. When I am angry, I ask: "Do I have an underlying fear or hurt?" "Do I blow this up right now?" "Do I wait for a more opportune time?" "Is there a future benefit if I preserve the relationship (I always assume there may be a future benefit)?" These are strategic questions that you need to assess in the moment. I can use the information gained from this self-questioning to understand myself and others better and to make better decisions. If you don't make this assessment, your anger will take over, and you'll blow up the relationship. Containment is a key part of my strategy. In the Wright Developmental Model, anger is a key emotion, and if we react in anger, we tend to make a mess. I developed an ability to hold back; by waiting and transforming the power of reaction into highly intentional, outcome-oriented moves, I was guided by positive intent rather than reactivity.

I'm able to assess without letting my anger get the best of me because I believe in the value of trust. Things happen for a reason, and I trust that the world wants the best for me. I remind myself that I'm not omniscient. Even though a given interaction seems negative, I can't read minds or see the future—I don't know the full implication of what just took place. Therefore, I trust there's a reason for negative events, that problems will resolve, and that opportunities will surface.

This trust helps me overcome another problem entrepreneurs face: the overwhelming need for speed. Entrepreneurs get caught up in a crisis-a-minute mentality. They feel that if they hesitate for even a moment, they're lost. I tried to keep my eye on the prize and orient to outcomes that contribute to my higher purpose. We all get distracted by squeaky wheels and brush fires, but the challenge is to focus on the most important matters and our key priorities. This takes us back to Ohm's law, and V=iR. Reduce the resistance that gets in the way of getting the most important things done.

I know this is a challenge because, on any given day, I've had a sense of being rushed, facing countless seemingly critical tasks to perform. Even though the demands on my time were significant, I never rushed. This was one of my most challenging lessons as a salesperson—to never promise what I could not deliver, including start dates. We learned to walk away from deals when we could not start as soon as the client wanted. We ended up, in many cases, getting these accounts back when the company's initial firm didn't work out. Eventually, we reached the point that we never went over budget or missed a deadline 94 percent of the time; a statistic almost twice as good as our largest competitors.

Though I didn't rush with any of my decisions, I also couldn't tolerate moving too slowly. At one point, I told Norm I wasn't going to slow down sales when we were operating at peak capacity, and, fortunately, he responded by always finding a way to unearth resources and outsource some key tasks. To avoid moving slowly, we implemented procedures and training that helped us operate more efficiently—we could do more with less and didn't have to move at a slower pace. We also did a better job of training our people, and when necessary, we formed partnerships or other alliances with external groups so we could maintain our pace.

Slowing down based on capacity drove Rich nuts, and his commitments demanded he maintain the company's speed and agility—he was focused on providing his current clients an optimal level of support. Norm, as COO, helped a great deal. Norm was able to service accounts and partner to fix problems and refine systems so Rich could play the critical role of company visionary and keep selling. He and Rich developed mutual respect and trust that allowed them to keep their word to clients at a remarkable level.

There's a difference between going fast and rushing. Famed UCLA basketball coach John Wooden has a great quote about this: "Be quick but don't hurry." He is also quoted as saying variations on, "If you aren't quick in today's world, you're done. If you hurry, things are poorly done or not done at all." One of the skills that we work on in the developmental element of our work is moving from reactivity to assertion—taking increasing responsibility to intend desired outcomes rather than react. This is the mastery that Rich is talking about right now in these passages.

I would never do anything without thinking it through. At the same time, I'll act quickly if a window of opportunity opens. I assess if it's the right opportunity for us, and then build consensus before acting.

I have never forced things on people with whom I worked. Before promising something to a client, I would talk it through in a process that I called "socializing an idea." Dr. Bob taught me to be defensively offensive and have pre-meet meetings. I sought to reduce unpredictable elements by harvesting thoughts and concerns before meetings, integrating them, and working toward their solutions before I presented an idea in the meeting. I included people in the meetings as well as in conversations before the meetings—and after the meetings. This was the same approach I followed with our clients.

My persona as a leader was "we," not "I." This inclusiveness was critical, and I took several actions to make it a reality within LYONSCG. We invited people in, both literally and figuratively. We created a participative culture that valued hard work and also fun.

We had Christmas parties, summer events, happy hours, and an annual holiday brunch. This wasn't just for employees and clients but also for their families.

Rich understood the value of thanking and "selling" the families on the great work LYONSCG was doing. He knew from his own upbringing, and from Norm and Dave, how important family was to everyone. Many leaders talk about how their people are family, but Rich made a consistent and astute effort toward this goal so that it was more than talk.

Family was important to me, and the holiday brunches especially allowed me to thank the moms and dads for all their hard work, and to thank their kids for understanding when their parents were away on business trips or working late. My former boss, Bob Bernard of Whittman-Hart, used to take pictures of his employees' kids and put the photos on a wall. I decided to borrow that idea, but instead of a wall, we built a structure with three big steel squares. On one square, we put our core values. On another, our customers' logos. And on the third, we posted pictures of our peoples' children. It communicated: This is why we work so hard.

Once, someone told me that the company would be more successful if I worked harder and didn't spend so much time coaching my kids' soccer teams. This individual maintained that you can only have one or the other—personal or professional success—but not both. I said, "Screw that! I'm not sacrificing my family." That represented a fixed versus a growth mindset. An either-or versus a both-and mentality.

I believed there was a better way for the company and for myself as a leader. I didn't take credit, and I didn't dictate. In certain instances, I planted the seed of an idea and let it germinate in others. When it bloomed, it felt like it was their idea, not mine. They owned it in a way that they never would have if I had just told them what to do.

Most entrepreneurs succeed based on "I," not "we." They come up with a great idea and tell others how to implement it. But I didn't want "yes" people beside me. We allowed conflict between the delivery and the salespeople at the beginning of a project, but by the end, we brought everyone together.

I wanted my staff and our clients to be invested in a decision and move forward together. Even though I knew the direction I wanted, my people had to own the decision and buy into it. I was always selling, and the best sales are those where the staff or the client comes to the desired decision themselves, with a little help via conversation. We would still move quickly, but we all needed to be aligned on these opportunities.

One of the best examples of this happened when we eventually opened our London office. At the time, Demandware had a lot of business in London, but didn't have a company like ours to partner with that could consistently deliver the quality it wanted. It seemed like a great opportunity, but our team was not unilaterally in agreement that we should do it. I presented the idea to my leadership group and our advisory board and asked them to think about its potential. I wanted them to arrive at the conclusion that this was an opportunity worth pursuing. I wanted them to own it, to feel responsible for making it a success. If I had just said, "This is what we're going to do," I wouldn't have made the sale. Or rather, it would have been a superficial and forced sale because people were only going along with the boss's idea.

From my coaching perspective, this was the riskiest and most demanding investment for Rich, as well as the one with the longest return. For more than a year, he spent a good part of sessions asking himself hard questions. Dave and Norm questioned the move repeatedly. When the staff member Rich planned on sending to London was not allowed to stay in the UK, Rich took on that job. He was holding himself accountable for making the sale, practicing consensus with his leadership by inclusion and at the same time asserting his leadership vision in the greatest period of doubt and uncertainty he experienced before selling the business.

He heard a lot of criticism, but he never stopped including others in this accountability process, even when they disagreed with him. Rich is particularly good at not getting stuck out on a limb; he was adept at getting himself out of a jam by selling, and they all knew it. Too often, we entrepreneurs tend to be spontaneous, creative problem-solvers, and it is very easy for us to get ahead of ourselves. In skiing, we talk about being out over our skis, which can lead to us taking a header into the snow. I cannot think of one time that I ever saw Rich do this.

Ultimately, the London move was a result of my vision—I had a bigger vision for what our company might become. The move to London was not just about profit and loss; it was about supporting our US customers abroad. Many other companies had failed to support Demandware in London. I needed to keep my commitment to Demandware and make it work.

The New Norm

It wasn't that we knew from the start that Norm was the solution to all our operational problems. It's fair to say that his value emerged to us as the company began emerging. His planning expertise and financial acumen became increasingly obvious. Norm, with his forecasting crystal ball, was able to predict and plan with uncanny accuracy. Initially, we brought in Norm once every year to help us with our annual planning. Then we increased the frequency to once a quarter. His structured planning exercises and SWOT analyses helped us develop our first three-year plan—a discipline that was critical to our survival because we needed to be accountable to my mother who had loaned us a significant sum of money. Norm helped us develop metrics and track our numbers quarterly, and as good as this was, it wasn't enough. We needed to measure our progress against goal more often if we wanted to optimize our performance.

We asked Norm to come in monthly, and his work helped us gain greater insight into our key performance indicators (KPIs). With this knowledge, we made faster and better decisions about major business issues. We could also change on the fly because we had real-time data that told us the pros and cons of making any change.

Given the enormously positive effect Norm had on our business, we talked about bringing him on board full time. Norm was an expensive addition. He was a very senior businessperson who had founded and run multiple companies. This wasn't an easy decision. Norm had been helping us as a consultant for three years, and as a consultant, he was a huge bargain. If we made him a full-time employee, we would have to pay him a sizable salary and pay him benefits. We knew at our size that we couldn't afford Norm. We had no idea if this would be a good move, and if we could make the investment pay off in the long run.

But for the long-term health and growth of the business, it seemed like the right thing to do, just as stretching into the UK would prove to be a good move in the future. Our head of recruiting, Kathleen, was on our management team, and she pushed hard for us to hire someone like Norm to run the business operations. Ultimately, we decided that if the move could free Dave and me up to sell more, it would help us to make a quantum leap. We believed that there were no better salespeople in the industry than Dave and me, and we could sell more and train more salespeople and scale the business if we were freed up.

And that's exactly what happened.

Norm quickly began overseeing operations in general. He helped Rich in the constant refinement and expansion of service delivery. Norm never lost sight of putting the customer first. He implemented Rich's vision repeatedly in the face of the implementation and development teams' inclination to design systems to make their lives easier at the customers' expense. He was that unusual operations, finance, and strategy professional who was good with customers. His sensitivity to the importance of sales caused him to take on increasing responsibility over time.

Norm was also very good at overseeing all aspects of human resources from hiring, to employee development, to firing. He provided an assertive style that complemented Rich's much more easygoing and sensitive demeanor. This freed Rich to focus on mission-critical responsibilities, even though it was not always comfortable for everyone. As a note: Rich being "easygoing" refers to how he appears to people, not to his core self. Think of the old saying about ducks appearing to move serenely on a pond while their webbed feet are continually paddling underneath the placid surface. Rich is more like a nuclear power plant that keeps many electronic ducks moving.

The Tension Between Sales and Delivery

Entrepreneurs have a wide range of responsibilities—hiring, delivering products and services, managing operations, setting policies, and developing a direction and vision. For all these responsibilities, however, they still need to sell. They're selling all the time—or at least they should be. They understand what it means to sell a product or to sell a potential client on their services. But they must also sell internally—to employees, vendors, or the community. Hiring Norm freed Dave and me to be able to leverage ourselves better and sell alongside our developing sales team.

We intended there to be a healthy tension between sales and delivery. Typically, you have conversations daily with a variety of people that, on the surface, have nothing to do with selling them something. In reality, however, you have a goal for the conversation to establish rapport and to achieve a desired win-win outcome. You must think in selling terms. That's why I'm super-strategic in my conversations—what am I giving them and what am I trying to get? I do this as a parent, too. As my children grew, I was always selling them on their capabilities, on their potential, and on what they could achieve.

At work, I sold my people on how they were part of the best organization, part of the best team in the industry, and we kept the statistics and metrics to prove it. I sold them on how they were going to deliver the best results for clients, that no one in the world could do it better. It became part of our culture. While that may not have always been true early on, it became true over time. I was selling a vision and a way of being, and if

I didn't get our employees to believe it, how could I expect it to ever become true?

But you can't sell crap; you must deliver on what you sell. Honesty and integrity are critical. This was true for me as the company's leader, and it was true for all of us concerning our clients. We never sold products or services we couldn't deliver, but we always pushed our delivery organization to deliver things that were challenging and complicated.

Rich would never say this, and he might disagree with me, but Rich is also always selling Rich. I'm not saying that he is some sycophantic butt-kissing embarrassment to himself. Not at all. But Rich is acutely aware of potential judgments that might come from others and rarely does anything actively that might turn them off. I'm sure he doesn't even see this as sales. However, over the years, I have learned that those of us with sharp elbows are often setting up inhospitable environments into which we might sell. Rich does not work against himself much at all.

Norm helped us with the delivery part of the equation. He was the one responsible for partnering with me and the delivery organization in creating the delivery methodology. And it wasn't a one-and-done effort. We upgraded the methodology continuously through project postmortems. We assessed even the best projects, determining what we might have done better. We integrated that insight, making improvements in our quoting process up front and in our delivery systems. With this delivery methodology, we could quote projects more accurately for our staff and clients. These advantages improved our sales process, and we felt more comfortable with what we were selling and our ability to deliver on time and on budget.

We began to agree to fixed-bid projects where we guaranteed a result at a specific cost. This gave us a significant advantage. Our One Team methodology was a core principle that gave us an edge; it required that we function as a single, cohesive unit with clients as well as internally among our various practices. It helped us achieve our 94 percent on-time and on-budget performance, and it became part of our sales and marketing pitch.

Dave and I dedicated ourselves to doing what we did best—selling! We often sold beyond our capacity, knowing that Norm and Brian Wolfe (Norm brought Brian on as our CTO), and the delivery organization had our backs and worked with the customers' best interests in mind. We always seemed to overcome roadblocks, and we never put the brakes on. This is the advantage of being a sales-led organization.

Rich is not only a businessman. He has always been a student of business, and his learning allowed him to understand the importance of adding Norm and having a solid delivery organization. Rich's study of business began with his grandmother since she ran the family business. It continued with his participation in the sales and leadership groups where he had exposure to a wide range of businesses, from carpet cleaning to high-end consulting and manufacturing. These lessons offered him insights, providing perspectives that allowed him to make bold moves and deliver the excellent services he promised; they also helped him to become a selling CEO.

During this period, Rich put his visionary leadership into practice with increasing effectiveness, and Norm aligned with him. Rich led by articulating a compelling vision for the company and directing the company's selling efforts brilliantly with Dave, while Norm took over the daily responsibilities that allowed Rich to do what he did best.

Outcomes

After hiring Norm, and implementing our methodology-based programs, our company matured. Like a child who becomes a young adult, we stopped searching blindly for an identity and started trusting our substance, becoming who we genuinely were. When that happened, we attracted even better talent than we had in the past. Part of our attraction was our reputation in the industry (we had great projects and great people), but part of it was our culture and experience. We would hire someone, and he or she would say that they had never been a part of such a cohesive, smart, and productive team. Our new people would also comment on the maturity of our methodology. Even consultants that we hired from much larger firms would comment on its sophistication. Our new employees valued our culture, our methodology, and our work-hard, play-hard attitude.

In many ways, I think the company reflected who I was. One thing I haven't discussed yet is my desire to do something important. For a while, I was skeptical of our business—I wasn't solving world hunger or curing cancer. A certain amount of cognitive dissonance existed between my desire to make an impact and our focus on eCommerce. Over time, and with the help of the Wrights, I grasped the impact. The more the company grew, the more jobs I provided to people—good jobs in a good environment that helped them support their families. I realized that creating a win-win culture—a win for all of us who worked at the company and a win for customers—was a good thing.

Rich just articulated a key to transformational leadership, as described in the book of the same name by Bernard Bass and Ronald Riggio. This type of leader is concerned not only about himself but also about all the others in his orbit. Transformational leaders possess vision—Rich had a vision for his company, and he helped others share this vision. These leaders walk the talk—Rich lived and worked according to his principles. And they want people to be engaged with their work—to embrace it completely rather than just competently.

Rich wasn't born this type of leader but worked hard to become one. He worked on internal and external relationships with Judith and me for years. He turned to Judith for help with his hurts, fears, and anger. He turned to me for business coaching.

I had learned to trust the world and myself more fully. No longer the scared little boy of my youth, I had reached the point where I knew I could handle being hurt—even bad behavior from others wouldn't change my view of the world as a safe, trusting place. Similarly, pilgrimages with the Wright group to sacred sites around the world opened my eyes and cracked open my brain. As I learned about different races and religions and observed various cultures, I became more tolerant and accepting of differences. This helped me become more inclusive as a leader.

As we emerged to become the company we wanted to be, we shifted our focus both externally and internally. When we started out, we had to search high and low for the right people to hire, and even then, we made mistakes. Now, we were flooded with applications from the best people in the field, and this allowed us to raise our talent level another notch.

Looking back, I can see how we were able to move from a body shop to eCommerce. When we started, our business cards read, "The single point of contact for all your IT needs." In 2009, eCommerce was our focus, but then we expanded our services, adding creative, hosting, digital marketing, and strategy into the mix. People were starting to buy everything online, then they started to return online purchases to stores, and then they bought online when they were in stores. Just as consumers were breaking down traditional silos, we were integrating services that had once been separate.

If I saw a window of opportunity that could help customers, I'd jump through it. In business terms, we expanded organically—every move was related to our core competencies.

The principle of service and customer-first drove LYONSCG's expansion. LYONSCG's deep partnership with customers was critical, helping it evolve in ways that its competitors couldn't. Because its partners were teaching the company about the marketplace, it possessed insights that others lacked. As a result, LYONSCG had a high level of credibility among its customers because it seemed to know more sooner than anyone else.

We had always talked about ourselves as an eCommerce company, but we were more than that, and so we eventually dropped the "e." We became dedicated to helping our customers realize and maximize their commerce potential, online and in-store ... and helped our employees maximize their potential as well. Commerce Realized! was born.

WDM Takeaways

- See yourself clearly and tell the truth about your skills and your best use for the company (Level 4). Hire people around you who are stronger than you in complementary areas.

- Don't act out of fear and scarcity, either by acting too fast or too slow. Try to engage in a "both and" mindset vs. "either or." Choose to trust (Level 1). Make sure it is the right time to make big moves. Act out of positive intent, not reactivity (Level 3).

- Accept and create healthy tension to push your organization to grow and evolve. Conflict is not always negative and can be productive and used to gain alignment around purpose (Level 5).

- Strive to be your best (Level 5). All the best athletes in the world have and use coaches. Hire a coach. Don't kid yourself—you will never develop your full potential and be your best on your own.

- Develop a keen sense for all your feelings—fear, hurt, anger, sadness, joy. Own them or be driven by them. Awareness is the key—with awareness comes choice. And with choice comes more requisite variety and more personal power.

CHAPTER EIGHT

GROWING PAINS AND PLEASURES

We were keen observers of the market and our selling environment, and we shifted our practices to align with the changes emerging all around us. The markets evolved as technology developed and services consolidated. If we didn't adjust, we risked becoming stuck in unproductive, unprofitable, and unsatisfying routines.

In hindsight, it's obvious how necessary these changes were. When you're running a growing business, however, you can become so caught up in the daily tasks, the immediate problems, and the myriad of opportunities that it's not easy to see the longer-term changes that are necessary or the short-term changes that will have long-term effects.

For us, one of the major changes involved our decision to sell two different eCommerce platforms rather than just one—a choice that was anything but easy.

Demandware and Magento

Starting in 2005 and up until 2009, we were working with Demandware exclusively, a continually evolving platform that began focusing on the upper end of the market. Hosted in the cloud and with certified cartridges (integrations to third-party software providers), Demandware was (and still is) a great platform for us to sell to our larger, more mature clients. Demandware, though, used a revenue-share model with a minimum monthly fee, which often did not appeal to our smaller customers. We were missing out on the smaller and middle market segments because some of these customers wanted to host their platform in-house rather than rely on the cloud, and they also preferred a licensed over a revenue-share model.

Magento, as a licensed, open-source platform, met these requirements. The company had just come to market with Magento Enterprise, which was the first paid version of Magento, and it fit our market segment and our need. While this platform could help us capture clients in the middle and lower ends of the market, forming a relationship with Magento had two potentially negative consequences:

- We had a great relationship with Demandware, and we knew the company wouldn't be happy with the addition of a competing platform.

- We would have to devote resources to this new platform—training our technical staff and salespeople on how to use, implement, and sell it.

Dealing effectively with seemingly unsolvable problems has allowed Rich to win the trust of many people. Rich believes in coopetition, a belief that requires Rich to maintain trust. The obstacle for Rich was to communicate to each of his partners openly and honestly that they were adding another platform, and it could be a win-win solution for clients and all parties. Demandware liked being the only game in town, and so Rich had to engage in some difficult conversations. He understood and empathized with Demandware's vulnerabilities. He accepted the company's reticence, discussed its concerns in depth, and outlined the parameters for how LYONSCG would operate. His listening skills allowed him to recognize his partners' fears and to negotiate win-win outcomes for all.

He made it a point to keep Demandware informed of what he was doing and when. Demandware began to trust the process, and Rich respected its territory, never introducing Magento to a customer that Demandware had referred to LYONSCG. Demandware referred a lot of business to LYONSCG, especially early in the relationship. As Rich's company grew and began sourcing more of its own deals, this was to prove highly beneficial to both Magento and Demandware; each received more business than they could source on their own.

This business relationship was the "loose tooth" from our earlier analogy (when Rich addressed the loose tooth, it eventually paid off as LYONSCG was able to source its own deals). This sourcing advantage was just part of the company's maturation as a sales organization, which included hiring new staff and eventually adding a strong inside sales function. As it developed its account management function, the company was growing stronger and less dependent on any one business sourcing channel.

This was a critical moment in LYONSCG's history, foreshadowing many cooperative changes to come.

Demandware preferred that we be exclusive to it, even though it wasn't exclusive to us. When I broached the subject of Magento, and Demandware objected, I said, "Fine, we'll be exclusive to you as long as you don't have any other implementation partners and are exclusive to us." I was clear to both Demandware and Magento that when they brought us into a deal, we would never "flip" the deal and sell the other competing platform. I promised that if we entered a deal together, we would win it together or lose it together (unless either company told us it was disqualifying itself). I laid out the ground rules of our relationship in the most transparent and detailed manner possible. I told Demandware that if it brought us into a deal and the prospective customer asked us to quote Magento, we would only do it if Demandware gave us permission first.

Transparency matters. Honesty counts. Full disclosure is crucial. Anything less, and Demandware would have resisted more strongly.

It also helped that we had made a practice of partnering deeply with sales reps at all our partnering companies, including Demandware. My rationale was that when Dave and I started, we were small, and a company like Demandware had a ton of salespeople. If we could somehow leverage that sales force, it would be a huge boost for us. To that end, I began coming up with ways to help the Demandware sales reps close deals, providing them with references, turning around quotes quickly, connecting existing customers to prospects, etc. As a result, the company's reps became loyal to us. Even after Demandware became a large company and used much larger competitors like Accenture, its reps still brought deals to us (even though, technically, management frowned on this practice).

But our partnering went beyond helping the reps close deals. Part of our metrics involved having our outside salespeople meet with the sales reps for these platforms, establishing relationships through lunches, reviewing the pipeline and account lists, and engaging in other partnership-building activities. Sometimes we would do events in their markets where we invited both customers and partners.

Many times, companies in our field don't recognize how important partnership relationship development is. This is especially true of the larger companies that adopt arrogant attitudes of "they should be kissing our ring." They don't see the value in making the effort that partnering requires.

But I was always asking myself and our people: "How can we be a better partner? What can we do better? What are we missing?"

This open and honest approach helped us cement our relationship with Magento. We worked our way into deep partnerships with the company's internal staff—always making them look good and helping them succeed. In the "bowling shirt company" story, we had some challenges with the early performance of the Magento platform, and we ended up returning the customer's check. To this day, Bob Schwartz, Magento's president at the time, tells this story with fond memories—but also with respect. If the company had any doubts that we were a company with integrity, returning a customer's check banished them. I also communicated in no uncertain terms that we had returned the check partially because its product was struggling and partially because the bowling shirt company was having business issues, but I was still going to hold Magento's feet to the fire. I expressed my interest in continuing to invest in its product, but I made sure the company understood that I didn't expect this to happen again.

Stability in software platforms was a significant issue back then. Magento Enterprise was still new and was not yet a totally stable product. It lacked many of the features that customers sought. Magento needed a good-faith partner, with experience and a proven track record, like LYONSCG. The integrity of LYONSCG was on the line, and Rich was committed to maintaining this integrity. He would do whatever it took as a leader to solve what seemed unsolvable, thereby earning even more partner and customer respect and trust.

We got into the business of trying to save implementations when they didn't work, but this also created problems. In some instances, people would have up to fifty extensions that they integrated into the Magento platform to handle specific functions or features. Because the extensions were not tested together, they frequently failed to work well together and would crash the customers' systems. It was a mess.

Change is messy. We had spent years with just Demandware. Bringing in Magento changed the script. Even as our business was evolving, our bedrock principles remained the same. Part of our decision to add a second platform was that it communicated our lack of bias—our independence and our commitment to doing what was best for the customer. We could tell customers the pros and cons of both platforms without customers seeing us as slanting our sales pitches to favor a preferred provider. It also allowed us to capture more of the market and serve more customers, as I didn't want to focus only on the upmarket and large customers. We would no longer have all of our eggs in one basket.

In doing all this, I had the advantage of knowing our business better than anyone—the various markets, products and services, different types of customer relationships, and so on. This deep and wide knowledge of the business proved to be a sales advantage. It would lead to many of our advances and innovations—Magento, Hybris, the London office, our digital strategy, and much more.

Demandware and Magento appreciated our knowledge, honesty, and reputation as an unbiased third party, and we closed many deals for both of them. Our integrity and customer focus are what helped us navigate change successfully.

Rich was skating on thin ice. He represented both firms but needed to maintain a neutral posture. Each firm needed to trust that he would represent them fairly in conversation with the customer. This became increasingly complex when some of the sales originated from Demandware, while others originated from Magento or LYONSCG or still other sources. The potential for hurt feelings and distrust was great. Coaching Rich was a delight as he sorted out the fairest solutions, keeping Magento and Demandware fully informed and maintaining their trust.

Unlike me, Rich is concerned about "looking good." I don't mean he just wants to be liked. He wants to build rapport with others, which certainly helped in his relationships with Demandware and Magento. He senses what drives other people and uses that to bring depth to relationships, to get to the heart of the matter. His customers greatly appreciate this ability. Even if a deal doesn't happen, he maintains that person as an asset. He's an asset collector.

As I am fond of saying, "I don't like to burn any bridges." The market was evolving quickly, and I was leading the business with finer and finer distinctions. I had to not only understand people but also understand the products and services for each customer and situation. As I look back, I was aware of relationship management then, but I now grow increasingly aware that I was learning my business from the inside out for many different markets.

Our customers told us what other products and services they were considering, and their trust in us gave us industry perspective. Serving our customers fully became a road to market research. Just in the course of doing business, our customers gave us insight into what the competition was doing and how they were going to market. This opened up a world of opportunities as we expanded our network and found more folks with similar needs with whom we could partner.

We were getting so good at understanding our market and services that we could see how even competition could become partners and help us.

Master of Alliances: Knowing Every Deal in the Market

We have already discussed how Rich is an exquisite networker who threads the needle of seemingly conflicting interests to find the win-win for everyone. With his established willingness to partner with competitors at times, he was becoming a coopetition specialist. Implementing eCommerce platforms required relating to many different service and software providers, many of whom became friends with Rich. This ability to form partnerships became a critical part of LYONSCG's success and helped it to maintain a strong and independent position. Rich often found common ground with all, whether sitting across the desk or discussing a lie on the twelfth hole of a golf course. His ability to sense and respond to the heart of others' concerns won diverse and lasting friendships that provided the foundation for long-term partnerships.

His strong relationship ability was seeded early. Growing up, he was confused and upset because of his family's financial shortfalls and conflict; he was also concerned because of his mother's seemingly constant distress about money and other issues and how they affected her relationship with his father. One of Rich's biggest fears is mess. His mastery in relationships and the avoidance of messes—skating on the razor's edge—blossomed where his early childhood trauma had plowed the ground.

Rich is always defending against potential conflict by finding creative solutions to seemingly impossibly messy situations. We've already seen his ideals in service delivery. Now let's examine one of his more focused strategies—to know every deal going down in the marketplace.

Knowing every deal in the market was an impossible task, though one worthy of our BHAG. As our company evolved, we set our sights high. We didn't do what a lot of growing companies in our position do—wait with our hands open and constantly ask partners for leads. We recognized that it was just as important to give as to take. Everyone wants to be your partner, and the subtext of partnership for many companies is, "Give me access to all your customers." That's not a partnership; these opportunistic companies are just looking to feed off you like leeches.

We didn't like this model because it created inequitable relationships. We also didn't like it because we wanted to control our fate; we didn't want to be dependent on our partners telling us the deals in which we could participate. Every partner wanted to box us in and know what we were best at, in what industry, and what size company. I don't like boxes. And I had lost enough deals on my own—I didn't need my partners deciding which deals I should or should not be in.

We created an inside sales team and gave them the mandate to network and learn as much as they could about the market, especially whenever a company wanted to re-platform and implement a new eCommerce system. We established alliances that went beyond the usual suspects (the platform vendors). Every eCommerce implementation requires a large variety of service providers—tax providers, email providers, payment gateway providers—as well as a plethora of integrations to multiple systems such as ERP, OMS, DAM, PIM, POS, etc. Don't worry about their definitions; just know that this mishmash of acronyms means confusion and complexity for an implementation! We encountered anywhere from ten to twenty third-party vendors in every deal, and all of them were much larger companies and had much larger sales teams than we did. They had many, many clients and knew the clients interested in re-platforming or that were unhappy with their current implementation partners. We established relationships with all of them. This gave us an ear to the marketplace, allowing us to discover prospective deals before our competitors. As we realized a greater volume of deals than anyone else, our alliance expertise developed rapidly.

I didn't want to be dependent on Demandware (or anyone else) for business. I also didn't want Demandware to lose deals for us because they decided we were too small or too busy or lacked the right expertise for a prospective client. Pushing to be in on every deal gave us a degree of control that we otherwise would have lacked. We wanted to be the ones to decide if a given client was right for us, not to cede this control to anyone else.

Our partnership mentality was critical because we couldn't afford to develop a huge sales force. Having varied, numerous alliances, however, is almost better than having a mammoth sales staff—you get the business without having the huge salary and management overhead.

Most people are social or reflexive networkers, but Rich's intentionality was a huge advantage. Rich intends benefit and keeps an eye out for opportunities for himself and those with whom he is working. This intentional attitude motivated people to give him leads on deals that they might not have offered otherwise.

People didn't understand how I could be friends with my competitors, including Thomas Obrey (TJ) of PixelMEDIA and Adam Grohs at Sapient. It wasn't unusual for Adam to call me and say, "We can't do this deal; it's too small for us, but you guys should go after it." Too often, people view competitors as the enemy, precluding any type of friendship. In my view, there are plenty of business deals to go around—my competitors will win some, and I'll win some. And, in terms of friendship, I like being with people I like, regardless of who they work for.

Hunters and Farmers

One of the most significant structural ways our company adapted as we grew was with the creation of an account management team. Some people are hunters, and others are farmers or gatherers. In sales, some people are great at opening doors and acquiring customers, while others are great at growing and nurturing these relationships and accounts. As our relationships became more complex, we needed to have and manage both types of salespeople and to use their skill sets to our best advantage to grow our accounts optimally.

In a way, our business expansion dovetailed with our move to account management. Our account managers were bringing us information from the market and customers, and we responded with services to meet market and customer needs. We knew that customers wanted an integrated approach, and that's why we pushed so hard on Demandware to partner with us. Demandware was used to working separately from firms such as ours, but we made the case for going in together as a single team offered a better customer support strategy. Eventually, Demandware adopted our model.

We designed our sales compensation system to incentivize people to get new accounts. Typically, salespeople received a diminishing percentage from accounts they brought in over a three-year period—as an example, they'd receive 6 percent the first year, 4 percent the second, and 2 percent the third. After that, they received 0 percent. It was in their best interest to bring in new accounts rather than sit and milk existing ones.

As we brought in customers that became long-term accounts, we developed a large pool of active customers in need of attention and love. Who was going to take care of this customer now, or after the second or third year, if we encouraged salespeople to bring in new business? That's where the farmers came in: account managers.

Dr. Bob and I had many discussions about account management before I took any action. The organization had to be ready for this change and for this investment. I had always thought of salespeople as door openers, their key ability being to bring in new customers. Account managers, on the other hand, are relationship-oriented. Their primary roles are to keep customers satisfied and happy and to resolve conflict. Was it worthwhile to hire people for these roles, especially because we were not going to charge the customer for them? From a financial perspective, could they generate sufficient revenue directly or indirectly to justify their salaries? With more attention to and a deeper relationship with customers, could account managers resolve conflicts before they escalated, increase customer retention, and upsell or cross-sell additional services?

We started slowly. My first account management hire was Katie Dunlap, and it was essentially an experiment. A highly successful project manager in the digital agency space, Katie had taken time off to raise her children and was just deciding to come back into the workforce. I saw that she was driven and high-powered, but I also knew that she wouldn't make a cold call to save her life. Her skill set was different from any other salesperson I had hired, but I saw her value almost immediately. She was brilliant at building and strengthening relationships and at establishing trust. We began traveling together, and I introduced her to all of my accounts.

This was critical for one of my goals. I didn't want problems with clients continuously escalating to me. I wanted to spend more time selling (as well as other management responsibilities, like evolving our strategic vision, our culture, and our growth), and I wanted Katie to become our clients' trusted advisor. If clients needed me, she would bring me in, but if she could be successful with these relationships, I would have more time to lead, manage, and strategize.

The broader goal was to develop our account management to the point that our hunters could hunt, and our clients could feel that there was someone at LYONSCG that they trusted to troubleshoot, answer questions, and do whatever needed to be done. We positioned these account managers as our customers' advocates, and we brought them into the sales process early (rather than after the sale had been made) to demonstrate how much we valued them—and hopefully, how much customers would value them. It became a competitive advantage.

I should emphasize that our account management strategy didn't happen overnight. Like many new methods and strategies, it started as a test that we then implemented incrementally until it started growing exponentially. When I brought Katie in to work with me, her original job was to take care of conflicts and other issues, making sure I wasn't called into an account problem unnecessarily. Katie did such a good job that it made sense to bring in another account manager, Jennifer Conklin, to work with Dave. Katie and Jennifer saved us a lot of time and enabled us to sell more. In addition, when we were pulled into account issues, it was appropriate, since our involvement was strategic rather than random.

From there, we brought in other account managers, and these account managers grew their own accounts and addressed key issues effectively. Katie and her account management group functioned as customer advocates, but in this role, they also sold new services to customers. We learned that the happier the account people made customers, the more they could sell.

Hiring professional account management was a need Rich saw, one we discussed repeatedly for more than four years. As was often the case, when he moved strategically, he seized the opportunity in his network to hire an established star. Katie and Rich became a dynamic team. She understood the industry deeply and was unusually good at making friends, problem-solving, and penetrating accounts. Her understanding of the industry allowed her to identify client needs. As the company grew, the accounts became increasingly complex. She and Rich became joined at the hip in the service of customers; when a storm needed calming, Katie could bring Rich in. Most of the time, however, she was very capable of dealing with a great deal of complexity on her own. Her dedication to client satisfaction was profoundly aligned with Rich and the company's values.

Katie's goal was to never have a client issue escalate to me. She was great at building client relationships, and she knew when it was a good time for us to visit clients to give them some "Rich love" and attention. On one such trip in the LA area, we were checking in with some clients, communicating how important they were to LYONSCG. I always asked Katie if there was anything I should know to avoid surprises. We visited one account, and we happened to be there for the weekly status meeting with the client team, with our support team on the phone. During the meeting, the CEO wandered in and started yelling at his team, and then continued on to my team. My heart rate went up quickly, and I chose to respond to protect my people. This is where we learn to harness reactivity into assertion. I told the CEO that if he wanted to yell at someone, he could yell at me. "But never yell at my team," I explained. This sounds like I calmly delivered this message, but I admit I may have thrown in a couple of f-bombs to communicate how upset I was. He stopped yelling. More to the point, this became another iconic story within the LYONSCG culture, letting everyone in our company know that I had their backs.

A postscript. I saw the CEO at the airport that night. We were both going through the priority line, just the two of us. He apologized to me and rationalized that he had to be hard on his people, blah, blah, blah. He wanted to buy me a drink, be friends. I don't drink, but we spoke civilly, and I had earned his respect by protecting my people.

Our account management team became a huge asset with Demandware as well. LYONSCG was held up as the example of how to work together with Demandware on an account. It took some time and some fighting over whose account an account really was. In the end, we would agree an account was "our" joint account, and we partnered closely to bring the best of both companies to the client to make them successful.

At the time, our competitors weren't doing this. Instead, they were there to implement an eCommerce platform—end of story. While it took me a long time to commit to account management, when I did, it sent a clear message to customers that we were there to make them successful, grow their business, and bring them best practices. We increasingly brought account management in early in the sales process. It was a key differentiator for us, and although others have subsequently adopted our account management approach, our willingness to be first significantly boosted our growth. In fact, over time, our account management team brought in more revenue than our outside sales team. With more than one hundred active support accounts providing us with best practices across the customer spectrum, we had a great view into what was happening in the market and could serve our customers better by identifying upcoming trends and reacting quickly.

Change always has ramifications, and in this instance, we knew that introducing account managers into the mix could create internal conflict. The salespeople who opened up the accounts might resent them: "We do the hard part of getting an account, and they just have to babysit it."

One of the biggest potential points of conflict involved compensation. Too often, management can fail to appreciate how difficult it is to open the door—to find and bring in a client. As a result, they pay commission for the first year and then cut off that commission in the second year. We wanted to communicate to our salespeople that even though we were bringing in account managers, and bringing them in early, we recognized the long-term value of the account that they brought in the door. That's why we structured the commission system to compensate them not just for that first year, but for the next two years as well in diminishing percentages. We would even pay them on everything sold into the account, even by the account manager, and protect them by making sure they received their full commission for the big project, which was usually the implementation. Imagine a scenario where we did an assessment or provided a small amount of digital services for a year, then did a big implementation in year two. We made sure the sales rep got the higher commission rate for the big project.

Rich had experienced and complained about many compensation systems as an employee; as a manager, he was challenged to view these systems from an owner's perspective. For him to operate as a business owner and not as a salesperson took time and many different sales structures. One error he never made that his former employers had often made: trying to nickel-and-dime his sales and account management folks. He knew that when they made a lot of money, it translated to company success.

We also recognized that we had to structure a compensation system for our account managers that was different from our outside salespeople. When we hired Katie, we gave her an excellent annual salary as well as commissions, but her commission rate was lower than that of our outside salespeople—so she was still incentivized to sell additional services as part of her work with clients, but the rate wasn't so high as to distract from customer satisfaction responsibilities or to alienate our existing salespeople. We even provided a quarterly bonus to make sure we were setting goals based on customer satisfaction, penetration, and retention in addition to being referenceable.

My motivation to implement a strong account management system was as much internal as external. The more self-aware I became through my training at Wright, the more aware I was of my and other salespeople's reflex to grab all the credit and compensation. Years earlier at marchFIRST, I'd experienced the conflicts between sales and account management, and I saw how sales would take 100 percent of 0 rather than share $1,000 fifty-fifty. This mentality made an impact on me, and it guided me when I designed a more equitable compensation system.

We added more account managers until they were generating 50 percent of our revenue. This 50 percent represented account managers expanding and selling services to our existing accounts. This was a revelation. It was as if we had discovered a secret source of revenue and growth that no one else knew about. Retaining customers long term provided a much easier path to growth and profit goals than having to find new customers annually. We also became efficient at "taking over" support from our competitors' clients, because we offered a better solution, a better relationship, and the best ongoing support experience in the market. We created measurable results for our clients.

This epiphany changed our view of the business. We'd sometimes compete against big organizations such as Accenture, and these competitors would tell us that they would never want to do a deal for less than $1 million or less than $5 million. We would laugh at their myopia. We understood that if you did a deal for, let's say, $800,000, you might be able to earn $2 million annually from support services for the next three to five years. We wanted to keep our customers for life.

LYONSCG's value proposition was, "We'll really get to know you and conform to you rather than force you to conform to us." This was a huge value-add for its customers, and they were willing to pay more for this value. It allowed customers to retain staff who would have otherwise become redundant, as was often the case for a customer with one of the one-size-fits-all conglomerate consulting firms. Tapping potential synergy with their customers, LYONSCG brought best practices to its customers, and its customers brought best practices to LYONSCG, resulting in a partnership beyond anything that the behemoth big-name consulting firms could imagine.

Building a Data-Rich Customer Base

With more than one hundred customers to support, we had a great foundation for learning what worked and what didn't. Even though these customers represented a wide variety of business sectors, we could apply the lessons we learned across industries. One new customer, for instance, was Hibbett Sports, an online sporting goods marketer. It partners with Nike and other major brands, and we helped the company launch its eCommerce site. As we worked closely with it to develop the site, we discovered that people are hungry to learn when the latest version of a given shoe is being released. They wanted to know if they could buy it immediately or if they needed to put their name on a lottery-based list. To help, we created an innovative calendar that satisfied customers' needs for different types of information.

Shortly after launching this site, we brought in another new prospect, GameStop, which sells video games and related accessories. Though we had never worked in the gaming industry, we found that we could apply the lessons we had learned from Hibbett (and other customers) to this completely different business sector. Like the shoe aficionados, gamers wanted to know when a new game would be available, when they could order it, and so on. The games, like the shoes, had a cult-like following, and both groups of customers relished online calendars. We won the pitch for GameStop despite having no experience in gaming because we demonstrated how we might apply our calendar experiences working for Hibbett to GameStop's business. Because of the depth and breadth of our customer base, we understood eCommerce and had developed many innovative features and functionalities, and that helped us win GameStop and many other new customers.

Companies often sell robotically. They don't exhibit any curiosity or share any wisdom as part of the selling process. They're so obsessed with making the sale that they don't find out what the customer wants or suggest proactively what might benefit the customer. To counteract this tendency, we instilled the value of independence in our culture. Our strong customer base helped us engage proactively with organizations and actually provide best practices and consulting. We defined our independence as the ability to say yes and no. We would provide healthy pushback, and we would appropriately question our customers, a quality many of them desired.

We made it our business to develop a data-rich customer base, and we did it in part because it enhanced our selling pitch: No one else was supporting one hundred eCommerce customers, and we drew from this wide and deep base to understand what practices worked best. We invested a lot of time and expertise in mining and sorting this data. For instance, we looked at customer conversion rates on laptops versus mobile devices; we assessed when people were prematurely leaving sites; we evaluated recommendation engines and determined, when people had a product in their carts, if we could recommend other products based on those preferences and past purchases. This type of data put us ahead of the curve and allowed us to offer services we termed "Commerce Realized!" I used to tell customers, "We'll get you implemented, but the real work starts after that." We provided our customers with our trainers to teach their people how to use and optimize their platform, which was a major point of differentiation.

Another growing part of our business was providing support for sites that other companies had implemented, and as part of this support, we questioned assumptions and assessed the site design, recommending many enhancements and improvements. Assessments became a great way to get our foot in the door and obtain a new customer.

At one point, a company that sold golf clubs contacted us. It had implemented a new promotion, but the promotion accidentally limited how much a customer could purchase online. Why? That was the question we asked immediately that its previous offshore vendor hadn't. By questioning the company's strategy and goals, and applying our knowledge of buying behaviors (and some common sense), we helped the company create a highly effective site that sold more products. The company appreciated our approach and how we drew from other implementations and customers to offer insights, something that other partners neglected. This strategic support translated into a significant bump in revenue and contributed to our continued growth. We were more expensive, but we added more value.

Part of their tremendous growth was Rich establishing massive credibility because of all the customer knowledge he and LYONSCG had gathered. He'd talk to customers matter-of-factly but would say things that were revelatory. Each added to the other's knowledge of the industry. He helped establish reciprocal relationships with customers, an uncommon occurrence. By reciprocal, I mean that they just weren't "taking orders" but were providing feedback, questions, and insights. LYONSCG had developed a thorough understanding of what worked on sites because they were deeply partnered and invested in their customers' success, not just throwing up sites.

One reason Rich knew more than anyone else was because his customers told him what was going on in the marketplace. He made friends in his customers' companies, and they became Rich's eyes and ears.

In sales, you always want to be the OEM guy—the original equipment manufacturer. Let's say you're an engineering company selling auto parts. You want the automobile company to bring you in to design the original parts, giving you an inside track on manufacturing and supplying those parts. That's what LYONSCG did. The company's intimate knowledge of sites prompted customers to depend on its expertise in "manufacturing and supplying" their sites.

Our mantra became, "We're going to put ourselves in the customers' shoes. We're going to do what's best for them and see things from their perspective." In sales, it's easy to lose sight of the relationship element.

Some organizations are scarcity-based, and all they want to do is have their customers write them checks. Others become so enmeshed in what they produce, they lose sight of the end goal. Engineering-based companies sometimes become enamored with their products and aren't always thinking about how these products can meet customer needs—they sell features and not benefits. Customer relationships are like marriages—they require a lot of work to be successful. We vowed to put in that work to make the relationships last by providing value and keeping our eyes focused on the customers' goals.

If at First You Don't Succeed ...

Rich walked away from a number of deals, or deals walked away from him based on price and his honesty. Rich was selling on value and results, and he was never going to be the low-cost provider. He would meet with clients, see what they wanted, and if he didn't think he could do a good job given the parameters, he'd refer someone else and walk away. In some cases, prospects would hire other firms to do the job based on price, and Rich has a lot of stories where the other guy wins—at first until the problems arise and the client turned back to LYONSCG. What's unusual about Rich is that he's not afraid to find new business. Many salespeople have a scarcity mindset—they're convinced that if they miss out on one deal, another one won't come along. Rich was never desperate like that.

I never wanted to be motivated by scarcity or feeling that I was not enough; I endured enough of both feelings during my childhood. At LYONSCG, we always tried to believe in karma and trusted that if we did the right thing, the right result would emerge over time. I determined early on that we were going to do the right thing for the customer and that if we adhered to that philosophy, things would work out. When we lost deals, we believed that they would come back.

Unlike churn-and-burn cultures, Rich was committed to being what he called, "100 percent referenceable." That meant even deals they lost would speak well of them. This was an extension of his never-burn-bridges philosophy—a difficult philosophy for some of us with sharp elbows.

We maintained a high level of integrity throughout the sales process. If we believed customers needed certain elements to make their site successful, certain integrations, or even a separate system like an order management system (OMS), we'd detail exactly what they were and the cost. We developed the most detailed quotes in the industry, outlining integrations and customizations and giving the customer as much detail as we could. We told customers that we were not going to be the least expensive company you could hire, but we would be the best. Some prospective customers met with us and wanted to hire us but couldn't because they couldn't afford it. Our meetings created an aspirational feeling—the smaller companies aspired to work with us at some point. And sure enough, some of them would return and hire us when they could. We created a halo effect in the marketplace—we possessed an ethical, trustworthy aura.

Rich's integrity came at a short-term cost. It killed Rich to have to tell clients that they couldn't do an implementation within a given time frame and lose the business. As much as he was compelled to be honest, as a sales guy he wanted to win the business. But for Rich, it was more important to do what you say you're going to do than to make a sale based on unrealistic time frames.

We learned to schedule implementations at a doable rate. I pushed Norm and the delivery team extremely hard to adhere to our schedules, and they became disciplined to adhere to committed dates. For instance, we had a board in the middle of the office that listed the next available start date, and we didn't deviate from whatever date was on the board. Under certain circumstances, we might have two separate kickoffs with two different teams to meet customers' schedules, but we made sure we didn't overcommit and fail our customers.

Salespeople sometimes say to customers, "Sure, we'll start whenever you want." They tend to overpromise and under-deliver. This might make customers happy in the short term, but when you can't deliver what you promise, it creates long-term disappointment and anger. I preferred to under-promise and over-deliver.

We had to be realistic about resource allocation. In doing so, we not only helped our customers but also our own people. We didn't want to kill them with work, to give them so many projects and deadlines to meet that they'd be overwhelmed and perhaps quit—we had really good people at this point, and we didn't want to lose them.

Besides demonstrating our integrity, this scheduling discipline also gave the customers a sense of urgency; they understood that they needed to make a commitment and sign a contract to secure the dates they wanted. We explained that if they didn't choose the first date available, the next date might not be for another two or three weeks. I should point out that these were real dates, and we were being completely transparent with our customers about them.

Coaching Through the Changes

As our company grew, I faced numerous, and difficult, decisions. As Dr. Bob noted, it killed me to have to turn down business. But it was more important to operate with integrity and be successful with a client than to make a sale. On these and other issues, I had two competing impulses, and it wasn't always easy to know which one to obey.

That's why having a coach like Dr. Bob was so valuable. As you've probably noticed from these chapters, my relationship with Dr. Bob could be filled with conflict at times. But it needed to be that way! I didn't have anyone in my organization who was going to take me to the mat on these tough choices, who was going to push me outside of my comfort zone to be the best me I could be.

You need this type of healthy relationship with a coach where you don't always do everything your coach says. Dr. Bob would advise me that I had to consider putting an account management system in place, and I'd sit with it, trying to wrap my mind around it until the idea was no longer Dr. Bob's but mine. It took Dr. Bob years talking about account management before I embraced it and implemented it.

Rich resisted things until they absolutely clicked into place for him—I'd often rub his nose in the fact that the business was missing an account management component when problems would arise, and he'd tell me to go screw myself—but that's the dynamic of a good coach-client relationship.

Dr. Bob and I were painting a vision of what LYONSCG might be, and he held that vision for me. In the day-to-day chaos and noise that often exists in fast-growing entrepreneurial companies, we all need reminders of what we are doing and why we are doing it. Dr. Bob didn't forget, and he never let that vision go. He would remind me of it continuously. I wasn't ready to commit to account management for years, but when I did commit, I went all in, and it was tremendously successful.

WDM Takeaways

- Stay true to your highest vision, in all interactions, including with employees and customers. Open and honest communication is critical in all relationships, including employees and partners (Level 4). Conformity and fitting in and wanting to be liked are hungers we all share (Level 2). But the damage you can do to relationships by not telling the difficult truth may be irreparable. Have the courage to express the truth.

- Don't be a loner, a norm for many entrepreneurs (which is why we work for ourselves). Choosing to trust (Level 1) and creating alliances and partnerships can accelerate your growth and provide nourishment for your life.

- Monitor your reactivity and anger (Level 3). Don't burn bridges and try to maintain beneficial relationships with everyone. You never know when you may need to ask someone for help. Use your anger intentionally to get what you want. When you act with intention, seemingly negative events can lead to breakthroughs.

- Be clear on what behaviors you are incenting—compensation plans work with behavioral clarity. Don't fall into scarcity and demotivate your most important assets, your salespeople (Level 1). If salespeople make a lot of money, you make a lot of money.

- Remember that sales is service and should be about helping your client to succeed. Prioritize your purpose for selling and stay focused on the customer (Level 5).

- Develop a strong sense of self if you use a coach. It is easy to become reactive (Level 3) and not listen or conform (Level 4) and blame later. A coach is just that, a coach. You must own each perspective and piece of advice for yourself.

CHAPTER NINE

CLIMBING TO THE NEXT LEVEL

Approaches to selling evolve as the marketplace changes and as sales professionals develop. You can't sell the same thing the same way for a long time and expect to be successful. The best leaders and entrepreneurs adapt and change their approach to changing conditions—they don't just maintain what they've created—to grow and succeed. This change can include everything from adding new products and services to restructuring to entering new markets. Successful sales professionals turn selling into a continuous learning and challenging process.

LYONSCG evolved by adding the Hybris platform and opening a London office. These two moves were part of our ongoing efforts to learn, change, and grow. Just like adding Magento to Demandware and placing greater emphasis on account management, we were crossing boundaries that were literal (geographic) and figurative. We were testing new ways of doing business, and though these tests were absolutely necessary, like all experiments, they entailed a certain amount of risk—no risk, no reward.

An Opportunity-Driven Decision

With Demandware and Magento, we had the enterprise and middle markets covered for business to consumer (B2C), but we lacked a platform for business-to-business (B2B) clients. B2B is a huge market—some estimate it to be roughly four times larger than the B2C market—and a market that we hadn't capitalized on yet. Though we were capable of handling simple B2B accounts—ones that mirrored the B2C process, where people paid via credit card—we lacked a platform for more complex B2B transactions. The complications might include using a purchase order, determining if a new customer should be given credit, handling very large orders, and so on.

As we analyzed the market, we recognized that we were missing out on significant opportunities. If we had been a large company with deep financial pockets, we might have responded to these opportunities by acquiring a company or by hiring and training an implementation team to take advantage of the opportunities when the time was right. But without these financial resources, we didn't have the luxury of hiring a new team and allowing them to sit on the bench indefinitely while we worked to generate new business.

During our analysis of the B2B market, we identified how we might make this transition. We saw how other companies utilized independent contractors that possessed B2B experience and had them go on sales calls and develop proposals. A few of our competitors were also starting to make forays into this market, and one of them was using the Hybris platform.

Hybris looked like an ideal addition to Demandware and Magento. Just as we had established account management as a way to serve our existing customers and diversify our direct sales focus, Hybris seemed like another way to broaden and diversify our business. We were always worried about putting all of our chips on one number, and Hybris would allow us to have more options to attract a wider variety of customers.

In addition, Gorilla was a competing company that had partnered with Magento and had been successful with Hybris in this B2B market, and the company had tried and failed to get into the Demandware market. Acquity Group was another competitor that had done a lot of work with Hybris. From a purely competitive standpoint, we needed to enter this market, and since we had done well competing in the past against Gorilla and Acquity, we thought we would do well.

We realized that our future was based on these partnerships, and Hybris represented the third time we had expanded our offerings based on a new platform.

This was an extension of Rich's alliance way of living. He possesses the capacity to negotiate conflicts of interest in order to achieve coopetition that helped him ally with Demandware, Magento, and Hybris. With the marketplace consolidating, we knew that traditional brick-and-mortar companies were going to shift online, and tools such as search engine optimization would be key to a successful transition. Rich had been observing all this, waiting for the right moment—he doesn't do things prematurely. He considered forming an alliance with Hybris for a long time, and when he established that relationship, it was well-timed. He managed the potential conflicts expertly, communicating with Demandware and Magento about how they could all work together beneficially. Once again, he needed to deal with the perceived threat for Demandware and Magento. He showed them both the win-win-win proposition while dealing with platform overlap. His previous negotiations now became even more complex.

Initially, I remained focused on Demandware, while Dave became our in-house Hybris guy and pursued B2B deals. From the beginning, I was concerned that we lacked B2B experience. We had evolved our company from its general positioning of eCommerce implementations, adding experience design, digital strategy and marketing, hosting, and other support services, but we had always focused most of our efforts on the B2C market. Hybris, a more complicated platform that allows users greater customization options, was the right platform to help us serve enterprise B2B customers.

To implement this platform, we needed to create a new process—one that required expertise that was different from what we used to implement B2C. In the latter case, many elements remained constant from customer to customer—home page, product detail page, cart, checkout, and my account. Though companies can vary in how all of these elements are designed and implemented, some uniformity and best practices exist that facilitate the process. With B2B, much more variation is required based on the industry and the unique business and its business requirements. The flow is different from project to project—a business customer's journey through the site can involve a wide range of options. To customize the implementation and meet a given customer's needs, we had to learn how to "flex" our process or how to make it sufficiently agile to work in different situations.

To make this expansion of our business feasible, we had to accept the risk—risk that was coming in multiple ways. There was the obvious financial risk—we had to hire and pay people, including a practice leader and a technical architect, and we had to move some of our salespeople away from Demandware (our financial bread and butter) and Magento toward Hybris. There was time risk—we had to invest a lot of hours training our salespeople and engaging with the Hybris alliance people and salespeople in the field. Finally, there was the risk of offending Demandware (Magento wasn't threatened because it wasn't operating in the enterprise B2B space back then).

Demandware did have some B2B customers (when B2B looked very much like B2C), and we recognized that it might object to Hybris. Given that 80 percent of our business was Demandware, we were taking a serious risk. Yet it was a necessary one if we were to continue to evolve, serve our customers, and become the company I envisioned we could become.

Ultimately, it boiled down to this: We turned away many B2B prospects as the market continued to evolve. Demandware could not serve most of these complex B2B customers. Demandware had many other partners besides us, justifying our desire to have other platform partners. As long as we defined the rules of engagement and communicated honestly and proactively, we were good.

Once we started working with Hybris, we had to manage its expectations as well; Hybris wanted us to partner with it on the B2C market. We made it clear that we weren't going to do this. And we reassured Demandware of this fact. It helped that we'd kept our word when it came to Magento. Demandware recognized at this point that we'd be a stronger partner because of our lack of bias.

Still, the shifting market made things complicated. We had several tough conversations, as we danced around delicate situations. The following story illustrates this situation best.

We had a customer requiring a great deal of customization on the platform, and we were bidding on a project. We sent one of our technical architects to visit the customer, and he was getting on a plane when I decided that this was wrong—that winning the deal wasn't worth the risk and having an unhappy customer in the end. I didn't think the project was right for Demandware, but I didn't want to get in Demandware's way. I called the architect as he was walking down the aisle toward his seat and told him to get off the plane and cancel the appointment.

We backed out of the project elegantly, explaining to the customer that we didn't have the resources necessary to handle it right now. The customer apparently accepted our explanation without rancor, since subsequently it called us back to bring us into another project. Still, navigating these waters was difficult. We needed to be ethical and above board to maintain our strong relationships.

I insisted on transparency. We wanted Demandware's people to hear about our deal with Hybris directly from us rather than from someone else. I explained to Brian Callahan, Demandware's head of sales, that he and his team would soon be seeing a press release announcing that we had signed with Hybris for its B2B capabilities. We reiterated our promise that if Demandware brought us into a deal, we wouldn't flip it (to Hybris or Magento) unless Demandware wasn't interested in the deal. We defined our go-to-market strategy and our swim lanes, as well as how we were positioning each platform. While Hybris wanted to be in the B2C market, too, and was targeting Demandware in that space, we made it clear that we were taking Hybris to market as our enterprise B2B solution exclusively. We defined Demandware as our enterprise B2C solution and Magento as our middle-market solution (Magento would eventually add B2B, which served us well). We were segmenting our ecosystem.

Rich managed his partners' expectations effectively by informing them of things to which they might take exception. This is a critical skill in any service industry, and it became even more essential given the complexity of the Hybris move. Rich empathizes and anticipates with great sensitivity, incorporating these traits into relationship management.

By reassuring Demandware that our rules of engagement remained the same and that it was still our number one platform partner, we hoped that the company would accept this change. Demandware was concerned at first, but it responded positively to the open communication and the trust we had built over the years.

You always have to pull the trigger at some point. Rich had known his company was weak at B2B, and he spent time helping his platform company executives and senior staff grasp the value of going with Hybris. As with so many things, Rich lived with the discomfort until he and his staff were ready to go into new territory. He limited the domain of the Hybris business he would chase. He wouldn't give Hybris everything it wanted, but he did give it a high-integrity partnership.

His method of developing the Hybris relationship represents his strategic approach to alliances that has allowed him to operate with coopetition. Any of his three platforms could easily have said no to Rich representing the others, but he generated a win for all. The Hybris alliance was a new adventure for Rich, and he had to take a risk by hiring people who could work with the Hybris platform, knowing that it would take many months before the investment would pay off. To innovate and move into new territory, though, you have to pay the price. Rich's finely tuned sense of value helps him know when the price is too much. The price in manpower and investment dollars was high, but he was determined to make good returns with this new platform, as he had access to new customers in a new market.

Rich is highly intentional. In most instances, he doesn't go into meetings without knowing the outcome. Through casual conversation, he plants seeds and takes the temperature of the group. As an excellent leader, Rich valued the contributions and consciousness of those with whom he worked. Despite all his abilities, he knew he couldn't do it alone. I had Rich read Machiavelli early on. He learned the lesson: The prince exists at the pleasure of the peasants. Rich didn't have peasants, but he knew his success was dependent on others, so he socialized with intentionality.

A lot of Rich's success, too, is due to his continuous work on problematic issues. The shadow of Rich's father's failures hung over his head. His pride in LYONSCG being the best in the industry goes back to the core early family issues that he would work consistently to resolve. Rich challenged his core belief that he was fragile and a failure—that he was an imposter—through the work he did at Wright. By resolving these issues, he was able to move forward with clarity and without the unconscious baggage that would weigh him down. For instance, Rich has a cocky side, which could get him in trouble, but he learned to rein in that cockiness. For him, there's always a tension between this cockiness/self-satisfaction and working hard. As Rich's business took off, he worked extremely hard, recognizing that transformational change is discontinuous. You keep working, working, working and then bam, the breakthrough happens. Hybris wasn't an overnight success, but the result of a long, steady effort.

After Dave closed our first B2B client, Steel and Pipe Supply, we began building our Hybris practice. While we hired a practice leader, we soon learned that there was more to B2B than just having the right platform. We needed a new database of customers that our salespeople could sell to, and that meant going to different types of trade shows than we had in the past to develop these relationships. The demands of B2B meant that we had to evolve our marketing strategy—buying new databases and establishing relationships with the Hybris salespeople and alliance team (much as we had done with Demandware's and Magento's sales forces) to partner on new leads and pursuits.

All this took time and effort. Our board tracked our performance on traditional SWOT measures. When we planned, we performed a risk/benefit analysis. The result of one such analysis was the decision to make this inroad into the B2B market. We knew we'd have to endure some downtime and cost when ramping up our internal team. Some clients wanted to know the team that would be serving them—without a team, we would have little credibility. If we didn't hire and train at least a handful of people in advance of obtaining clients, we wouldn't obtain the clients, and we wouldn't be prepared to do a good job once we started getting customers.

We viewed our B2B moves as part of a strategic investment. Based on our analysis, we were willing to tolerate five new people not generating revenue for a short period of time. We trained them and kept them busy with internal projects and asset development, but until Dave closed that first deal, they went a little crazy sitting on the sidelines, and we went a little crazy worrying about the investment and the cost.

Taking these risks tests your mettle. It tests your appetite for investment. And it tests your intention. We were going to be losing money on the bet for a while, and if we didn't get a project relatively soon, the Hybris-focused people we hired might quit. But we intended to create a positive outcome and to see it through no matter what.

I've found these types of moves are always more difficult than they appear. You start with great confidence that a strategic investment will pay off since you've done the planning and analysis and all the signs point up. The reality, however, is a different story. Nothing happens as fast as you think it will. You start questioning your decisions. You wonder if you should back off. As former heavyweight boxing champion Mike Tyson said, "Everyone has a plan until they get punched in the face."

When Rich decided to move forward, he was resolved to do so but was also battling uncertainty. He dug in deeply during coaching sessions with me. This helped him maintain his resolve in management conversations with Norm and Dave. They had an unusual trust in and respect for each other, creating a tight executive team that allowed them to vet their thinking repeatedly in challenging conversations. This doesn't mean that Rich always knew exactly what to do. Rich is often uncertain, but he covers it up so others don't realize it. This quiet uncertainty is a strength, allowing him to listen carefully to Norm and Dave and consider their perspectives.

You can't talk to anyone about this uncertainty besides your coach. As a leader, I couldn't show it. I needed an unconflicted consciousness to project confidence. Everyone has uncertainty, but it's how you process it, come to terms with it, and do something about it that matters. Can you make the choice to trust even when you're feeling fear and uncertainty? If you're not in touch with that fear, you can make poor decisions. If you try to "muscle" through it, you can force the wrong action. I learned to embrace the fear and uncertainty. I asked myself: Why am I uncertain? Is the risk worth it? The answer would often lead me to a path forward.

All this helped us enter and remain in the B2B market. Despite many soul-searching conversations and the need to initially spend money with little to no immediate return, we stayed the course, in large part because of my burn-the-canoes philosophy. If you're going to do something you believe in, you have to be all in. I was absolutely convinced that we needed to diversify into B2B—the market opportunity was too great to pass up.

It took nine long months before Dave landed that first client, but when he did, it gave us confidence—if we did it once, we could do it again. And, in the coming months, we did it a number of times, building our B2B practice successfully and positioning ourselves for future changes and success.

London Calling

A few years after partnering with Hybris, we contemplated another strategic investment. In 2015, it became clear that the global market was not just for large corporations anymore; in a digital age, a wide range of companies could be successful as global players.

We had helped launch global sites for some of our enterprise customers before contemplating opening an office abroad. Working with Jarden Consumer Solutions, which owned kitchen brands such as FoodSaver, Mr. Coffee, Oster, Crock-Pot, Sunbeam, and many others, we launched twenty-six sites in the US, then expanded to Canada, the UK, China, Japan, Latin America, among others locales. We also worked with GoPro to launch sites in the UK and Hong Kong. We even had a large Magento customer in London, Warner Music Group, and launched and hosted more than 350 artist sites around the world for the company. And we had established a long-term partnership with a company in Ukraine called Speroteck, to serve clients in that area of the world and be able to provide 24/7/365 support for our customers globally.

Demandware came to us and told us that its business in Europe was going gangbusters; the company could use a strong go-to partner in London. When it suggested it would steer deals our way, it was a no-brainer to establish an office there, especially given our experience and our reputation. We could better support our existing US clients with their Demandware sites in Europe, and we could win new customers while we were there.

The parallels with our launch of Hybris should have been instructive. In both instances, we had tested the waters of a new market with existing clients—we'd done simple B2B projects using Demandware, and we'd launched global sites. When looking at B2B and global expansion, we saw tremendous opportunities and were optimistic about our chances for success. In both situations, we had to make strategic investments that entailed a degree of risk—risk of time, money, people, and focus.

Initially, after our chosen staff member could not move to the UK and run the office because of visa issues, I considered relocating my family to London and establishing the office myself. The timing, though, was bad since my younger daughter was a junior in high school (and I wanted to be around to help with college visits and decisions). Still, when I talked about a London office with my people, we all agreed that I needed to be involved to make it work; Dave had small children and was even less able to spend time away from home than I was. We decided to do it for many strategic reasons, and I decided to do it in my typical fashion—all in and burn the canoes.

I had learned the importance of stepping out of my comfort zone continuously. I had to keep evaluating opportunities, and, sometimes, I had to take the more difficult path. It would have been much easier to remain in Chicago and keep doing what we had been doing. But if you want to take advantage of new opportunities and continue to grow, then you've got to take on challenging and uncomfortable tasks at times.

Transforming a business requires three investments: time, money, and many forms of upsetting discomfort. Rich has the remarkable ability to live with inconvenience and discomfort; this is unusual. A lot of entrepreneurs want to buy their way through growth phases, but they aren't willing to pay the tougher price. Some borrow money and go deeply into debt. Jack Stack, the father of open-book management, tells stories about people with MBAs and money coming to him for help; they don't realize they need to prove a concept to succeed. They do what they were told in school or follow other conventional wisdom, but they don't realize the difference between using money and resources effectively and using them wastefully. They hire people and throw money at problems, but these actions don't lead to an integrated solution.

Rich's moves in London demanded money and time. They also caused discomfort with his family and his staff in the US—they complained that they were not getting enough of him. Rich put his highest-value asset, himself, where it needed to be—in London. He invested his time in being away from home, and for Rich, this was a difficult but necessary investment, one he often discussed in our coaching sessions.

I questioned this investment frequently because I was traveling and not home for half the year, two weeks every month, but ultimately, I saw the immense potential value of this investment. We were the first among US companies in our category to try and establish a European hub, and though others would follow our example in the coming years, we were the pioneer. While this was the right thing to do from a business standpoint, I had to make personal sacrifices.

Entrepreneurs need to possess the discipline of evaluating opportunities, a discipline that requires seizing the right opportunities. Contrary to what some people believe, the best entrepreneurs don't just rely on instinct, chasing after every opportunity—we certainly didn't. They require an overarching vision and pragmatism that allows them to evaluate opportunities. Because our vision was to be the best company of our kind in the world, London fit our requirements for an opportunity worth pursuing. We had a larger strategic mission for our London office—it was a key piece to becoming a global company. From the outside, it may have seemed like a precipitous move, but it was the result of a larger, carefully considered vision.

Dave and I deciding to stop selling accounts on our own parallels the London move, in that both were difficult, uncomfortable choices that made absolute sense within a larger, strategic framework. Right before making this decision, Dave and I were responsible for 70 to 80 percent of the business. We were both star salespeople, but we were never going to grow the business to the extent we envisioned if we were spending all of our time selling. We realized that we needed to build a good sales team and trust them. Still, giving up all our accounts was both difficult and scary. We had to give up doing something we were really good at and delegate this job to other people who might not be as good as we were.

So one of our first tasks was to hire good salespeople. Once we did that, we bit the bullet and stopped selling directly into our own accounts. We could have transitioned to this new model more gradually, but once we made this decision, we didn't want to delay putting everything in place.

Remember, working with a coach does not always mean warm and fuzzy support. I argued vehemently against this move. I thought that it was precipitous—they could have made this change in stages—but Rich and Dave proved me wrong. They realized that they were the narrow neck of the bottle and kept work from flowing—they couldn't scale while the company was so dependent on their selling.

It bothers me that I was so wrong. This doesn't happen often, though I was also wrong about hiring Norm—I saw it as premature. But Rich viewed things differently—more like the high school running back he once had been. He saw a gap in the line that I did not see, and he shot through that gap for extra yardage.

Dave and I decided to spread our support over as many people in our company as possible. We shifted our focus from direct selling to training our people, helping them close, and going on calls with them. We hired a sales manager for the first time to facilitate this transition and shifted to a geographic model with assigned territories. And it worked.

Similarly, London required us to make a transition, one in which we implemented several changes in how we operated. I also needed time to adjust to these new circumstances.

We devoted many coaching sessions to these issues, questioning the viability and necessity of each move. Norm constantly reminded Rich of the revenue deficit and the opportunity cost of Rich not selling in the US and the company's need for "more Rich." I was most concerned about Rich's well-being, given all the travel and business challenges he would encounter and the physical and mental toll these challenges would take on him. Fortunately, he had an ace in the hole in his MBA friend, Harvey Spevak, who was the CEO of Equinox Fitness Clubs. Equinox had just opened its first gym in London, close to the hotel where Rich was staying. So Rich had a portable personal training plan and did the same workouts with trainers in both countries.

Thanks to Dr. Bob, I learned the trick of leaving clothes to be cleaned at my hotel in London, freeing me to travel efficiently, only bringing carry-on luggage when I traveled—a small but meaningful convenience. I knew I had to tend to myself since it was a highly stressful arrangement and environment. Once again, my networking and friendships paid off; Harvey's high-end gym, Equinox, allowed me consistency in trainers and facilities.

I also made the best of a challenging situation from a family perspective. My wife Gertrude and I had to make a conscious and consistent effort to communicate because of the six-hour time difference. I also scheduled trips for my daughters Hannah and Morgan to visit London, and the four of us had memorable times there. Recognizing that the separation would be difficult, I and my family were alert to this difficulty and figured out ways to capitalize on the positives of me being in Europe rather than passively accept the negatives.

In the US, we would win about one in every three deals we proposed, a very high percentage in our marketplace. In London, I was losing every deal initially, and I wasn't used to it. My ego took a hit. The only way I could persevere was through sheer force of will and intent.

This is a key point. Rich doesn't engage in self-doubt very often. This was, however, a time of serious questioning because it took a long time for the London investment to begin paying dividends. Rich was not bullheaded.

He listened to Norm and Dave and took in what they said, but he had a greater vision for LYONSCG and was the guy on the ground. He was deeply invested, as his rugged travel plan represented. He did not allow doubt to disable his performance as so many entrepreneurs do. Instead, he used intentionality and strategy to keep himself moving. I've had several opportunities to be present and watch Rich in a meeting and observe how focused he is on outcomes. I find it to be a thing of beauty to see his capacity to sense what the right actions are. He constantly weighs the pros and cons to avoid confusion and problems—another benefit of the reaction to his early childhood messiness.

Rich is particularly effective because of his silent consideration and containment. He'll remain quiet, observe, and let information and ideas develop and emerge. His internal computer is constantly entering and recalculating this emerging data. When he talks, others listen.

The London office tested Rich brutally. At times, nothing seemed to work, but could he remain steadfast and intentional when he lacked an applicable knowledge base like he had in the US? Sales hires failed until he found the right person, and that took a long time and a lot of investment. Still, it turned out that although Rich questioned and re-analyzed, he rarely wavered.

But that doesn't mean that I was worry-free. I didn't articulate my concerns, however, to anyone in the company. I used Dr. Bob to vet my concerns. I told him about Dave wanting to pull the plug on the London operation and how Norm had serious questions about its financial viability. Dr. Bob helped me analyze the situation rationally and allowed me to express my anxiety, always offering a sounding board and a support system. To everyone else, though, I remained unwavering in my belief that we could and should make London work. My vision was wide—I saw us serving not only our US-based global clients but also new customers based in Europe. Others had failed to achieve this type of vision and pulled out, even the large consultancies. I said we would not be like them, keeping my word to Demandware and the market that we were in it for the long haul. If I wanted to sell everyone—not just prospective clients but my own people—I had to take this stance.

Obstacles, Wrong Turns, and Finding Our Way

We had shared office space in Kensington with Regus, a workspace company, similar to WeWork. This venture abroad may not seem like a big deal, but it represented a significant risk for our business—the two weeks I was spending in London meant two weeks away from our US business.

Still, I thought that our success would be quick and easy. After all, Demandware was bending over backward to help us. I established relationships with Demandware people in London, went on sales calls with them, and started to chase deals.

It was more like chasing my tail. Part of the problem was that Demandware already had partners in the market, and many of them were low-cost offshore or nearshore partners, making it difficult for us to compete with them on price alone. We would beat them in the US market, as they were offshore. But now we were offshore and more expensive. Second, Demandware's business had slowed down from the previous year, and the slowdown coincided with the opening of our office. Third, I was a guy from the US who said *pra*-cess, not *pro*-cess. My Midwest accent was a problem, and the first question every prospective customer asked was, "How many customers do you have in the UK?" I would list all the US-based companies for which we had launched UK and European sites. The question would shift to, "No, how many UK-based or London-based customers do you have?" The answer was always zero. Nothing seemed to be working.

I met a lot of people, established relationships and trust, and made a lot of pitches, but I was getting nowhere close to closing our first deal. To suggest I was getting frustrated is putting it mildly, and I did begin to question myself. I was not used to losing deals. The contrast to our success in the US was significant. There, we were Demandware's number one partner, and in London, prospects didn't care how good we were or about any of my US customers; they looked at us as if we were unknown novices (to be fair, we were unknown in this market). On top of that, my business partners in the US were growing restless; Dave wanted me in the US because my presence would help him sell more, and Norm was concerned about whether our current and projected results justified our investment.

Rich was in London a lot of the time. His employees missed him and wanted more of his presence, but they couldn't have him. As a positive result, his staff and the company grew in some ways because they were forced to become a little less dependent on him during this time. Like any loving father, Rich was torn—he was pulled by his responsibility to the US operation and this family. His vision of making the company stronger as a global operation and his LYONSCG family stronger catalyzed his reorientation.

I wondered if the organization was strong enough to survive if I was physically absent and mentally distracted by our London issues. As I did when we were struggling to make our B2B effort work, I asked, "Should we be investing in this London office?" It was a big expense that wasn't giving us any return, and I was not devoting as much time as I should to our main business. I was convinced, however, that we needed to have a presence in Europe. Only by having a physical location there would we be perceived as a global company. I was also answering another question: Were we just building a support office for our US customers, or were we also building a European sales office?

I favored the latter, and to achieve this more ambitious goal, I made another investment. I hired a European guy, Danny Rippon, to be the London office's general manager. Unlike me, he wasn't burdened with a Midwest accent; he spoke with the right British English accent. Danny had worked for Oracle and Sapient, and he knew the European market. We built the office around him and moved some of our experienced delivery people from the US to London (we had tried to hire people who lived in the UK, but they struggled to follow our LYONSCG proprietary process, so moving our own people seemed like the best alternative). We hired other part-time employees—a technical architect, a project manager, an account manager, and others—and soon we started closing deals.

Danny was the right guy. He partnered powerfully with Rich. When you have an asset like Danny who knows the game and knows a lot of people, you don't want to lose that asset. Still, he cost a lot. And the London office lacked a project manager for many months. On top of that, LYONSCG was an unknown entity in London, and people were wondering if Rich could really get LYONSCG known as an elite company in the London and European marketplace.

Rich was wrestling with a lot of issues, and part of my job was to think all these issues through with him. Fortunately, I was familiar with cross-cultural issues, having done business in Europe and studied in Germany and France. I was acutely aware of the varied biases, both earned and unearned, against Americans. Despite Rich's Midwest accent, he was free of most American disadvantages. European business people may have hurt his feelings. They were testing him. But Rich kept it to himself and processed the issues without blame, an unusual trait for someone who suffers the hurt of doors being slammed in his face. He was drawing on his years of sales insight and SEI education, and he digested this often hurtful data with remarkable equanimity.

This was the first time that I faced cultural resistance. In the United States, we started from scratch. Our principles and values guided us to an outstanding reputation. Going to another country, where we were recognized as an American firm, was totally new. And devastatingly frustrating. We were facing understandable marketplace skepticism. There was a legacy of other companies saying they'd invest in and stay in the UK market, then leaving when things got tough.

When we would call on prospective customers, they'd tell us that many US companies enter the market and then depart. They would ask, "If a company much bigger than you couldn't make it here, why should we believe you'll stay?" I would insist that we had the best team in the world, not just in the US, and while some believed me, others didn't. The latter group was wary of a bait-and-switch tactic, sure that we'd "show" them highly experienced, highly skilled people and then we'd put someone else on their account who was inexperienced. This was a major obstacle, and to overcome it, we needed to build trust.

LYONSCG was not a typical American firm. Too often, American firms act arrogantly without a history of actual excellence to back up those superlative claims. LYONSCG was simply excellent. Its level of excellence was difficult for others to understand when the firm's mythology and ethos were not confirmed by others in the host culture.

Rich was not just facing the unfamiliar and often valid skepticism based on unpleasant experiences those firms had with American service providers; he was facing the all-too-common experience of other countries when working with Americans. Please understand that I am only discussing the experience that Rich was facing in the UK as an American representing an American firm and finding his potential customers incredulous about his team delivering the excellent, superlative experience they promised.

Rich has an amazing ability to negotiate across cultures. He wasn't arrogant; he was confident. There's a big difference between the two. I'm the scary American. I speak quickly and freely, and I appear arrogant. Rich doesn't.

I'm confident, but I choose to contain it. I sit back and listen and wait for my moment. I've been told that I come across as intriguing. People can't figure me out, and I suppose that intrigue served me well—it wasn't off-putting to Europeans, and it was one of many elements that helped us in London.

To overcome cultural biases and a preference for cheaper offshore competitors, we embarked on a multi-threaded strategy to communicate our commitment—the hiring of Danny, opening an office, and transferring some of our best US people to our London office.

Intentionality helped Rich find solutions. He recognized that he had to earn his way into the market. Not many smaller American firms succeeded the way LYONSCG did in London. It was a painful process, and part of the pain was the significant amount of money Rich had to invest with no certain return. Part of it, though, was emotional. Rich's staff in the US wanted him to return; they often made him feel guilty about "deserting" them.

Other obstacles emerged. Competitors got wind of our entry into "their" market, and they told our customers to request a tour of our office; the competing companies knew we didn't have our own office and were operating in a shared space. No doubt, we lost some deals when people took competitors up on their suggestion and discovered that we lacked our own office (this was before WeWork and other similar types of shared spaces became an accepted part of the business landscape).

Our first major customer win in Europe was Hotel Chocolat. When I met with the company's CEO, he asked how many customers we had in Europe. I said, "You'll be our first customer," and added, "I will personally guarantee that you will be successful." I wanted to convey to him how important he was to us, and that despite our lack of experience with London or UK-based companies, we would bend over backward to make sure that our efforts paid off for his company. He trusted me, negotiated hard (we deeply discounted the deal to obtain our first customer), and we got our first win in the UK. Hotel Chocolat being a well-known brand made it even better.

Despite my guarantee, our relationship with Hotel Chocolat and the management of the project's scope didn't always go well. This provides a cautionary lesson that every salesperson should heed: just because you make a deal doesn't mean you have it made. Especially when you make the deal with the CEO, but then have to implement the project with other employees. Our people were complaining about Hotel Chocolat's people, and their people were complaining about us. We became hopelessly stalled, unable to lock down the final scope and unable to get the site up and running because of miscommunication, conflicts, and inertia. Some of my people were threatening to quit over the difficulty of working with this account.

Finally, I decided to meet with the company's CEO again, and I made him the same offer I had made to our bowling shirt client. I told him I would give him his money back, everything that he had paid to date, that he could keep the code we'd developed for the company's site, and that I was sure that he and his company could make it successful with another partner or on their own. I emphasized that we could not continue on the current unproductive path.

Again, this was an offer fraught with risk. Hotel Chocolat had spent $1 million with us up to that point. More importantly, if we stopped doing work for Hotel Chocolat, we would be back to square one without a successful European client—a key to building credibility.

Rich's offer was unheard of—it just DOES NOT happen in business. But Rich knew what the dramatic impact of the offer might be. He was not blaming, but he was communicating powerfully and in a nuanced manner that the Hotel Chocolat folks were a problem while owning his own side of the problem and responsibility. He was willing to make good on his initial promise and was saying that success was impossible if nothing changed.

This kind of integrity-based bold move was not uncommon for Rich. However, his ability to assess the situation, calculate the options, and come up with a move like this is remarkable. Most of us would have reacted out of frustration. He was, indeed, frustrated to the max and we went over the situation quite a bit before he made the move.

Just imagine the enormity of this risk! At the same time, calculate the cost to LYONSCG. A loss of $1 million puts the company behind and at best, takes it back to where it started. It might even foreshadow an exit out of Europe. I have seen Rich make this kind of move two or three times over the years. First, he expects that the person will not take him up on the offer. Second, he is quite willing to do what he says. Third, he realizes his credibility with his staff is essential, and he must stand up for them. Fourth, he realizes the client could not do any better. You might imagine that this is Rich's way of yelling at a client—with profound effectiveness.

I was sincere in my offer, but I also knew I had to say something that would jar the CEO and force him to take the problems we'd been having seriously. The CEO was an entrepreneur like me, and entrepreneurs tend to think differently from other businesspeople—I was taking a risk, a calculated risk, but it was a risk to which entrepreneurs can relate. I made my offer to the CEO in the type of come-to-Jesus meeting that could have gone either way. Fortunately, it went the way I'd hoped. He acknowledged that we needed to lock down the scope and could not continue to accept any changes. He and I committed to becoming more engaged in the project through weekly calls, and together we created clear definitions of working methods, deadlines, and so on. It became a great account for us, and it served as a great lesson for everyone: The sale doesn't stop when you sign the contract, and it's only finalized when you implement successfully.

It's also worth noting that my money-back, code-back offer also had a positive impact on my team. They felt supported by me and that I was listening to them. As frustrating as it was for me, it was at least that frustrating for them. They felt that if something didn't change, the project would drag on forever and drag everyone down with it. No doubt, at least one and probably more of them would have quit. We had to do something radical to grab Hotel Chocolat's attention and change the trajectory of the project. Too often, when there's this type of conflict between customer and supplier, both parties engage in the blaming game: "Your team sucks." "No, your team sucks." The way we approached the problem allowed both of us to orient to a higher value and purpose.

Though the relationship flourished from this point onward, and Hotel Chocolat remains a customer today, we were still not out of the woods. To get this first UK deal with Hotel Chocolat, we had to make compromises financially; we didn't charge as much as we normally would have. It took a long time before this account was profitable. We needed a referenceable customer, though, so we were willing to accept less-than-favorable terms. This is an example of a time when we subordinated our "always sell value" proposition to enter a new market.

Back to Start-Up Mode

Hotel Chocolat was a victory, but it would have been a Pyrrhic one if we didn't acquire more customers. We weren't winning, and we were still investing. Our future seemed to be leading more to a break than to the break-even point we hoped and planned for. For the next two years, it was touch and go. We weren't living up to the financial expectations Norm had for our London office. I made the argument that you couldn't measure our results only in terms of the new business in Europe, since we were generating business in the US because of our London presence—our US clients wanted our help in Europe now that we had an office there. The revenue from US customers may not have counted on a balance sheet toward the break-even point in Europe, but it counted for something.

For a while, it was one step back, two steps forward. We got scrappy and started to pick up Magento support customers in London, and we even expanded to pick up some new Magento customers throughout Europe. We hired a salesperson from a competitor, but that didn't work out. Then we hired one who did. We hired other people and started getting more deals, but the project managers didn't understand our implementation process. For this reason, we decided to import two more people from our US office to London for two or three years so they could help train the people we hired in the UK.

I believe that we all can learn from Rich and how he went about this. He trusted himself despite facing headwinds in his own company. He was able to harness his hurt and anger toward creative direction. Check out Level 3, harnessing anger to move from reactivity to assertion, in the Wright Developmental Model. He never took his hurt and anger out on anyone. He was willing to pay the price personally by going to London for two weeks every month—a brutal pace he maintained for more than a year. He needed to believe in himself and honestly and vulnerably persist in engaging his team, listening to them, affirming their concerns, and despite it all, continuing in his chosen direction.

If I only trusted the evidence and not my instincts, we would have shut down our London operation. We lost more deals in London than we'd ever lost before, and it was a contrast with how we kept winning deals in the US. On top of that, Norm and Dave were questioning the benefit of remaining in London, and I valued their opinions. I also recognized that sometimes you have to say, "It's not working" and end a project. But in this instance, my gut told me that it would work eventually. More than that, I was committed to making our company a truly global operation, and without the London office, that wouldn't have been possible.

Gradually, however, business picked up with clients like Hotel Chocolat, and soon our gamble paid off. I began weaning myself away from London, spending less time there as we attracted more business. More importantly, I saw that the Demandware people and our customers were recognizing our unwavering commitment to the UK market. Danny was getting up to speed, combining his knowledge of the market with our implementation processes and differentiators.

Still, Dave wasn't convinced that we should stay in London. We had many discussions about the financials and where my presence would serve the company best. Though Norm was more supportive of the London office, he suggested it might operate more effectively as a delivery office rather than as a sales office.

We were also adjusting to a competitive environment that was somewhat different than the one in the US. One of our competitors in Europe, Astound Commerce, had the advantage of being offshore (or nearshore) and low-priced. Another competitor possessed a partnership with a locally based design firm. We had to learn how to position our products and services against the low-cost competitors, and we needed to establish a partnership with a local designer we could use on projects. On top of this, we had to deal with all the language difficulties. In the US, all our various markets spoke a common language. This wasn't true of Spain, Portugal, Holland, Germany, and other countries where our UK clients had business or where we were seeking to serve new clients; it was just one more vexing challenge as we tried to sell throughout Europe.

Rich sorted through these various challenges with remarkable objectivity and developed even more friends and partners everywhere he went. With Dave and Norm, he examined how he might best be used in the face of their doubts. His ability to listen and empathize kept him humble and objective and earned major points with the Brits. He used coaching to sort through options and to strategize. He remained conscious of the problems. Too often entrepreneurs turn their back on problems, thereby missing opportunities and solutions. Rich steadfastly faced the challenges. He discovered options where, I am convinced, others would have been blind to the opportunities.

His relationships with companies like Demandware (which became Salesforce) bore fruit and added to his credibility at this and later points.

While these challenges were frustrating, they motivated me to be more intentional in my way of operating. It doubled my resolve to find a way to make our London office successful. I refused to accept that we might fail and instead started thinking of a way to "crack the code."

And we were cracking it, albeit at a slower pace than I wanted. Part of the problem was that my people in the US lacked the perspective I possessed because I had boots on the ground. They just saw that we were losing deals. They didn't see the incremental progress we were making as we built our office and gained experience. They didn't see how positively people responded to our physical presence in London and how it marked us as a global company.

We continued to build slowly over time as we closed some deals and added a digital marketing person who was working for one of our customers outside of London—this helped accelerate our deal-closing rate.

We then had a small epiphany: we were in a totally different market than we were in the US and had to go back to start-up mode. This may seem obvious, but it's anything but when you're enmeshed in the details of establishing an office. Logically, we had been in start-up mode ten years earlier when I began the business, and we were now an established company opening a branch office.

But that branch was so distant from our roots that we had to learn to think and sell differently. This start-up mindset was critical. It helped me become more agile in my strategy and make investments in the office without an immediate financial return. Hiring Danny, for instance, was exactly what had to be done, even though it was a costly investment in the short run.

As salespeople, we're conditioned to evaluate our performance based on the numbers, and certainly, the numbers are important. But I was learning to think beyond the numbers. How were our moves in London affecting the LYONSCG brand? How were we differentiating ourselves from our competitors?

This start-up mindset paid off. Finally, we had a well-known brand we could talk about to other prospective clients. Our work with Hotel Chocolat and other European-based clients opened doors. We furthered our relationship with Demandware. We began working with Magento and some of its customers in London and Europe. Just as we had evolved our services from B2C to B2B, we had grown from a domestic to a global operation.

WDM Takeaways

- Make fear your friend. Let it inform your moves and not shut you down (Level 1). Without fear, we lose our edge and can become cocky and arrogant. Be willing to go back to a beginner's mind and learn things anew.

- Never forget your responsibility to your employees and customers, no matter how much knowledge and experience you might possess (Level 6). As transformational leaders, we must be willing to put in the time and effort and be willing to do anything that we would ask our employees to do. And it is our job to protect our employees and have their backs.

- Tend to your own needs as leaders and keep yourself in good condition (Level 2). We need to be on our own side and find others to be on our side. We cannot expect our employees or customers to pat us on the back or make us feel good. That is our job—to tend to our own needs so that we can tend to the needs of our customers and employees.

- Express anger and intent in different ways (Level 3). Awareness is the key, as it gives us choice. Sometimes we must choose to initially contain these emotions, so we can evaluate the situation and strategize on the next best move to obtain the desired outcome. Never let reactivity get the best of you. Regardless of how you feel in the moment, choose how you want to respond and the desired outcome you are trying to achieve.

- Let all of your feelings (fear, hurt, anger, sadness, and joy) guide you to the right action. Our feelings are all going on all the time, whether we choose to be aware or not. And life can be so much richer with the awareness of our internal emotional states. No one knows but you, and you have the secret to understanding yourself and everyone else. You get to then choose how and who you want to be. It all starts with awareness.

CHAPTER TEN

WHATEVER IT TAKES

Nothing takes place in a vacuum. The events I've been describing—the growth of our business, adding platforms, adding people, expanding to a London office—occurred during an era when everything was changing. In 2005, when we began working with *Playboy* and it chose Demandware as its platform, we simply wanted to be a successful eCommerce company. We had no thought at the time of going global, of adding other platforms, of creating a number of creative and digital marketing services, or of acquiring or being acquired.

Back then, the world and our industry were simpler places. Since then, the digital universe has morphed. If we had continued to sell as we did in 2005, we would no longer exist. Just as you need to change in anticipation of or in response to changes in your life, companies need to alter their sales and go-to-market approach as their environment evolves.

And that means doing whatever it takes.

The Larger Context

Rich hates letting go of business. His can-do philosophy led him to accomplish whatever companies asked him to do: staff augmentation, infrastructure work, portals, ERP implementations, custom programs, and website design. If he didn't have the people to do what clients wanted, he'd go outside the company to bring in expertise. His Playboy implementation with Demandware began as a can-do project. Unlike some entrepreneurs, Rich was able to expand his vision beyond his business, seeing the events and trends that would shape many marketplaces. Most people didn't see the huge potential of online selling and how to monetize it; brick-and-mortar stores were dominant, and, though companies didn't ignore online tactics, most saw it as a secondary tactic.

Over time, LYONSCG grasped and took advantage of the almost unlimited potential of eCommerce.

This was the beginning of an ongoing process in which Rich adapted new services, always at the level of best practices. As online sales matured, LYONSCG needed to do the same. This was not only a time of new technology but also of changing customer expectations. Customers expected more because of companies like Amazon and its quick checkout process. Customer experience became increasingly critical. Businesses went into online selling with multiple uncoordinated siloed systems—separate inventory, ERP, order management, marketing, in-store point-of-sale, and eCommerce systems. Customers were frustrated with the result. A customer would buy a product online and then try to return it to the same company's store, and the store would refuse to take it. This is unheard of now, but back then with all the unintegrated systems, it was common.

Rich and I had frequent conversations about consolidation in the industry and the strategic implications for LYONSCG. Just as LYONSCG was adding services, major providers were acquiring companies that specialized in those services. Even warehousing and shipping were becoming extensions of eCommerce. eCommerce was becoming the core pillar of many, if not most, B2C and B2B businesses. If somebody bought it online, the entire process needed to become automated so that people experienced no delays or inconvenience. Seamless integration of former siloed functions from order to ship to payment to returns was essential. New terms like "on-demand," "just in time," and "nimble" were not only becoming common but also defining a new kind of marketplace—rapidly expanding, transforming, and highly demanding.

As companies struggled to tear down their silos to meet customer expectations, we took a holistic stance. We helped our customers integrate all their disparate systems so their customers had a seamless experience. In keeping with this holistic approach, we expanded services to include digital marketing and strategy, experience design, analytics, hosting, and ongoing support—and we did it adaptively, using the staff and systems the customer had wherever we could. This approach was more challenging. As we added services to compete, we still partnered with our clients, using what they had and working with them. We embraced the complexity and guaranteed our customers support for their entire commerce enterprise. We partnered to help them realize the potential of their online business. To provide this support, we built our account management team and a separate high-response 24/7 technical support team.

Perhaps even more importantly, we applied this integrative approach in deep, holistic partnership, recognizing that helping customers achieve their goals was crucial to our success. If they did not win, neither did we. As opposed to our earlier staff augmentation focus, eCommerce projects demanded collaboration across the company and into the ecosystem. We needed to engage with customers at a higher level and also with their partners and providers, while always keeping the end customer in mind. Therefore, we had to deepen our commitment to customer success, taking more risk and responsibility. We pioneered true partnerships and met the expanded demands that came with it.

Deep Partnering

At the same time, we innovated repeatedly as we developed our alliances program to the point that it was second to none. Our strategic alliances, also known as partners or service providers or independent software vendors (ISVs), could plug into our commerce platforms. As online selling evolved, we needed all sorts of different services, from payment gateways to tax providers to recommendation engines. Companies wanted to personalize their sites, so they needed a platform with universal compatibility. Some eCommerce platforms, for instance, couldn't handle subscriptions, recurring orders, or payments; we took "doing whatever it takes" as our mantra and made even more friends and found ways to work with a wide variety of service providers.

Though we were far from the biggest company in our space, we kept ahead of many competitors by paying attention to what was happening in the rapidly evolving market. We tracked everything, especially our relationships with ISVs. As a result, we knew the new features and functionality and services that were on the cusp of being the next big things, and we let our customers know about them. Because our managed services had grown so big (at one point we were supporting one hundred customers), we had data and insights from our customers in terms of what was and was not working. No other company had anything like this. Many companies shied away from support work because of its difficulty, and they turned away from developing integrations for ISVs because the projects were too small. We embraced both as a competitive advantage.

For example, when Apple Pay was introduced, many companies didn't have it on their commerce sites or their road maps. We took our data to our customers and explained to them that they needed to make sure Apple Pay was on their sites, that a growing number of people would be using it, and that it would boost their conversion rates.

Rich's "yes, and" and "One Team" innovations continued to deepen customer and industry relationships and yield other benefits. As LYONSCG brought new perspectives to clients, the clients brought new information and ideas to LYONSCG, investing in their success. Rich was collaborating on many different levels, becoming increasingly masterful in win-win-win approaches, as was his staff.

We'd bring our partners like Demandware and Magento into deals, they'd bring us into deals, and soon we had developed a partner ecosystem that was of great value to everyone in our industry—it was a huge source of data, leads, and customers.

We had a partner with a skyrocketing business as subscription services became popular. The company's CEO called me and said that although it currently did all its own implementation services, the company needed help—it wanted to focus on being a software company and develop partners to do its implementations. We started working with the company and proving our value by subcontracting with it on projects that it primed. Based on the skill and experience we gained partnering with the company, we soon possessed the capability to do our own implementations. This was the same lesson we learned when we started working with Demandware, and we began applying it to other software companies. Demandware realized that it made sense to let us focus on implementation, allowing it to concentrate on the company's software. Because of this decision, Demandware developed its partner program further and expanded to many more implementation partners.

This was a great model. Not only did it help us grow our business, but it also created closer ties with our partners. Many of our partners had no interest in building a services organization, and when they realized that we could support their customers, they were excited to hand this job to us. Many times, we would build and certify their integrations to Demandware and Magento. Other companies did not want this "small" work and saw it as a distraction. We saw it as an opportunity. As a result, our partnerships strengthened significantly.

Rich's agility, his ability to make transitions and anticipate the future, all helped him move his company to a deeper partnering model. When Rich worked with his friend and client, Playboy's Scott Stephen, that work helped transition LYONSCG into the eCommerce space. This story illustrates Rich's prescience about where the industry was heading and the changes he needed to make.

Before arriving at Playboy, Scott Stephen worked for a number of companies, including Yesmail, a pioneer in consensual marketing—it was a response to people's growing irritation with receiving unwanted emails selling various things. I coached Scott, and I watched as he had success after success. Playboy recruited him, and he eventually was in charge of both its print and online businesses. When Playboy chose Demandware for its online selling platform, Demandware wanted to do the implementation. Scott insisted that they use Rich's company, and this led to Rich's ongoing relationship with Demandware.

But just as important, it provided Rich with insight into the future of online selling. Rich's friendship with Scott opened a window to new opportunities. Scott had done a study of online selling platforms and providers, and it helped him conclude that Demandware was the best platform for Playboy. He shared this study with Rich, which provided him with insights about the market and the direction in which it was heading.

When Scott showed me his study, he told me that this was going to be the next big thing, and I should get into it. As a firm, we had a technical background—we were doing ERP implementations, for instance—and it helped us evolve as eCommerce took hold. Selling online can be complicated, requiring many integrations, and we had a leg up because of our background.

I have a slightly different take on this story than Rich; I was struck by his commitment never to alienate people and how his loyalty resulted in

Scott fighting for him. Rich was consistently able to transition his company to meet an evolving market because he always picked the best and brightest contractors, vetting them thoroughly. He possessed the connections and expertise to do well in this new space. Part of it, too, is that Rich is so good at envisioning the future. And part of it is that Rich is a master salesperson. Rich's competitors weren't owned by salespeople, so he had a significant edge—he understood how to convince people to take a chance on his company in a way that others did not.

Perhaps underlying everything was that I had done my personal work—the social and emotional training at Wright allowed me to establish rapport with people and to form deep alliances. It was four years of intense personal development and many years of leadership development (more than thirty years as of this writing). None of this would have happened if my wife hadn't "dragged" me in to see Dr. Bob to discuss our impending wedding and marriage.

You have to put in the work. People always ask what's the one thing they should be doing, and Dr. Bob and I always laugh. There are hundreds of things, from developing social and emotional intelligence to becoming a conscious and principled leader. But everyone wants a magic solution, a quick fix. The strong partnerships I built with others were a result of all the work I had done on myself. This ability became a superpower.

Rich didn't just develop deeper partnerships. His training in understanding others and having meaningful relationships paid off as he focused on assessing a partner or client's strengths and weaknesses, not just on selling them something. It added a depth and intimacy to the relationship that was a much stronger bond than other companies enjoyed. When Rich started, he couldn't always deliver what people wanted at the exact time he sold it—his capabilities were limited, and he needed to reach outside his company for assistance from others, some of whom were competitors. This experience, though, taught him to be careful about not overpromising and to focus on delivering on time and on budget. Delivery transparency became a foundational, prioritized value for Rich.

His approach was also less threatening to staff at client companies. LYONSCG adapted to customers, whereas larger firms tended to make the customer adapt to them. Rich was not interested in replacing people but in forming a true partnership with these companies, committed to their success. He was perceptive about assessing a partner's assets as well as its liabilities, and then he created a strategy for working with the partner that met its needs—this is what creates intimacy. When you add all this up, you come up with a variety of high-quality distinctions about how his company operated. Rich and his company didn't just assess the client company's technical capabilities, LYONSCG evaluated the company's people assets as well. LYONSCG was, after all, a person-to-person business, not really a technology business. It specialized in technology serving people, not people serving technology.

We became the best in the industry at delivering on time and on budget, almost double the industry average. We had the best people and the best processes—Norm helped guide this evolution. We also possessed the best account management team under Katie, who developed the important relationships and managed potentially difficult issues with grace and finesse. All of these puzzle pieces combined to help us develop trust with our customers from the beginning. This was the foundation of our relationships. We did not overcommit, and we even developed systems to determine ensuing kickoff dates. We sold with our customers, not to them. We talked about co-development, something most of our competitors avoided because it required a lot of communication and collaboration. We embraced these tasks through our One Team approach, working with our clients' creative and technical teams.

Rich and his account management team were deepening their partnership with clients in ways that developed career-long relationships.

Everyone wants to work with the best. As a company, you reach a tipping point where people say, "I know Rich. I know his tech people. I know his account management people. I want to work there." And when they get there, they say, "This is amazing."

Not only was LYONSCG attracting the best people, but Rich was also making moves that many entrepreneurs miss. He was allowing his clients' needs to drive his company's development. His account management team was his market research. Notice how he adapts to clients and then takes what he's learning from each client to lead other clients into increasingly profitable directions.

When Rich got a new account and began implementing his processes, people at the client worried that Rich would replace them—it's what a bigger competitor might have done. Instead, Rich communicated to them that his company's approach would empower them. As the many stories we've told about Rich demonstrate, he finds a way to work with his client's people rather than pushing them aside.

Our Customer First philosophy started with our client companies and extended to their employees. From the LYONSCG point of view, we were all on the same team—our culture-based One Team principle evolved to include our customers. We needed to be One Team internally and externally—how we engaged and operated and how we fit into our clients' cultures. This gave us another competitive advantage, making our partnerships deeper and more effective. It helped us form our own efficient ecosystem within the Demandware ecosystem.

We were both agile and customer-focused—not just focused on the size of the deal but on the potential lifetime value of a deal, allowing us to work on smaller accounts that didn't interest our larger competitors. In many instances, we were able to build these into big accounts over time. We did it by making customer satisfaction our top priority. That's why we gave them a satisfaction-or-your-money-back guarantee, and that's why we always had a budget for accommodations rather than a budget for lawsuits. We strove for what was fair, doing the right thing for the customer and the relationship.

Too often, companies draw boundaries between themselves and their customers. Our view was that we were all on the same team, and this gave us another competitive advantage. Employees of our clients became de facto market researchers for LYONSCG, providing us with insights on what other firms were offering so that we could better plan and prioritize expanding our services.

We also developed cutting-edge approaches that helped us compete. Employees we hired from competitors couldn't believe the sophistication of the processes we had in place—we were doing things that were more innovative and effective than companies many times our size. Working with the best people, customers, systems, and processes, we had great employee retention rates and morale.

The benefits of this approach were intangible and tangible. Deep partnerships, the One Team concept, and other customer-focused tactics created a bond with clients—a bond that motivated them to do more for us than they would for others. They would be willing to spend more with us, forgive mistakes, and do a hundred other things because of the trust and commitment we established. These intangible rewards were as valuable as all the ones spelled out in a contract.

Invasion of the Giants

Given all this, we set lofty goals rather than rest on our laurels. We wanted to be 100 percent referenceable, an impossible objective but one worthy of striving toward. That means that our highest priorities were service and satisfaction. Whether we won the deal or not, we wanted to leave a positive impression and make new fans and friends. We also communicated to our people that we wanted to be 100 percent on time and on budget—another impossible but worthy goal. And we insisted on being customer-focused in everything we did. Every interaction must be a positive experience. We trained our people to be aware of our customers' feelings and not take angry or overly harsh responses personally. As a result, we were well-positioned for an industry that was undergoing massive changes.

One of the biggest changes we encountered was that the customer experience from client to end consumer was becoming paramount. Responding to this trend, the larger services and software companies decided they needed to get into the commerce game.

Those large companies, including Accenture, which had built a reputation for Hybris B2B implementations, and Sapient, which had concentrated on larger B2C implementations, began looking to develop deeper expertise in smaller B2C commerce as well. They didn't have this down-market ability yet, but they were looking at acquisitions and moving quickly into Rich's territory. These large firms lacked a sense of the customer's needs. Closer to the ground, the smaller firms could see details, respond to these, and create an increasingly sensitive customer experience. Personalized customer experience soon became the watchword for all eCommerce.

Salesforce, too, decided to enter our market. It had done extremely well with a variety of services and clouds—Sales Cloud, Service Cloud, Marketing Cloud—but it lacked commerce. Adobe was thinking along similar lines. In 2013, SAP acquired Hybris, starting the consolidation in the market. They all recognized how the industry was evolving and wanted to be leaders in selling online. Rumors were circulating that a major company was going to buy Demandware—it turned out that company was Salesforce. In June of 2016, Salesforce bought Demandware for $2.8 billion. Having lost the bidding war for Demandware to Salesforce, Adobe acquired Magento in 2018 for $1.68 billion.

When we heard about the Demandware purchase, we were extremely concerned. We'd seen many great businesses decimated in just such an acquisition. Norm had lived through this at his last company, Laurus

Technologies. His company had been a major Sun Microsystems reseller, and when Oracle bought Sun, it decided it didn't want a reseller program. This destroyed Laurus.

Our nightmare scenario: a company buys Demandware, decides it wants to do all the services we provided as a partner in-house, and we lose 75 percent of our business overnight.

Fortunately, Salesforce was the acquiring company. Because its culture was partner-friendly, we greeted the purchase optimistically. Of course, we weren't the only partner, as Salesforce already had a well-developed partner ecosystem. Accenture, for instance, was providing services for Salesforce to the tune of $1 billion annually. As a $50 million company, we were a small player next to Accenture.

At the same time, we had maintained a strong, mutually beneficial relationship with Demandware for many years. Here's a story that illustrates the relationship and also will put my response to what happened next in context. Demandware gives awards to its partners annually, and one year, it named us Global Sales Partner of the Year. Demandware assumed that this would be the award that would be most meaningful to us, but then we heard it had given another company Delivery Partner of the Year. We immediately met with Demandware, and I said, "Who cares how much of your software we sold? To say we're not your Delivery Partner of the Year, that's killing me and killing my employees. We live for delivery excellence and are the best in the world. If you think Delivery isn't the biggest award, you're mistaken." Understand that this wasn't spoken in a cool professional tone. I was angry to the point of tears. The next year, and in subsequent years, we received the Delivery Partner of the Year award.

Rich would not have been able to deliver this fiery, heartfelt response without having done his internal social and emotional development work. Most remarkable to me is that his response would normally cause people to react and fight, but he imbued what he said with such force and emotional honesty that he maintained rapport and deepened the partnership.

In any relationship, there are times when you need to be brutally honest. The previous story illustrates one of these times. Here is another. A Salesforce partner executive summit was held approximately six months after the purchase of Demandware. At the summit, we sat down with the Demandware people (now Salesforce), and our conversation started promisingly. Demandware told us we were awesome and that we were responsible for 40 percent of the company's business globally. Then it added that it intended to triple its business in three years and become a billion-dollar Salesforce cloud business. All good so far. Then, Demandware dropped the bomb. As part of this ambitious plan, Salesforce intended to push more business to companies that did multiple clouds—companies like PwC, Accenture, and Deloitte. According to Demandware, it would be able to scale with these companies and sell bigger multi-cloud deals, while we were limited to only one cloud.

My response: "F*** off!"

I was even more upset than I was when I expressed my disappointment about not receiving the Delivery Partner of the Year award. Nonetheless, my profanity was calculated. I am a highly intentional businessperson. Certainly, I was angry, and my response reflected that, but I also wanted Demandware to understand why I was upset. I said, "We've grown this business together. I have no problem with scaling. We do 40 percent of your business, so if you're going to triple your 60 percent as well as our 40 percent, why mess with our portion of the business?" Demandware heard my message, and I heard its message—we needed to expand our cloud capabilities.

The story becomes increasingly complex at this point. Remember how we said that the Accentures of the world needed the smaller companies that could see consumer needs in finer detail? This was true at the beginning, but not necessarily once consolidation of technology started. LYONSCG had one significant advantage being a smaller player. As big as Salesforce was, the bulk of its clients were the smaller and middle-market firms. LYONSCG was in a surprise position, as you will soon understand, to partner with and align powerfully with Salesforce better than other firms.

Rich was engaged in one of his biggest sales efforts. He knows how to get attention when he needs it. Everyone was shocked to see the mild-mannered Rich Lyons so angry. Rich does not do it very often, so when he does, people pay attention.

My anger is intentional—I don't express anger often, but when I do, it's done for a conscious, strategic purpose. Many entrepreneurs, however, become angry without intention and far too often. They are not aware of their own reactivity—they just react to situations, sometimes inappropriately, and do not know when to contain. Many of these business leaders fail to get their hunger and affirmation needs met outside of work, and instead come into the office looking to get these needs met by their employees or customers. It's only when they're aware of their feelings that they can choose to express anger with purposeful intent.

Being CEO is a lonely job. You need to be surrounded by a lot of allies. It also helps to have a good coach. Often when I was feeling full of myself and on top of the world, Dr. Bob would kick my ass. When I was feeling down and questioning my value, he would tell me how great I was doing and to keep the faith. I'm exaggerating, perhaps, but my point is that you need someone outside of yourself to point out your strengths and weaknesses, to keep you in touch with your needs and hungers. Without this type of coaching, you're vulnerable to reactivity, poor decision-making, and chewing out employees for minor mistakes.

Anger is a result of being afraid and hurt and not being aware of these feelings. Some CEOs are unaware and end up competing in a way with their own employees. Rather than feeling good when one of their people does well, they're competitive and pissed. Or when an employee takes a suggestion from the CEO and turns it into a positive outcome, the CEO will declare, "That was my idea!"

When Rich was an angry young man, he was also a drinker. Over time and by putting in the work, he became sober, more intentional, and contained. Eventually, he became able to direct his anger toward a desired outcome better than anyone I've ever met.

The Growth Imperative

Our first step toward expansion was to register as a Salesforce Marketing Cloud partner, which we did right after the acquisition announcement. As an advantage, we already knew how to resell ExactTarget, which Salesforce purchased in 2013 (becoming Marketing Cloud). We then trained people so we could meet the requirements for having multiple clouds, starting with the marketing and commerce clouds. Thrown into the vast Salesforce ecosystem, we had a lot of new reps to meet and people to get to know. We launched an initiative to introduce ourselves to and establish relationships with these targeted individuals, assessing what they needed from us and letting them know of our cross-cloud capability.

One of the best decisions I made during this time was hiring Jennifer Kijek as our alliance manager. We needed someone who knew the market and the people in the ecosystem—and someone who reported directly to me. Jen not only helped us get our Salesforce certification quickly, but also managed the partnership with an astute understanding of its importance.

Like Rome, our relationships weren't built in a day. Three of our closest contacts at Demandware departed Salesforce shortly after all these events took place, including the CEO, the head of sales, and the head of partnerships. Things were changing, and we recognized that we needed to change; our willingness to do whatever it took to remain excellent and relevant and able to serve our customers guided our actions. Our most immediate concern was growing bigger to remain competitive. We had two options for growth. Either we raise money through private equity and pursue an acquisition strategy—acquiring other companies—or, as we finally decided, we get acquired ourselves. I talked with Dr. Bob and our board and decided to launch a formal process to examine our options. After a selection process, we chose William Blair in Chicago as our investment bank.

LYONSCG began as an implementer and then later added SEO, hosting, design, account management, customer experience, and many more services. In the meantime, logistics, order management, payment businesses, and others were getting into the consolidation game. We frequently addressed the possibility of adding services and making acquisitions and always decided to put this decision on hold. Acquisition seemed too steep a hill to climb in a rapidly consolidating and expanding universe. By the time a move became compelling, LYONSCG would have needed to be the highly excellent little fish consuming the whale to maintain its excellence.

Maintaining excellence was highly unlikely in either case. Rich began setting his requirements for firms that might acquire them. Any potential acquiring firm had to value LYONSCG for its excellence, its people, and its culture.

No one in the company besides Dave, Norm, and myself knew that selling had become an option. For years, I had reassured our people that I would never sell the company, and I meant it. But as the saying goes, that was then, and this is now. It would have been foolish to ignore the changes in the market. Since we had to get bigger to survive and remain the best, being bought by a larger enterprise was one way to do it. Recognizing that I needed to prepare people for the possibility of being bought, I began talking to them about how the market was changing and that if we wanted to stay relevant, we had to view ourselves differently—and that acquisitions or partnerships were options. It helped that people trusted me and that our business was doing great, and people were already concerned about the future because of Salesforce's acquisition of Demandware. By "breadcrumbing" various paths, I was ensuring that whatever we decided wouldn't come as a shock to our employees. I had experienced such shocking surprises, and I was sensitive to my people not experiencing the same trauma. Working with William Blair, we looked at both strategic acquirers and private equity firms, identifying more than fifty potential companies. During a tedious and grueling process, we narrowed the list down to three companies, including one private equity firm, but none of us was high on private equity, even though we wanted to keep this option in play. As we explored our various growth strategies, we kept risk in mind. Historically, we were aware that our reliance on Demandware had always been a risk. Our reliance on Salesforce was equally risky, but we decided to double down with Salesforce. We always tried to manage the risk in part by reinvesting in the business. But at this point in our company's life, it would have been irresponsible and risky to reject the possibility of being acquired.

LYONSCG was becoming increasingly interesting to Salesforce. It integrated two clouds—but that still was not enough. A lot of entrepreneurs and business leaders don't understand their companies' intimate relationship with the marketplace and their response to it. Most of them respond too slowly to a rapidly changing marketplace—and some respond too quickly. Rich has always kept pace with the market, and we generally discussed implications and options in coaching sessions. Despite feelings of impatience, he doesn't give in and act prematurely. A key aspect of our coaching has included me pushing movement, Rich agreeing on the direction, but not moving until he was ready. His previous employer, Whittman-Hart, didn't grasp the need to move at the market's pace—the company outpaced the market with over-financing, responding to investors and stockholders rather than the people who purchased their services.

Most people don't think of market knowledge within the context of intimacy, but it's a useful word. Only when you know something inside and out can you respond to it effectively. For most people, big marketplace changes are overwhelming and even terrifying. Rich, as a salesperson who makes and keeps friends widely, has always understood the marketplace deeply through his partnerships. His partners and affiliates have helped him grow by keeping him aware of what was taking place. As a result, people look to Rich as a market-maker; they understand that he knows what is happening and when. In investing, we talk about timing the market. Rich's intimate knowledge allowed him to display remarkable timing with his moves.

We really didn't have to sell, given that at this moment, we were Demandware's number one partner. We could have fought our way through this period. But the risk was that we would become decreasingly relevant over time. Salesforce and Demandware communicated to us that we needed to grow and expand our services to include other Salesforce clouds, or we risked becoming irrelevant as a Salesforce partner. And though there was no way of anticipating the COVID-19 period—those two or three years of business shutdowns would have made life very difficult for us—being part of a much larger organization offered a degree of protection. We had received offers to sell in the past that indicated our value and now seemed a time of peak value, where expanded capacities could allow us to provide even greater services to our existing customers and to even more and bigger clients.

The easiest decision would have been to do nothing. I was aware, however, that many entrepreneurs get caught in the trap of inaction, resting on their laurels rather than evaluating risks and opportunities continuously. We were always striving to maximize our potential, to be a learning organization. Selling the company increasingly seemed to be a way to stay true to these foundational principles.

WDM Takeaways

- Pay attention to risks, and allow your fear to guide you to the next right action (Level 1). Evaluate your fear to be sure it is a real fear versus an imagined fear before taking action. Use objective counsel.

- Keep in mind that sales is service. To be successful, salespeople must commit to the success of their customers, beyond themselves (Level 5). Beyond striving for wealth, status, and success, there lies a purpose in serving another that makes selling—and life, for that matter—different. This is the concept of life is sales. Value friends first, integrity second, and profit third. Profit is important but never at the expense of friendship and service.

- Guard against feeling superior (Level 6). Once we get really good at something, we can rest on our laurels and not see the signs of change. Be vigilant to changes in the market. Track risks and opportunities as if your life depended on it—because it does.

- Use anger carefully and effectively (Level 3). One can be very assertive and intentional without ever expressing anger. Sometimes containment is the best option, regardless of the tornado that exists within. And other times, carefully thought out and strategic times, anger can be a great weapon and tool. Use it sparingly and wisely. Be capable of kicking ass. It may be rarely needed, but it's also necessary when people are too self-satisfied.

- Express the truth. Conformity is useful, but there are times when we must choose to be honest with others (Level 4). It is nice to be liked and to get along with everyone, but at what cost? Let people know who you are and what you believe, but do it responsibly and be aware of the potential consequences.

CHAPTER ELEVEN

TRADING INDEPENDENCE FOR IMPACT

We didn't have to sell, buy other companies, or change anything. We considered doing nothing at all and continuing our current growth. After all, LYONSCG was highly successful—we were Demandware's number one partner and had excellent relationships with Magento and Hybris. We could have sustained the company for years by maintaining the status quo and doing what had always made us successful—focusing on our customers.

Rich is also not talking about how deeply he had collaborated with Salesforce. As he noted, the bulk of Salesforce's original clients, especially for commerce, were small firms. LYONSCG had never abandoned smaller firms, but they were a stretch. Rich's understanding of Salesforce's business model let him serve the company's client base even further as LYONSCG began developing very inexpensive, high-quality, entry-level eCommerce QuickStart solutions that addressed many of the frustrations and problems so many of Salesforce's smaller customers faced.

The top executives at Salesforce all knew who Rich was. They expressed appreciation for what LYONSCG was doing as Salesforce was expanding into new clouds (realms of business and engagement). They trusted him enough to invite him to address the Wall Street press and investors with them in their annual meeting. There was no way that LYONSCG was going to go away; however, life was going to become increasingly challenging, and the wins were going to become increasingly competitive and costly. Salesforce desperately needed the first commerce cross-cloud services to demonstrate the power of Salesforce beyond sales support. LYONSCG earned huge respect and gratitude as the company developed cross-cloud services.

But maintenance and status quo weren't what we were about. We had always pushed boundaries and explored new approaches and opportunities. We always wanted to be the best, and we had become the best—we were willing to burn the canoes to keep that position.

With the changing marketplace, if we wanted to remain the aggressive, growth-oriented, customer-centric company we'd always been, we needed to find a buyer. The road to acquisition was too slow, and there were several bidders pointing out synergies between us and them long before we decided to sell. The challenge, though, was selling the company without selling our soul. We didn't want to lose our identity; some acquisitions suck the life out of the bought company. Rather than look for a buyer that would offer us the most money, we were searching for one that valued our culture and skills and would enable us to become bigger and better in service of our customers.

A Time of Consolidation and Low-Price Competition

It was becoming increasingly difficult for smaller players to compete in the rapidly consolidating market unless they possessed a broad array of services. LYONSCG's place in the market was limited to eCommerce.

That's why the initial idea to acquire other firms was compelling—an idea that we pursued for a while but eventually decided wouldn't result in an optimal outcome.

The industry consolidation was like a slowly approaching tsunami, with pressure building as it moved with increasing velocity toward land. LYONSCG's value proposition was at risk of eroding. We were seen as the high-quality but pricey option, especially as offshore competitors arrived—competitors that charged considerably less than we did.

Customers cannot always assess quality and value, at least initially. When Rich would lose a deal, companies would often come back and say, "We should have picked you." They had a prospective customer that justified the low-cost, low-quality option this way: "If they screw it up, they can do it over again, and even if they have to do it three times, it's still less than what I would be paying you."

Rich served as an educator and ombudsman for potential customers, but sometimes they still opted for cheaper or inferior competitors. When they discovered that the services they'd purchased fell short, they often came back to LYONSCG sadder but wiser.

My response to this type of thinking was, if you have a toothache and go to the dentist and he pulls the wrong tooth three times in a row, are you happy? It makes a lot more sense to pay a bit more rather than endure the pain, not to mention the cost and time, of multiple mistakes. And that's why I tried to avoid burning bridges. Dr. Bob had a good phrase to describe this approach to customers who decided to go with competitors: bless and release.

Despite the unsettled market environment, LYONSCG was still in a good position. Financially, we were doing well, our culture was great, and our alliances were stronger than ever.

We knew that Marc Benioff, the head of Salesforce, had a strong relationship with Paul Hermelin, the head of Capgemini. What we didn't know at the time was that this relationship foreshadowed what was going to happen next.

The Search for the Best Fit

In evaluating prospective buyers, we weren't operating in sell-and-run mode: getting the most money we could and then running off to an island to sip piña coladas. Norm, Dave, and I wanted to continue working in our business, to continue to be the best, so we wanted to make sure a company would give us this opportunity. We were intent on maintaining a significant amount of control over the business. And we hoped to ensure that our people were protected.

We met with a number of companies, including our large competitors, and what we learned was enlightening. As much as we may have thought we were different from other businesses, these discussions confirmed it. They told us about their policies and practices, their strengths and weaknesses, and how they sold and went to market. Compared with our larger competitors, we were much more agile. Unlike most of the companies we talked to, we were also more aggressive in our partnering and selling strategy. Multiple companies told us they lacked a direct sales force—they depended on executives or partners for this task. That we had made a strong effort to develop both our inside and outside sales groups was another distinctive trait of LYONSCG.

What was discouraging, however, was that some of the big businesses we talked to were never going to allow us to remain whole. They saw us as bodies to put into their current operations and had no appreciation for the unique culture and business model we had developed. Though they were willing to pay a premium for us, they intended to break us up and absorb us into their much larger organizations.

Early in the process, it looked like one of the major Indian IT companies would be the likely winner among the potential candidates. It wasn't just that it said all the right words, praising our culture and our capabilities. As the highest bidder, the company's offer was also extremely attractive—clearly, it valued us. Unfortunately, the company didn't value us enough to avoid burying us in the organizational structure. I had been concerned about who I would report to, and when I broached this subject with the company's leadership, it was obvious that I would be reporting up through dense hierarchical layers.

For a while, we thought some of the other big strategic consulting firms might be a good fit for us, but we became aware of what happened when they bought other companies around our size: the acquired company's senior leaders departed, and the rest of the company was broken up and distributed within the larger system.

Another major Salesforce partner engaged us in deep conversations about an acquisition, and it had recently purchased another Salesforce partner—a purchase that seemed to have benefited both companies. The partner came on strong and talked like it would move heaven and earth to make sure the acquisition happened. But then it never put in a final bid. We're not sure why the bid never came through, but after this failure to bid, the company began aggressively trying to poach our people, with success in recruiting some of our employees. I was livid; it seemed morally wrong that it had acted as if it was intent on purchasing us and then switched gears and started picking off our employees.

After our hopes were raised and dashed, we thought again about private equity and growing by making our own acquisitions. But Dave, Norm, and I considered the amount of time this would take and all the unknowns that would be part of this approach. How many years did we have left? Did we want to spend them focused on acquiring and integrating other companies? The risk seemed too great.

The European Superpower

We knew Capgemini was different from our other potential buyers. French-based with more than 300,000 employees, this leading technology company didn't do much eCommerce. Earlier that year, Capgemini had purchased a smaller company in France (Itelios) that did some Demandware work, and it wanted to expand more into this area. Capgemini also possessed the multiple Salesforce Cloud practices we lacked. Right off the bat, the strategic fit seemed good. Even better, Capgemini told me that I'd report directly to John Mullen, who was the leader of North America—that meant we were important enough not to be buried beneath multiple reporting layers.

Dave, Norm, and I agreed that Capgemini could be the one. In fact, throughout this process, we were aligned, minimizing the tension that can arise between partners during this exploratory period. As 10 percent owners of the business, Dave and Norm wanted to be part of the new organization, motivating them to find the best fit rather than choose the highest offer.

It also helped that Rich is a facilitating leader; he facilitates what needs to happen without asking everyone's opinion. He really listened to what Dave and Norm had to say, but he was focused on making the sale happen.

Rich may appear laid back but that is because he's an observing/analyzing person, waiting for the right moment to make a move—he knew what he was doing bringing Dave and Norm into ownership, and they justified this decision when they voted to continue working with the wonderful teams they had developed.

I can be a bit manipulative, at least in the sense that I know where I want to go and can help others share that vision and get them to feel that it isn't just my idea but theirs. Perhaps I did that to some extent with Dave and Norm during our discussions of possible suitors and especially Capgemini. But more than anything else, I knew we had to sell. The market had changed so much that we had to get bigger or we'd become irrelevant. I had put my heart and soul into LYONSCG for fourteen years, and I wasn't going to allow anything bad to happen to it and the people who worked there. Capgemini seemed like it provided the best path for becoming bigger and better and able to serve our customers more fully.

But many times, big sales come with big obstacles. William Blair warned us that we would feel like walking away or that the deal was not going to happen at least three times. As we talked with Capgemini, we hit number three—their bid was almost 50 percent lower than other companies' top bids. Still, we agreed to meet with Capgemini, and the first meeting was with its mergers and acquisitions group.

It was a terrible meeting. The group leaders didn't seem to understand what our business was about, and they didn't ask good questions. I told our Blair contact that based on the meeting, it seemed like a waste of time talking to them. My contact, however, convinced me that I should at least talk to John Mullen and hear from the businesspeople before making a final decision.

We were becoming increasingly anxious as we attempted to make the right match. We were second-guessing ourselves, thinking we had set our price too high—we insisted on a bid that was at least three times our revenue—and had scared away some viable suitors. Though I had tried to prepare our people for the eventual sale, I hadn't made any definitive statements and was worried about how rumors might start affecting their morale.

Meeting with John Mullen was key. He was based in Chicago, his kids went to the same high school as my children, and he was a great guy who placed a high value on our company and its culture. But I told him and Capgemini's leadership in Europe that they had to increase their bid substantially.

When they finally met our minimum offer (still substantially lower than other bids), we held a meeting in Blair's conference room with LYONSCG's leadership and our advisory board (via phone). During the meeting, we laid out the deal with Capgemini, and a moment of clarity occurred. All of us experienced the same realization simultaneously: this was the right deal for us. Everything had come together. Not only were we pleased with the reporting structure and the focus on culture, but we also negotiated a good fund for employee retention, ensuring we wouldn't lose many of our key people.

Despite all this, it was extraordinarily difficult for Rich to sell his company. In fact, when I told Rich it was time to sell, he became angry, even though we had discussed this possibility for years. Rich was feeling like he was in a car racing two other cars toward a narrow gap, and that only the first to get there would make it through. It wasn't that Rich wanted to sell the company to Capgemini but that he had to do it. The only other possibility was to acquire other companies, but why would he want to buy their inferior businesses and try to combine cultures? Capgemini didn't really do what LYONSCG did, so he had a clear field if they became a part of the French-based company—or so it seemed. While Capgemini made great sense, it still was a difficult and highly emotional decision.

We weren't naive. We were aware that the challenge of integrating would be significant—Norm had integrated companies in previous jobs. But we just couldn't continue grinding as we'd been doing. Dave might have been able to handle it because he is younger than Norm and I. But it was time to sell, and Capgemini was the right company, and we went into the contract signing without any doubt.

The moment of clarity was marked by silence—there was nothing left to argue about or discuss. I signed the paperwork right there, and the deal was done. It was a moment of excitement and sadness at the same time. We were coming to the end of an era. As I signed the contracts, I wept.

When I announced the deal to our employees, the most frequent question was this: If the acquisition doesn't work—if it turns out to be a bad fit for us—can we leave and become LYONSCG again? Of course, the answer was no. But I understood the fear. We had created a great place for employees to work, and we were asking them to trust that when we were part of Capgemini, it would still be a great place to work. Though I thought it would be, no one knew for certain.

Before the acquisition became official, we needed to meet with Paul Hermelin, Capgemini's CEO. He flew in from Paris, and he wanted to have dinner with us before he gave his final approval of the deal. John Mullen and Dee Berger from Capgemini North American leadership had a bit of trepidation about this meeting. They coached us about Paul's concerns, nervous that one of us might say or do something that would blow the deal at the last minute; they told us the story of another acquisition the company was pursuing, and when the CEO of the about-to-be-acquired company talked about how he wanted to work from home, Paul killed the deal. Fortunately, our dinner with Paul was great; he was smart, kind, and asked the right kind of questions. The deal was finalized, and LYONSCG became a wholly owned part of Capgemini.

Transitioning

The acquisition didn't come as a surprise to our people because we'd prepared them in our regular Monday morning all-company calls. Still, once the deal was done, we conducted a conference call with our entire company informing them of the details, using slides to illustrate what Capgemini was and our place within the larger organization.

John Mullen visited our offices, and in a reversal of his words of warning to me before our meeting with Paul, I suggested that he not wear his usual suit and tie—I was concerned that his formal dress would clash with our more casual culture. He said that he didn't know if he had a pair of jeans that fit, but he did end up wearing jeans and assured everyone that we would have an impact on Capgemini despite having only 400 employees to its 300,000 plus. In his words, we would "punch above our weight."

Though I was sold on John, I had to keep selling him on our capabilities. As anyone who has ever reported to a powerful boss knows, this isn't always easy—it involves a degree of risk. I insisted to John at a meeting of all of Capgemini's North American leaders that he show a video we had made. At first, he resisted. The video was a take-off on *The Matrix* movie, with Mullen as Morpheus and me as Neo. As you might expect, our video called for us to act in silly ways. In our culture, we embraced having fun and not being serious all the time. In Capgemini's culture, it was more about power and control. The video wasn't aligned with Capgemini's culture.

But I insisted that he show the video since it delivered the message that LYONSCG was all about global domination, and it showcased all the weapons we possessed to achieve this goal. It was funny, but with a serious message. After John agreed we could show it, everyone loved the video.

A great deal of what Rich and I worked on was how Rich had to sell to make a desired strategy happen, no small matter for Rich. People I coach are people who are committed to creating businesses that are a blessing to our world. That meant a blessing to Rich and his family, his employees, his clients, his market segment, and the rest of the world. After more than a decade of piloting his own ship and building a company filled with people he cared deeply for, Rich was profoundly disturbed, largely out of concern for his people—as people first and employees second. He negotiated as good a deal as he could, but the reality that he was facing was undeniable—they were the little fish and would have to work hard to avoid being digested by the stomach acid of the whale. Neither the Whittman-Hart/marchFIRST nor the Divine bankruptcies were as disturbing for Rich. Even though he was going to be financially well taken care of, he worried about his people. Finances were never Rich's primary concern.

Rich's impulse is to elevate the people around him. He has a huge drive to belong, and he doesn't want anyone to feel left out. Rich is acutely aware of other people's deficits—whether it's financial or social or anything else—and he works hard to address these issues.

When I was a kid, I never felt like I fit in. I was conscious that I was more emotional than other kids, and different, and other boys made fun of me because I had long, curly hair. So because I always wanted to fit in, I became driven to help others fit in.

During our transition into Capgemini, I was intent on helping LYONSCG people and strategies fit in. I recognized, however, that this wouldn't happen immediately. Until Capgemini acquired us, it was focused on the technology side; its audience was primarily chief information officers or information technology managers. Capgemini needed to make a transition to digital transformation and eCommerce, and our people needed to make a transition to working under the umbrella of a large company. Capgemini was especially eager to develop its eCommerce capacity in North America and shift the conversation to the chief marketing officers, an obvious motivation for the acquisition. Interestingly, during the first year, Capgemini left us alone. We discovered this was due to a previous acquisition, where it flooded the new company with far too many leads (good leads and goose chases), running the purchased company's people ragged and eventually hurting the business more than helping it.

Being separate but equal, however, wasn't ideal. On a practical level, we were both operating on different systems, preventing us from accessing Capgemini's internal portal easily (because of security protocols). We kept our @ lyonscg.com email addresses. We also couldn't take advantage of Capgemini's training materials and other valuable information. In hindsight, it probably would have been better to start the integration process sooner.

No doubt, the company wanted to leave well enough alone. Over time, as we succeeded in business, Capgemini told us that we were its most successful acquisition, and we were making our numbers. Still, multiple Capgemini executives started pushing us to pursue new leads they provided, and many times, we had to say no. Anticipating that we might be inundated with leads as their previous acquisition had been, we set up a process to ensure that the leads were real and qualified before we had our people chase them. Dave and I spent a good deal of time vetting the leads we received. We recognized that if our salespeople wasted a lot of time on bad leads, we would never make our numbers.

While this helped us have a good first year, it alienated us from some of Capgemini's managers, prompting us to start trying to repair relationships. We conducted trainings and tried to communicate more effectively what the LYONSCG approach and go-to-market offerings were all about. We represented a new space for Capgemini, and we realized that we had to educate the company's leaders about what we did and how we did it.

A Multifaceted Sales Campaign

Up until this point, I had done a lot of selling in my life, but in many ways, this was my biggest challenge. Not only did I have to make a strong pitch to external and internal audiences, but also many of the sales were strategically complex.

Shortly after we were acquired, for instance, we accompanied some Capgemini executives to a meeting at Dreamforce (a major Salesforce conference). We ended up meeting with Salesforce's COO—a meeting that would never have happened when we were LYONSCG but was facilitated by Capgemini's size and prestige. Top Capgemini executives flew in from France, and we had thirty minutes with the COO.

Because I'd built our business on alliances, I normally talked with partners about how we could become a better partner and asked for input about how we could improve—no matter how much we might have accomplished for a partner in the past. But our French colleagues had the floor to begin the meeting, and they started talking about the importance of verticalizing products by industry; they hadn't known that Salesforce had already verticalized. The Capgemini people spent most of the meeting boasting about their capabilities, talking about how great of a partner they were in France.

I was only able to speak during the last five minutes of the meeting, and I tried to sell them on our present and future synergies—the progress we'd made in the past, the direction of our partnership, how we might improve.

But the damage had been done. It was a ridiculous meeting, and it should have served as an early warning about how difficult it would be to sell Capgemini and its customers on what we had to offer.

Just as we started to sell Capgemini on LYONSCG, we began selling our own people on Capgemini. People on our staff who had gone through acquisitions with other businesses were understandably anxious. Our finance and administrative people probably had the most difficult transition, in that they were the ones who were absorbed into the larger Capgemini system first. We held many conversations with individuals and the whole company, and we convinced most of them to give us a year to assess if things were going to work out. During that first year, we had low turnover, though some people did leave to pursue other opportunities and work at smaller companies. I was upset that they left, but Dave put the situation in perspective by telling me that not everyone wants to work for a big company. He described our journey from Whittman-Hart to marchFIRST to Divine, and how these series of changes caused us to start LYONSCG. "Look at how many companies grew out of that one company (Whittman-Hart)," he said. "Our people who have left will talk about LYONSCG the way we talk about Whittman-Hart, how it was a great company with a great culture."

In hindsight, I know that selling the company was the right thing to do on many levels, and I would do it again. Strategically, it made sense because of all the consolidation in the industry and the price competition occurring in our space. Just as important, though, being part of a much larger business afforded our people a certain measure of protection during tough times. We hadn't had that buffer during the tough years of 2007 to 2008. The economy was struggling, and we had to let some people go through no fault of their own. We chose to keep the business alive, but achieving that objective meant sacrificing some good people. As part of Capgemini, I hoped we wouldn't have to face that difficult choice again.

Though our first year as part of Capgemini went well, we were all going through a grieving process; we had to learn to let go of LYONSCG and become ourselves as distinct individuals, parts of a much larger enterprise.

The period leading up to the sale was marked by gnawing uncertainty. You have to know yourself and work on yourself to get through it productively. Through the groups at Wright and on my own, I did that work.

Not everyone does the work. In our leadership group, we had a member who had been with a global company and came home to take over the family business when his father died. His brothers and sisters owned the bulk of the business, and they didn't want to make this individual the CEO. The group knew this person well, and we asked, "How many of you would vote to make him CEO?" He didn't receive a single vote; he hadn't done the work, and failing to do so is a recipe for business disaster. But that woke him up—he asked humbly for a chance to learn, grow, and prove himself and ultimately succeeded.

I'm proud of how we ran LYONSCG. We had a great culture, and we were enormously successful and served many customers. We were authentic as individuals and as an organization. We never overinflated our pipeline, pretending we were something we were not.

If companies want to maintain their quality and if their reputation is of paramount importance, they will opt for measured growth. Rich understood that if they had made numerous acquisitions it would have been difficult if not impossible to integrate them into LYONSCG. It was remarkable to watch Rich go after bigger accounts. He never overpromised during a bid. If he made a promise, he kept it.

In our leadership group, we have this credo: "We don't care how big your company is, we want it to be a beautiful blessing to the world."

LYONSCG was a beautiful blessing.

I remember when I first started working with Dr. Bob, he would say, "Be the biggest blessing you can be." At the time, I thought to myself that I could never use those words in business. At Capgemini, I remember telling my people, "We want to be the biggest blessing we can be with our customers."

The Integration Challenge

One of the stages of grieving is acceptance, and after that first year, we accepted that we needed to do the right thing for Capgemini. That meant letting go of the brand (LYONSCG) and integrating our people and systems with those of Capgemini. The goal was to build Capgemini's digital and commerce expertise and reputation if we wanted to compete with Accenture, Deloitte, and others. In the LYONSCG culture, we always spoke about One Team, and now we needed to create this at Capgemini.

But it was a challenge, in part because our earnout was based on delivering good numbers. We feared that if we integrated fully with Capgemini, we would lose our unique selling proposition and our numbers would fall.

Capgemini was more of a body shop when it acquired LYONSCG: It threw a lot of people at mega-assignments for a relatively low cost. A mega-assignment could have been a $500 million contract over multiple years. Imagine how many bodies Capgemini needed to dedicate to that type of job, given the cost. LYONSCG and Capgemini were two very different types of companies. Because Rich's company occupied the mid-market, Capgemini was unfamiliar with the service requirements. During the integration phase, Capgemini's large-account focus threatened to disenfranchise the LYONSCG people from this core client base. Big companies frequently do this; they buy companies they don't understand and ruin them. Fortunately, Rich's strong relationships with Salesforce and other key groups gave him the credibility to stop Capgemini from getting rid of mid-market clients.

Still, he had to fight to help keep the mid-market. Around this time, I had coached an entrepreneur who had completed a multibillion-dollar acquisition of a company with a unique product. Through this experience, I learned that everyone who is not succeeding in a large corporation sees the acquisition as an opportunity to latch on to something good. They're like leeches, and they suck the life out of the acquired company. Or, to use another metaphor, the acquisition is like a rare plant, and it would die if not properly tended. The acquiring company often fails to admit it has no idea what it takes to nurture its new acquisition. Rich determined "Until they do, we're not letting anyone mess with it."

Because Capgemini had two failed acquisitions before us, it was aware of how big companies can destroy the businesses they buy. From the start, Capgemini's leadership acknowledged its past mistakes in this area—how it spread those companies too thin and killed them. While Capgemini allowed us a lot of freedom during that first year to operate separately, everything began to change when we started to integrate the second year.

Rich was working on being on his own side during this period, independent of his external identity. He needed to maintain his principles, values, and sense of purpose in the face of ubiquitous challenges. There was a lot of drama—think about a sense of victimhood or self-pity—while Capgemini attempted to integrate LYONSCG, and Rich had to overcome his own drama and assert himself, speaking up forcefully and repeatedly in ways that he never would have spoken up before. His first major assertion was that Capgemini couldn't have Dave and Norm for other functions in these first two years. Large companies often fragment the businesses they acquire, and it was a big deal when Rich refused to allow Capgemini to fragment LYONSCG by giving Dave and Norm new positions, positions at which they ultimately succeeded—but only after the first two years.

Dave eventually left our core business for a great opportunity to transform the Capgemini sales organization. We all discussed this and decided that it was the right thing to do for the larger organization. Although we were afraid of the disruption to our core business, we allowed it to happen. But we had other concerns—we had to learn how to exist within a large corporation.

A man of action, one of Rich's first challenges was to get out of being dragged into a lot of bureaucratic internal meetings, ones without outcomes. He is a gifted salesperson and partnership-maker, and having him focused internally and not client- or partner-facing was a waste of his gifts.

After we started integrating into Capgemini in the second year, I ran the Digital Customer Experience (DCX) practice. This was a nice extension of the LYONSCG Commerce business, combining marketing, sales, service, and commerce. While we had always aspired to offer these end-to-end capabilities, running a practice within Capgemini was a different experience than I expected. There were a lot of time-consuming internal meetings that didn't help us advance the business, and I was facing challenges on several fronts.

As the company's global leader for commerce, I was trying to establish a foothold for us in countries such as Germany and Portugal. I was traveling a lot and closing deals—we landed Iceland Foods in Wales, and it was a great model to roll out through Capgemini in other European countries. I soon discovered that while I might be able to sell customers on commerce, I couldn't sell individual Capgemini country heads on following this commerce delivery model. It turned out that each country leader only cared about profit and loss in that given country. My idea of creating a global commerce practice would require a short-term investment that might affect the balance sheet adversely in the short term (though benefit it in the long run). Consequently, I was never able to turn this vision of a global commerce practice into reality.

Still, I kept trying to make it work. Once I committed myself to integrating LYONSCG into Capgemini, I had to educate myself about large businesses, specifically French businesses and culture. I had to learn the difference between managers who had power and influence and those who were just hangers-on. One organizational leader made a consistent effort to get to know me and work with me, and for a while, I couldn't figure out if he possessed real power in the organization or if he was just looking for someone to carry him. It turned out to be the former, and he came to possess even more power and influence within Capgemini than when I first got to know him. He was very respectful and brought me into great initiatives. He would tell his people, "Rich's relationship with Adobe is very deep, so we'll work together on this and meet with Adobe." Finding people like this at Capgemini was rewarding and one of the great benefits of the acquisition.

We were surprised that Capgemini had so many decent and substantial executives. At the same time, one of Capgemini's other acquisitions was doing territory grabs, and Rich had to go to leadership and say, if you make this guy (the leader of the other acquired company) my boss, I'm out. It wasn't a common move for Rich, but he was learning to assert himself in the larger company. And the company decided, wisely, not to make this individual Rich's boss.

We found a lot of Capgemini's managers and leaders to be rational, well-intentioned people. This doesn't mean they didn't make mistakes, but many of them were willing to listen when we brought up points that ran counter to their way of doing things.

Sometimes, however, selling Capgemini on making certain moves was an uphill battle. I had to overcome many obstacles—the hubris of some of our French colleagues, our unfamiliar (to them) commerce business, and the foreign (literally and figuratively) LYONSCG culture.

Once, I tried to sell Capgemini on an acquisition. Lev Digital was a terrific company, and I had an excellent relationship with its CEO. I heard that the company was in play, and I tried to get Capgemini interested in buying the company. Capgemini's mergers and acquisition people ignored my request, but others seemed intrigued, and eventually, Norm and I set up a meeting in Indianapolis, where Lev Digital was headquartered.

After this meeting, Capgemini sent two senior staffers to meet with the CEO, and I also attended the meeting at a restaurant in New York City. It was a disaster. It wasn't what was said that was the issue; it was the way it was said. During the meeting, the top Capgemini executive would turn to his colleague and voice asides in French. When this executive would speak to Lev's CEO, his voice was so soft and accent so thick that his words were frequently lost in the din of the restaurant. I tried to translate for the CEO, but it didn't do much good—the Capgemini executive appeared arrogant, and he obviously alienated the CEO.

After the meeting, I talked with the two Capgemini people, and the senior executive told me that he wasn't impressed with the CEO and that he didn't seem like a sufficiently skilled salesperson to run his own company.

I was furious. I hate doing end runs around people, but this was one of the only times I was compelled to do so. I was convinced that this would be a hugely beneficial acquisition, and for this reason, I decided to approach Capgemini's new CEO about the deal. Norm and I spent a lot of time going over the financials and produced a fair offer. I told the Capgemini CEO I felt strongly about the acquisition and that I could make it work.

When objections were raised about the Indianapolis location—Capgemini was focused on only having businesses in "hub" cities, and Indianapolis wasn't considered a hub—I explained that Indianapolis wasn't far from Chicago and that I would drive down to Indianapolis when needed; I also personally guaranteed that I would make the deal work.

Ultimately, we lost out to an India-based company that made a huge offer, one that Capgemini wasn't willing to match.

There's a lot to take away from the Lev Digital story. First, Capgemini lost out not just because the Indian company made such a high offer but because it didn't have a coordinated, aggressive closing—it made a classic Sales 101 blunder and was hesitant and uncoordinated in its strategy.

Second, I don't think Rich realized how much credibility he had within Capgemini, and I failed as his coach in helping him understand how he might have used this credibility to clinch this deal. One of Rich's great assets as a salesperson is his trustworthiness—people want to buy from those they trust the most. He could have leveraged this trust to pull off the deal.

In this second and now into the third year at Capgemini, my scope as a leader changed. At LYONSCG I was a doer/leader; I was the number one salesperson until Dave and I decided not to sell directly. Then, in the third year, I moved away from the LYONSCG core business and focused on alliances and partnerships for Capgemini in North America. It was a much more strategic leadership role and leveraged my gifts and relationships. Because I never burned bridges, now, I could focus on building more relationships with some of our biggest partners (Microsoft, AWS, Salesforce, SAP, Adobe, Google, etc.).

Here's an analogy that captures how Rich transformed. I knew a martial arts black belt, Nick, and he was testing for an advanced belt. In the test, a succession of people are sent out to fight Nick—first one person, then another person with a weapon, then two people, then two people with weapons, and so on until the sensei sends five people with weapons to fight Nick. As the number of fighters increases, Nick's form deteriorates, his legs are leaden, his arms like over-cooked spaghetti, and he becomes increasingly angry at himself for allowing this to happen. When the five people come out to fight him, he's furious, and he defeats all of them faster than he had beaten the smaller numbers of fighters. After the test, Nick is told he passed, and he asks the sensei how that was possible since his form was terrible. "It's not your form that we were judging," his sensei said. "You were eligible to take the test because of your good form. During the test, we were looking at your ability to harness your anger intentionally."

I continued my alliance role into a fourth year. Many events took place in the third year that were disillusioning. The COVID-19 pandemic and Capgemini's response to it was one of these events; the company chose to cut deep into legacy LYONSCG and much of the organization. I am not sure what we would have done if LYONSCG remained independent during this time, but it was very difficult. We cut back on alliance staff as well and changed plans and promises we had made to our partners. I started to become a highly paid babysitter, trying to convince great people to stay at Capgemini. It worked for a while, but during the fourth year, I reached a breaking point.

In my four years at Capgemini, I had never received a performance review. I was given the obligatory 3 rating, with no discussion of my goals, impact, or performance. In addition to my North America alliance role, I was also the global offer leader for commerce, defining the go-to-market strategy for commerce globally. I was still involved in lead generation through my relationships with Salesforce, and I still got to do what I loved most—be with new clients and sell. I was also involved with Forrester and Gartner and the other analyst firms, as they rated Capgemini on our Salesforce and commerce services in their Gartner Magic Quadrant and Forrester Wave analyses. We did great and helped move Capgemini forward—definitely "punched above our weight."

Then I got a worse rating, with no explanation; I didn't even know who did the rating, which meant no accountability existed. And my role in North America Alliances was eliminated.

Around this time, I was invited to play golf at the famous Augusta National Golf Club, where the Masters is always held. I of course decided to go (you don't turn down an invitation like this), and though I was determined to have fun and enjoy the opportunity, my game was off. I played terribly. Mentally and emotionally, I was devastated. Because of my poor rating, I was supposed to go on a performance improvement plan. Despite all that I'd achieved, my confidence was shaken.

With hindsight, I realized that I had not sold Capgemini's leaders on LYONSCG as well as I might have; or perhaps I had not factored their resistance to commerce into my pitches. I also wasn't used to playing politics as an employee of a large company. Politics is nothing more than selling ideas, convincing people to do X or believe Y. At LYONSCG, I never had to sell internally because of our culture—everyone understood that we were customer-focused. At a large organization like Capgemini, selling internally—or playing politics—was a necessity.

It was time for John Mullen and me to have another meeting. Once again, he asked me what I wanted to do. I told him nothing had changed for me—I wanted to be put in a role where I could add value and make a difference. Otherwise, I was wasting my time and talent. I was not there for the paycheck. I was still trying to change the world and help lead the best eCommerce digital agency in the world. John was honest with me, as always, and told me that he didn't think he could create a role like that for me in North America.

Part of the problem was that John had lost out in a power struggle with another French Capgemini leader. I was loyal to John—perhaps loyal to a fault. Again, I wasn't interested in playing politics.

During this period, I was pushing Rich to use his connections in Capgemini, go to Paris, and make his case to the top people. But Rich was used to working through people rather than going around them. Again, part of this was my fault. I don't think I was able to convince Rich of the gift he possessed, that he had earned a lot of trust and respect, and that he could use these assets to sell Capgemini's leaders on his ideas.

Many people were outraged by my negative performance rating and fought for me, knowing my value and offering me new jobs and other opportunities within Capgemini—times like this really show who cares about you. John Mullen himself left at the end of June. I was aligned closely with John for the almost four years we were together, and we had lost the battle. It was time to go. We structured a four-month transition plan and a flexible work arrangement, and I left at the end of October, almost four years to the day of the acquisition. When I decided to leave, it was a weight lifted from my shoulders. You can only hit your head against the wall for so long before the wall cracks or you do.

By the time I left, LYONSCG was once again broken out into its own group, Unified Commerce. We had free range to go after any accounts less than $5 billion in revenue. And we began building up again and rehiring after we had cut too deeply during COVID-19. We had integrated, then dis-integrated, so to speak.

At Capgemini, Rich became more intentional in harnessing his anger, learning to do what's right in the moment, and being increasingly on his own side in the face of seemingly overwhelming odds. He spoke up in ways that he would never have spoken up in the past. And people listen to him in ways they would not have listened to him before.

I left Capgemini after four years, and though I had positive experiences there, it was overly optimistic to believe that everyone would "get us." Some people understood pieces of what we did, but not everything. I recall that one executive at Capgemini thought of commerce as a commodity, rather than a personalized, tailored discipline. Or executives didn't understand how one person could work on five different projects—a common practice at LYONSCG. They insisted on a one-person, one-project approach and were unable to integrate our practice into their system.

There was a profound difference between LYONSCG and Capgemini that Rich couldn't have anticipated. It had to do with the value set of a company that does $500 million projects with a company like McDonald's. Capgemini is a $13 billion business, and as such, it didn't think much of the middle market, LYONSCG's bread and butter.

At the same time, the experience at Capgemini was essential for Rich's personal and professional development. His transformation completed itself with his exit from Capgemini. Most entrepreneurs, when they start a new business, keep doing what they know how to do. Rich is the only person I've coached, after a wealth-generating liquidity event, who has been willing to try what he didn't know how to do. That's a clear sign of transformation.

WDM Takeaways

- Monitor your emotions. Taking a company to market for a sale takes a lot of trust (Level 1). All kinds of feelings will be stirred up—fear, hurt, anger, sadness, and joy. Awareness is the win. Embrace each feeling and enjoy the ride.

- Communicate more frequently, more clearly, more intelligently. Communication may be the number one most important thing during a sale; in general, it is also the key to successfully running a company. Employees are hungry for knowledge and need affirmation (Level 2). No matter how much you think you have communicated, you can do more.

- Express the truth (Level 4), build rapport, and be on your own side. These are key skills for any leader. When to conform and when to express, when to contain and when to be assertive with anger (Level 2)—your awareness and ability to make these choices will change your life.

- Be responsible for being the change you want to see in the world (Level 6). And the change starts with you. Hint: It's an inside job.

- Be clear on the value that you want to create. And be on your own side in terms of the value that you bring, not just in terms of what you do, but also your presence and being (Level 5). It is your job to get affirmed and to feel valued (Level 2). Don't expect to get it from your boss, your employees, or your clients. Have good friends, life partners, mentors, and coaches to prop you up and clean up your wounds when you need it.

EPILOGUE

MOVING ON TO NEW HORIZONS— FROM SALES TO CULTURE

Life is sales has been my guiding mantra, and I hope it will become yours. Understanding selling in all its dimensions—from landing that first big customer to communicating persuasively as a leader—has provided me with an extraordinarily fulfilling life.

Another mantra, though, has emerged in recent years: Business is culture. Grasping the essence of culture and how powerful of a force it can be has been a revelation.

This message hit especially hard for me at Capgemini. I discovered that you can say your culture is one thing, but the reality may be something else. I'm sure Capgemini's leaders believed that their culture was all about people—it's what the company professed on its website and elsewhere. But culture is more than stating your principles—it's about living them. I realize that when you have a company of 300,000 people, it's a much bigger challenge to adhere to cultural values than when you have four hundred employees. Even then, it's a challenge. But it's a challenge worth meeting since culture can make an enormous difference, both in the lives of the people and in the company itself.

For this reason, I've been spending a great deal of my time working on culture. My work on boards, my graduate program, my consulting, and other activities have all revolved around cultural issues. As I've pointed out in these pages, everything you do—consciously or unconsciously—impacts culture. Leaders need to recognize that every conversation, policy, and decision they make help set culture.

It's a complex, crucial, and fascinating subject, and it will be the focus of my next book.

As I conclude this book, I trust that the stories I've shared about culture, selling, and entrepreneurship will help you in business and in life.

I believe that Rich's story will inspire people to look at sales as an exquisite opportunity to learn, grow, and serve the world. When you combine integrity and sales as Rich does, you do the right thing, not the easy or expeditious thing. You're willing to lose accounts, to say what needs to be said to clients, to walk away from deals that aren't right for you.

People are so busy trying to sell as much and as fast as they can that they lower their standards. Rich's standards never dropped from the time he started LYONSCG to the present.

Let me leave you with one more sales story—one that I haven't mentioned until now. It's about my first major sale.

I was working at Whittman-Hart, and I was struggling—I feared that I might be placed on a performance improvement plan. Then, finally, I closed my first SAP ERP deal for Benteler Automotive, a supplier to big automotive companies. We drove to its headquarters in Grand Rapids, Michigan. Bob Bernard, Whittman-Hart's CEO, arrived in a limo and told Benteler that we'd open a Grand Rapids office if we won the account.

We won, and we opened a Grand Rapids office. I orchestrated everything, and it was the first time that I "carried the bag." It was a turning point and led me to make bigger and better deals.

I mention this story here to make two points. First, you never forget your first big sale. And second, while there's the temptation to measure sales purely in account size, success means so much more than that. Selling is an opportunity to be the biggest blessing we can be. There's a karma to all of our work. If I treat someone well, I'll be treated well in return. Sales situations provide people with the opportunity to be better—to make a difference in someone else's life. It's about serving the world using your unique gifts.

At a recent leadership meeting, someone referred to me as a business mystic. And it's true—I believe it's possible for your work, personal, and spiritual life to come together. As I'm sure you understand by now, life is sales goes beyond transactions to who we are at our cores.

Before Judith and I left Wright, Rich helped us launch the Lyons School of Transformational Business MBA (which continues at Maharishi International University). This was Rich's way of giving back, of expressing gratitude, of being supportive of individual growth and development. I know he's grateful for how Wright has helped him as a salesperson, leader, and human being, and he wants others to benefit.

I am eager to pass on what I have learned successfully growing and running a business. While I valued many of the courses I had taken in my MBA studies at Northwestern University's Kellogg School of Management, the social emotional intelligence (SEI) classes at Wright were a revelation—they're what helped me grow as a salesperson, leader, and human being.

SEI is the key to the new model of transformational leadership. After COVID-19, people want more than money, and they don't want bosses who are bullies. They want leaders who can apply SEI to business functions such as teaming and staff development.

And they want to become transformational leaders. In my company, people felt my heart. I transformed from a stoic engineer to someone who cried at our annual meetings when I saw all those people I loved gathered in one place. The "transformation" in the Lyons School of Transformational Business is there for a reason. People need to learn to transform themselves before they transform others, and I hope the school will teach this incredibly valuable process.

I love business. My professional future seems to be as an advisor, consultant, investor, board member, coach, fellow student—and now author, with this my first book of a planned trilogy. I look forward to my expanding life as a friend and family man and hope this book, in some small way, contributes to your growth and success.

APPENDIX

WRIGHT DEVELOPMENTAL MODEL

OVERVIEW:

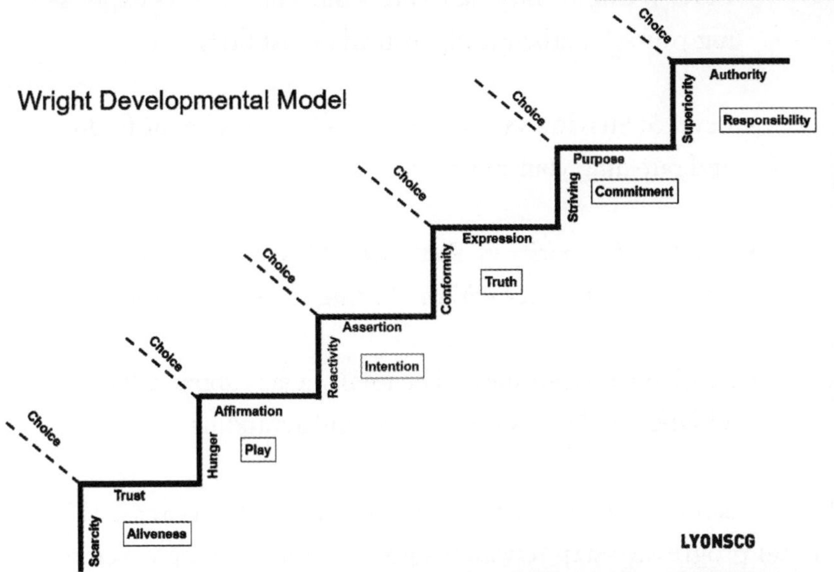

Rich has discussed how the Wright Developmental Model (WDM) is a tool that helps people understand their failure to perform at desired levels and to strategize and fill in developmental gaps as he has demonstrated above. He uses the model to understand himself and enhance psychological and behavioral growth. It breaks down this growth into seven stages that people go through over their lives. These stages are:

- **Level 1: Scarcity vs. Trust:** This is about learning to trust life and feel supported, rather than feeling like there's never enough.
- **Level 2: Hunger vs. Affirmation:** This stage is about seeking validation and feeling seen and valued.
- **Level 3: Reactivity vs. Assertion:** Here, the focus is on expressing your needs and desires assertively rather than reacting impulsively.
- **Level 4: Conformity vs. Expression:** This involves expressing yourself authentically instead of just fitting in.
- **Level 5: Striving vs. Purpose:** This stage is about finding and pursuing your purpose.
- **Level 6: Superiority vs. Authority:** This involves developing a sense of authority without feeling superior to others.
- **Level 7: Consciousness:** The final stage is about achieving a higher level of awareness and understanding.

At each stage, there are two sides like steps on a staircase. The horizontal progressive step represents growth and meeting developmental needs, while the vertical regressive step represents unresolved needs and immature responses.

People often get stuck on the immature side due to unresolved issues, which can lead to painful emotions like fear, pain, or anger when triggered by life events. For example:

- Feeling scared and not trusting (Scarcity vs. Trust)

- Feeling hurt and needing attention (Hunger vs. Affirmation)

- Reacting angrily without thinking (Reactivity vs. Assertion)

The model helps individuals identify where they might be stuck and work on resolving these issues to move toward more mature, responsible behavior. It's normal to go back and forth between and among stages as you grow and mature.

Key points to remember:

1. There are seven major stages of development.
2. Each stage has a side that represents growth and another side that represents unmet needs.
3. Life challenges can bring up unresolved issues from earlier stages.
4. Understanding the model helps you see where you are stuck and work on developing to the next level of maturity.

For example, at the first level (Scarcity vs. Trust), the main task is to learn to trust that life is supportive. People with unresolved issues (and we all have unresolved issues) at this level might have a scarcity mindset, always fearing there's not enough. Recognizing and addressing this can help build trust and support personal growth.

By understanding and applying the Wright Developmental Model, individuals can work on meeting their developmental needs and move toward greater personal fulfillment and maturity.

Level 1: Scarcity vs. Trust

Level 1 corresponds to the first six months of life, when keeping the baby alive is key—this responsibility to keep ourselves alive is gradually transferred to us as adults and the fear of our parents is unconsciously transferred to us to keep ourselves alive. At the first level of the Wright Developmental Model, people deal with the conflict between scarcity (feeling fear that there's never enough, and that death is around the corner at the extreme) and trust (believing life will support them). The main challenge here is to learn to trust that the world is a supportive place. Building this trust is essential for a successful and fulfilling life. Recognizing when you're stuck in a scarcity mindset helps you grow and overcome obstacles.

In real-life crises like famine or poverty, focusing on scarcity and taking protective measures is necessary and useful. However, many people unnecessarily imagine threats and limitations. This prevents them from taking healthy risks and living fully. Accepting responsibility for your feelings of scarcity allows you to build trust in yourself and the world, leading to growth and learning.

Scarcity is the most basic level where people can get stuck. When dominated by scarcity, a person lives in fear—of harm, loss, or failure. This fear can cause impulsive actions or complete inaction. Even in everyday situations like business meetings, a scarcity mindset can pop up, limiting satisfaction and growth. Facing irrational fears and accurately assessing real threats help build trust in your abilities and environment.

As you move past scarcity, trust becomes more dominant in your life. Fear becomes helpful, warning you of real dangers but not controlling you. Everyone has some unresolved issues at this level, but those who don't develop trust in childhood may lead anxious, defensive lives.

In the Wright model, trust means feeling safe to engage with life fully and honestly. It's about trusting your ability to handle whatever comes your way, not expecting life to be without challenges. In relationships, trust is based on truth and integrity, not on never being let down.

When you trust, you believe you can handle life's challenges. This repeated trust builds a stable belief that the world is generally good and supportive. You can then express yourself freely and take necessary precautions when needed. The key to trust is adaptability—responding well to your environment while expressing your needs proactively.

Level 2: Hunger vs. Affirmation

The second level of the Wright Developmental Model focuses on a child's need for connection and validation, which typically happens between six months and three years old. During this time, kids start forming their sense of self by seeking positive feedback from those around them.

Hunger in this context means the deep need to feel connected and validated by others. When kids get positive attention and playtime, they feel affirmed, which helps them grow into secure adults. If they don't get this affirmation, it can lead to issues like passive-aggressive behavior, extreme neediness, or acting like they don't need anyone.

Getting consistent, positive feedback during this early stage helps build a strong and positive self-image. The way children are treated shapes how they see themselves and the world. Extreme lack of affirmation, like in orphanages where children's needs aren't met, can severely impact mental health and even survival later in life.

As adults, recognizing and addressing these unmet needs can help continue personal growth. Asking for and receiving affirmation from others can refill emotional reserves, making it easier to give back to others. The goal is to internalize affirmation, so you don't need constant external validation to feel good about yourself.

Meeting these hunger needs through supportive relationships helps build a life filled with affirmation and nourishment. This solid foundation allows individuals to pursue meaningful goals, contribute to society, and live true to their values.

Key Points:

1. Hunger for affirmation is a normal, essential need, especially during early identity formation.
2. Unmet hunger needs can lead to adult issues, while adequate affirmation builds a positive self-image.
3. Taking responsibility for hunger needs as an adult supports continued growth and the pursuit of a meaningful life.
4. Play, unconditional positive regard, and attentive interactions are crucial for meeting hunger needs and feeling affirmed.
5. Fulfilling your own hunger needs enhances your ability to connect with and contribute to others and society.

Level 3: Reactivity vs. Assertion

The third level of the Wright Developmental Model is like the "terrible twos" stage in kids, around age two or three. At this stage, children start to set boundaries and figure out who they are by resisting and asserting their will. The main goal here is for kids to learn how to express their wants and needs in both good and bad ways, which helps them feel more in control of their lives.

Assertion is the progressive side of this level. It means expressing what you want and need in a clear, constructive way. It's about making conscious choices and feeling alive through your desires. Reactivity is the regressive side. It's a more basic response where you resist or push back against things. While reactivity can seem negative, it's actually important for setting boundaries and developing your will.

Reactivity happens every day, even if we don't always notice it. In personal growth, it's important to recognize and take responsibility for these reactive patterns. The goal is to understand the positive intention behind your reactivity and turn that energy into clear, strong assertion. This helps you get what you want and consciously shape your life.

The "terrible twos" can be tough for parents, who need to balance setting limits with encouraging their child's self-expression. Overcontrolling or shaming a child's reactivity can break their will, making it hard for them to develop a strong sense of personal power. If reactivity is squashed in childhood, adults might struggle with being passive, aggressive, or unable to assert their needs properly.

Healthy aggression, which means taking in what you need and pushing away what hurts, should mature into assertion as you grow. This involves learning to control impulses and express your will in a way that's socially acceptable and effective. If you don't learn to be assertive, you might end up being passive aggressive, overly dependent, or feeling disconnected from others.

As adults, we keep working on being more assertive in different areas of our lives. This is a key part of personal growth, along with accepting what we can't change. A strong foundation in assertion helps you act, create, and find peace.

Key Points:

1. Reactivity and assertion are both important for setting boundaries and defining yourself.
2. Recognizing and responsibly expressing reactivity helps turn it into clear, strong assertion.
3. Encouraging a child's self-expression while setting limits helps them develop healthy assertiveness.

4. Overcontrolling or shaming reactivity can lead to passivity, aggression, or trouble asserting desires as an adult.
5. Developing assertiveness means consciously meeting your needs, growing up, and creating a life that fits social norms and personal values.

Becoming assertive is a lifelong journey that helps you take effective action, express yourself, and accept things as they are.

Level 4: Conformity vs. Expression

Picture this: you're a teenager, trying to figure out who you are and where you fit in. You desperately want to belong, to be accepted by your friends and peers. But at the same time, there's a part of you that longs to express your true self, to show the world who you really are. Welcome to the tug-of-war between conformity and expression.

According to G. M. Durst, a whopping 70 to 75 percent of people spend their lives navigating this delicate balance between fitting in and being authentic.[1] Only a small fraction, about 30 percent, manage to live most of their lives expressing their authentic selves. This means disagreeing and offering unpopular thinking or actions while still working to belong and be accepted.

So what exactly is conformity? It's the urge to blend in, to adapt yourself to the group's norms and expectations, even if it means hiding parts of who you are. You might find yourself biting your tongue instead of speaking your mind, or going along with the crowd even when it doesn't feel right. The fear of being rejected or ridiculed is so powerful that you're willing to sacrifice your individuality for the sake of belonging.

---

[1] Delivered in seminar by Dr. Gary Michael Durst, author of *Management by Responsibility*, 0960255214, first edition date unknown, as he cited the work of Dr. Jane Loevinger.

On the flip side, expression is about boldly putting your true self out there, standing up for what you believe in, even if it means ruffling some feathers. It's about living in alignment with your deepest values and sharing your unique perspective with the world. The guiding principle here is truth—the raw, unfiltered expression of your inner reality in relation to others.

But let's be real: expressing your truth is easier said than done. The fear of losing a job, damaging relationships, or facing disapproval keeps us stuck in conformity mode, unable to let our true colors shine.

As a teenager, conformity serves an important purpose. It helps you break away from your family and form your own identity within a peer group. You might find yourself rebelling against your parents' values as a way of figuring out what you really stand for. But if you don't have a strong foundation of self, you can get lost in the process, losing touch with your authentic self in the pursuit of acceptance.

The danger of conformity is that it can lead to a false sense of belonging. By holding back your true thoughts and feelings, you might find yourself surrounded by people who don't really know the real you. It's like trying to fit a square peg into a round hole—sure, you might make it work, but it's not a comfortable or sustainable way to live.

The journey from conformity to expression is a gradual one. It's about developing the security to reveal more and more of your true self in your day-to-day life, even if it means risking some disapproval. It's a continuous unfolding, a process of getting to know and accept yourself on an ever-deeper level.

As a lifelong learner, your mission is to become increasingly aware of when you're selling out your authenticity for the sake of fitting in. It's about finding the courage to let your freak flag fly, to embrace what makes you unique, even if it sets you apart from the crowd. By consistently choosing to express your truth, you find yourself connecting with others on a more genuine level and living a life that feels truly fulfilling.

The road from conformity to expression isn't always easy, but it's a critical part of the journey toward becoming a fully actualized human being. So take a deep breath, summon your inner rebel, and get ready to show the world the singular marvel that is YOU.

Level 5: Striving vs. Purpose

When we come into adulthood, the urge for more and better becomes strong. Imagine you're at a point in your life where you're driven to achieve, to make something of yourself. You've got big dreams and even bigger goals, and you're willing to work your butt off to make them happen. Welcome to the world of striving, where the mantra is "go big or go home."

At this level, you're all about pushing yourself to be the best you can be. Maybe you're striving to be a moral paragon, or maybe you're chasing financial success like it's going out of style. Whatever your flavor of striving, there's a sense of being propelled by some invisible force, like a shark that has to keep swimming or it'll die.

Striving can be a double-edged sword. On one hand, it's a powerful motivator that can help you achieve great things. But on the other hand, it can lead to some pretty unhealthy patterns, like workaholism, perfectionism, or an overwhelming sense of guilt. You might find yourself running on an endless treadmill of accomplishment, never feeling like you've quite arrived.

In the midst of all this striving, if you have too many unmet early developmental needs, relationships can start to feel like means to an end. You might find yourself viewing people as stepping stones to your goals, rather than as valuable connections in their own right.

But here's the thing: Striving alone won't bring you the deep sense of fulfillment you're searching for. You can chase success until you're blue in the face, but if you're not addressing the underlying issues—like feelings of scarcity, hunger, or reactivity—you'll always feel like something's missing.

That's where commitment comes in. When you couple your striving with a deep commitment to your goals and values, something magical happens. You start to develop a sense of purpose, a feeling that your life has meaning beyond just racking up achievements.

As you lean into this commitment, you might find that your perspective starts to shift. Instead of being solely focused on the endgame, you start to find joy and meaning in the day-to-day actions that move you closer to your purpose. You develop a more balanced approach to life, one that allows room for both hard work and rest, for both ambition and contentment.

But purpose isn't just about blindly charging toward your goals. It's also about being willing to reevaluate and adjust when necessary. Maybe you realize that the goalposts you set for yourself are unrealistic or unfulfilling. Maybe you need to tweak your approach or even abandon certain goals altogether. That's all part of the process.

The key is to let your commitment guide you, to use it as a compass that keeps you pointed in the direction of what truly matters to you. When you act with commitment, you have a clarity of intention that cuts through the noise and distractions. You know what you want, and you're willing to do the work to get there.

Striving and purpose are like two sides of the same coin. Striving without purpose can feel hollow and exhausting, like running on a hamster wheel that never stops. But when you combine striving with a deep sense of commitment and meaning, you tap into a wellspring of motivation and fulfillment that can sustain you through even the toughest challenges.

So if you find yourself in the midst of a striving phase, give yourself permission to stop and ask yourself what it's all for. Do I have developmental potholes tripping me up? Dig deep to uncover the values and commitments that drive you. Then let those values and commitments be your North Star as you navigate the twists and turns of your journey. With purpose as your guide, there's no telling how far you can go.

Level 6: Superiority vs. Authority

At this level, the tendency to use our progress and success to look down on others is common. As you progress in consciousness, you reach a level where you understand more than most people. At this stage, you're in a position to serve and inspire others. The challenge is to fully own up to the gaps between your ideals and your actual behaviors. You blame no one for the gaps. By taking full responsibility for yourself in this way, you start living with true authority.

Responsibility is the principle of creating your own reality. The regressive side of this is superiority—when you learn and grow, you can start to see yourself as above others. This is counterproductive, as you end up focusing on others' flaws more than developing yourself. Once you embrace responsibility, you move toward the progressive side, which is true authority.

Authority means fully claiming ownership over the discrepancies between your ideals and actions. You stop making excuses and see yourself as the author of your own existence. This allows you to narrow the gap and live ever closer to your highest principles.

The programs at Wright are designed to help people learn to live with greater authority and responsibility. The goal is to support as much progress as possible on the path to higher consciousness and connection with the source of all life.

Superiority is often defined in terms of rank, status, or command over others. But in this model, it's more about an attitude or ego state where you feel superior to others, denying your shared humanity. Even when you're in a position to contribute, this superiority can mask deeper insecurities and unresolved issues.

Consciousness and authenticity help you accept your own frailties, allowing the shift from superiority to true authority. From this position of authority, you can take full responsibility for things like scarcity, hunger, and reactivity within yourself. Otherwise, the need to look good and attack others can become an addictive mental habit.

Many people have "authority issues"—a deep belief that their own needs and well-being cannot be met when dealing with authority figures. This leads them to either resist and rebel or submit passively. Overcoming these issues involves learning to assert your will, negotiate win-win solutions, and align with authority without a full-blown rebellion.

This growth process is challenging but important. As you address earlier issues around hunger, affirmation, and assertion, it becomes easier to confront and resolve these authority blocks.

Level 7: Consciousness (Non-Dualistic)

This is the level of transcendental truths. Non-dualistic consciousness represents the realm of transcendental principles such as love, compassion, grace, forgiveness, and unity consciousness. At this stage, the individual becomes a living embodiment of their highest ideals. While the Wright model does not attempt to map this level in detail, it suggests that the transformational principles of the lower levels—aliveness, play, intention, truth, commitment, and responsibility—lay the foundation for the emergence of these transpersonal qualities.

This is the real aim of the model—to help us become the most loving, gracious people we can become.

The Transformational Principles for Personal Growth Consciousness

The Wright Model outlines a progression of key principles that can guide our personal development and spiritual evolution. These range from the foundational to the most profound.

Principles of Identity Formation

At the most basic level are the developmental principles—core elements like ingestion, identification, and projection that shape our fundamental sense of self and identity.[2] These form the building blocks of who we are today. To become the person we could become, we use the transformational principles:

Transformational Principles

Building upon this foundation are the transformational principles. These are the guiding lights that help us grow into our most responsible, authentic selves. The transformational principles are:

- Aliveness—Allowing ourselves to be fully alive and expressive, rather than deadened by fear.
- Play—Engaging with the world in a spirit of curiosity, creativity, and spontaneity leading to nourishment.
- Intention—Directing our will and desires in a positive, constructive way.
- Truth—Courageously expressing our innermost experience and highest vision.
- Commitment—Dedicating ourselves to meaningful goals and causes beyond ourselves.
- Responsibility—Fully owning the authorship of our lives and experiences.

[2] Citation for further reading. I believe I learned this from *Introduction to Psychiatry* by English and Finch, 1957, Norton Press.

Mastering these principles is a pathway to the transcendent.

Transcendental Principles

At the pinnacle are the transcendental principles—qualities like compassion, love, grace, and forgiveness that represent the highest expression of human consciousness. These emerge naturally as we deepen our embodiment of the transformational principles.

The Journey of Growth and Transformation

This is not a static hierarchy, but a dynamic journey of growth and evolution. We're all works in progress, continually learning to live with greater aliveness, play, intentionality, truth, commitment, and responsibility. It's a lifelong process of self-discovery and reinvention.

The exciting part is that as we grow in this way, we don't just benefit ourselves—we become a greater blessing and positive force in the world around us. Our personal transformation translates into meaningful service.

Wright programs are designed to support people in navigating this profound inner journey. The aim is to help each person unlock their fullest potential as a conscious, purposeful, and compassionate human being. It's about waking up to the profound power we each have to shape our lives and make a difference.

So let's embrace this work with courage, curiosity, and care for one another. The rewards, for ourselves and our world, are immense.

Each level is associated with a key existential principle that supports the individual's growth from the regressive to the progressive aspect of that stage. For example, the principle of truth fosters the move from conformity to authentic expression, while commitment enables the shift from striving to purpose.

Engaging with these principles and developmental tasks is a lifelong journey. The Wright model encourages individuals to recognize and take responsibility for the unfinished business of earlier levels as it arises throughout adulthood. By facing one's fears, aligning with one's truth, and committing to a life of purpose and integrity, the individual gradually closes the gap between their ideal self and their lived reality. This ongoing process of development enables greater freedom, fulfillment, and the capacity to be of service in the world.

ABOUT THE AUTHORS

RICH LYONS is a renowned eCommerce pioneer and transformational leader, celebrated for founding Lyons Consulting Group, the industry's leading eCommerce/Global Commerce Services firm. His innovative work with clients like GoPro, Patagonia, and Herman Miller earned him and his company numerous sales innovation and achievement awards. Recognized for his expertise, Rich was named a "Top 25" consultant by *Consulting Magazine* in 2016, and his firm was listed three times as one of *Consulting*'s fastest-growing companies.

After Lyons Consulting Group was acquired by Capgemini in 2017, Rich spearheaded major growth initiatives for Capgemini's partners as leader of North American Partners and Channels. Since leaving Capgemini in 2021, he has been actively involved in board service, eCommerce consulting, and launching lifeissales.com, a platform dedicated to helping early-stage entrepreneurs refine their sales processes and expand their sales teams.

In 2022, Rich founded the Lyons School of Transformational Business at Wright Graduate University, offering accredited MBAs in sales, entrepreneurship, social-emotional intelligence, and principle-based leadership.

A graduate of the University of Michigan with an MBA from Northwestern University's Kellogg Graduate School of Management, Rich resides in Chicago with his wife, Gertrude, and they are proud parents of two grown daughters.

DR. BOB WRIGHT, a recognized expert in developing human potential and transformational leadership, is a master executive coach and trainer. With his wife, Dr. Judith Wright, he founded the Wright Foundation and Wright Graduate University for the Realization of Human Potential, offering accredited MA, MBA, and EdD degrees in transformational leadership and coaching.

Crain's Chicago Business recognized Bob as a leading executive coach, and over the years he has helped thousands of leaders and entrepreneurs push past artificial limits and achieve great success and find meaning and purpose. Bob has coached individuals and led workshops designed to help people reach their sales potential.

Bob has delivered talks about these areas of expertise throughout the world, and he has written two books with Dr. Judith Wright: *Transformed!: The Neuroscience of Changing Your Life for the Better, Forever* and *The Heart of the Fight: A Couple's Guide to Fifteen Common Fights, What They Really Mean, and How They Can Bring You Closer.* He is also the author of *Beyond Time Management: Business with Purpose.*